(handwritten inscription: To Tom, with best, [signature] 09-01-...)

There and Back Again

A NAVIGATOR'S STORY

IN CONCLUSION

Sixth Edition 2007

By
James Douglas Hudson DFC RAFVR
Honorary Member Battle of Britain Memorial Flight

(handwritten signature: Douglas Hudson DFC RAFVR)

First Published in Great Britain in 2001 by
Tucann Books
Second Edition 2002
Third Edition 2003
Fourth Edition 2004
Fifth Edition 2005
Sixth Edition 2007

ISBN 9781873257753

Produced by: TUCANN*design&print*, 19 High Street, Heighington Lincoln LN4 1RG
Tel & Fax: 01522 790009
www.tucann.co.uk

PREDESTINATION

THERE IS A DESTINY THAT SHAPES OUR ENDS

The destinies of two complete strangers, Alice Ormerod and an RAF navigator, were decided on the morning of 19th February 1943. Alice, travelling on the train from Aylesbury to Manchester, was joined at Loughborough by the young airman. It marked an occasion, which was to influence their lives for all time.

I dedicate this book to my parents, my wife and Edna Chapman my bomb-aimer's widow.

Their undemonstrative bravery, throughout times of great anxieties, epitomizes that of thousands of other brave people who made similar sacrifices. There were no medals for them in recognition of their stoical, silent service to their countries.

Future generations dwell on this. Strike for them medals of remembrance and thank them all for contributing to a great deliverance.

FOREWORD TO 6TH EDITION OF
"THERE AND BACK AGAIN - A NAVIGATOR'S STORY"
BY FLYING OFFICER JAMES DOUGLAS HUDSON DFC RAFVR

On Sunday 27th August 2006, along with my wife Alison, I had the great honour of representing today's Royal Air Force at the unveiling of the Bomber Command Ledger Stone at Lincoln Cathedral. On that marvellous, sunny day I met many of the brave men and women of the Bomber Command Association and other veterans, amongst them the author of this book, Douglas Hudson. I was deeply touched when he asked whether I would be prepared to write a foreword to this, the 6th edition of "There and Back Again - A Navigator's Story". I am truly delighted to do so.

This is one man's story - through family childhood, through training and early operations, through capture and privation, through many subsequent missions, and through the aftermath of world conflict; as such, it provides a deeply personal account of Douglas' experiences and thoughts, as well as lessons about broader society during times of combat. However, the book also captures other, wider truths, about camaraderie, about loyalty, about the deep sense of shared purpose and risk that pervaded those testing times, and about the fortitude of the human spirit. Of course, for an airman, it also captures the detail, excitement and uncertainties of combat air operations and, as such, the book remains a most important historical document. In all these terms, I commend it to all who have an abiding interest in aerial warfare.

But, perhaps overriding all else, the book stands as a tribute to those who served in Bomber Command during the Second World War, and particularly to the 55,888 men and women of the Command who paid the ultimate price. Those of us lucky enough to be alive now must never forget the deep debt of gratitude that we owe to those who endured so much in order to allow later generations to live in freedom. Their skills, bravery and sacrifice continue to inspire those of us still serving in the Royal Air Force today.

Sir Clive Loader KCB OBE ADC FRAeS RAF
Air Chief Marshal
Commander-in-Chief Strike Command

CONTENTS

THE SIXTH EDITION
of
There and Back Again - A NAVIGATOR'S STORY

This book, which includes the stories described in the Fifth Edition, is considerably augmented and written for the same purposes of tribute.

I was motivated to write it in recognition of a complete stranger, Mr RA 'Scotty' Scott from Welton near Lincoln. He pioneered the campaign to establish a Memorial Stone in Lincoln Cathedral dedicated to the men and women of Bomber Command who served during the Second World War.

There and Back again - A Navigator's Story - is entirely autobiographical. The stories relate to many of my forebears and continue with coverage of my own experiences from the day of my birth.

Apparently my chances of surviving early delicate childhood were remote. In spite of disturbing medical prognoses, worrying for my parents, I outgrew constitutional weaknesses and attained a high standard of physical fitness. With the blessing of an alert mind this has accompanied me throughout life to my ninety-first year as I write the present text.

Introducing Myself
AUTOBIOGRAPHICAL RECOLLECTIONS

By May 1916, after nearly two years of war, young British and Commonwealth soldiers had been slaughtered and wounded in their hundreds of thousands on the battlefields of France and Belgium. They were fighting, sometimes to gain only a few yards of territory from the German enemy, under the command of Kaiser Wilhelm II, Emperor of Germany and grandson of the late Queen Victoria of England.

In Britain, the accusing finger of Field Marshal Lord Kitchener, whose face appeared on national huge posters, exhorted young men to join the country's army. Many of these young men, merely boys, did not require exhorting. Their deep sense of patriotism was responsible for several to fake their age to enlist.

Under the command of Marshal Joffre, the French army faced a similar situation.

To express what is now a cliché, the pundits of the day convinced the general public that the country was fighting a war to end all wars! How misguided. It lay the foundation stone that would start the next war.

Controversy is dangerous. Nevertheless, I state with equanimity,

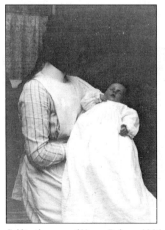 

Self in the care of Nurse Palmer 1916   *Self in pram Whitkirk 1916*

the combined ineptitude of the above mentioned commanders and their aides was profound, as was the avarice of many civilian 'entrepreneurs', who capitalised financially by industrial benefits arising from the manufacture and distribution of wartime necessities and black market activities.

Sunday 21st May 1916 marked the introduction of daylight saving, thereby achieving a longer evening daylight in summer months by setting the time an hour ahead of the standard time. The day had been warm and oppressive. Phyllis Hudson was lying uncomfortably in bed suffering from jaundice and in labour at the end of her pregnancy. At 7.30 in the evening, the pending storm broke with a vivid streak of lightning followed by almost unprecedented crashing of thunder. At this moment the child was born to an exhausted mother, who could relax now, knowing that her newly arrived son would be safe in the care of Nurse Palmer.

THE HUDSON FAMILY

On 23rd November 1871, George Hudson, son of James Hudson and Sarah Wade, married Mary Weeding, younger daughter of John Jessop Rust Weeding and Anne Neale, at All Saints Church, Aldwinkle, Northamptonshire. They had six children. Both Sarah the eldest and Harold Ernest the youngest married. Sarah moved to Argentina. Harold Ernest and the other three sons and a daughter, all of whom remained single, continued to live in the United Kingdom.

Mary Weeding's forbears were aristocratic and of Suffolk origin. She was brought up in Stepney and baptised at Whitechapel. After her marriage she moved to Yorkshire, where she lived until the time of her death in 1923 and was buried at Calverley.

Harold Ernest
My Father circa
1914

THE PILLEY FAMILY

Fred Pilley married Emily Gray in 1882 at Calverley Wesleyan Chapel. They had seven children. Arthur, the eldest son, emigrated to Canada and married a Canadian lady who was known to the next generation as Auntie Hattie. The youngest son died in infancy. The remaining son and three of four daughters married. The youngest stayed single to care for her parents who provided her with a permanent home in Calverley.

It is possible that Mary Weeding had certain difficulties coming to terms with living in Yorkshire. It

My Mother, Phyllis
Chestnut Grove Circa 1914

is also possible that some Yorkshire folk, but not all, had difficulty in coming to terms with Mary Weeding. After marriage, her problems were cushioned by a lifestyle of relative grandeur in the Gildersome area of Yorkshire. Supported by servants, she had no domestic anxieties. A carriage bearing the Hudson family coat of arms, drawn by a pair of well groomed horses, took George, her affluent textile mill owner husband, to a thriving business each day. It could be said they enjoyed living for many years in Victorian and Edwardian high society.

Shortly after the turn of the century a drastic change took place. The trade entered into depression, the mill closed and George and Mary ceased to enjoy the grandeur of living in high society. They became impoverished.

Their son James Weeding was appointed manager of Holly Park mule spinning mill at Calverley. Their daughter Maud became a teacher at a school in Greengates and the family moved to Chestnut Grove, a smaller but pleasing property in Calverley. George Hudson died in December 1920 and Mary died three years later. She was not autocratic, which was the impression of many local people. Born an aristocrat, she died an aristocrat. When asked by a local lady why she did not speak like them, she replied, "Because I wadn't." Of course she did not come to terms with Calverley and Calverley did not come to terms with her.

Towards the end of the nineteenth century the Hudson's elder daughter Sarah enjoyed living in a mixed high society in Rosario, Argentina. Lavish garden parties could be planned with safety months ahead. Her husband became wealthy and profited from buying and subsequently selling large tracts of land at exploited prices to the government, for building railroads.

The South American climate was responsible for the premature deaths of Sarah's earlier offspring, so her son Gordon Alan was sent to England and brought up by a governess before attending Rugby school. He went on to Sandhurst for officer training and passed out to serve and survive a few months in the Great War.

Sarah's daughter, with the charming names Marjorie Eileen Frances Murray-Hudson was also sent to England, initially to be taught by a governess. In 1923, two years after the death of her husband, Sarah, having earlier moved from South America, bought 'The Small House' in Berkhamsted. Marjorie grew up here with her mother and later completed her schooling at a nearby grammar school.

I am currently in touch with the present occupiers of 'The Small House', who found primitive artefacts in the attic like the tip of a ceremonial spear and a model of a simple hollowed out tree trunk canoe. From recent photographs these have been traced as belonging to my late cousin Gordon Murray-Hudson.

George Alexander moved to Whitley Bay. As an army officer he survived the war and with the armistice declared, provided a home in 1919 for his faithful batman, who worked for him part time. Alexander went on to become county surveyor for Northumberland.

James and Maud stayed at Chestnut Grove, where they continued to provide a home and support Horace Kemble, who at the age of seven had contracted an illness, which left him mentally impaired for life. In spite of his handicap, he was a man who displayed a great dignity, but never was able to earn a living.

Harold Ernest married Phyllis Pilley on 4th August 1915 at Calverley Wesleyan Chapel. They had one son, James Douglas. The marriage was conditional on Harold remaining relatively temperate.

He became almost an abstainer for the rest of his life. The second condition was that they should be married in the Wesleyan Chapel. This resulted in a divided family feud, which persisted for twenty-six years, as the Hudson family strictly pursued the doctrine of The Church of England.

Early in the story we left the newly born baby safe in the arms of Nurse Palmer. The baby's father Harold recovered from operations for appendicitis and peritonitis, whilst Phyllis soon regained strength health.

Aunt Sarah and Marjorie 1917

I was that baby. My first recollections, two and a half years later, were of the large Union Jack flag flying from the bedroom window next door in Carter Avenue, Whitkirk. I did not know of course that it was called the Union Jack, nor that it was flying to celebrate the armistice of 11th November 1918. The saga which now unfolds is based on my subsequent memories.

My cousin Marjorie with her son Simon 1940

My Mother and self Whitkirk, 1916   *Self whitkirk 1916/1917*

MEMORIES

Jimmy Tebitt was a neighbour's little boy, about my age. I remember him arriving at the back gate, having pushed a toy wheelbarrow completely lined inside with labels of gollies. For some reason we found it very amusing and from the faded photo you will see me running down the garden path in excitement to tell Mother. It is a memory going back eighty-eight years.

My last recollection of Whitkirk was shortly afterwards, probably late autumn 1919, holding Mother's hand whilst walking in the rain on wet cobbled stones to a railway station. I do not know which station, but it marked the beginning of a journey to Newcastle-upon-Tyne, in which area we lived for the next two years.

On arrival at Monkseaton, near Whitley Bay, I met George Alexander Hudson, who I then learned was Uncle Alec. Another faded photo shows him trying to coerce me into the sea. I was terrified and the water of the North Sea was cold.

We then moved to Forest Hall and Father entered into partnership

Self at Whitkirk late 1918

with a man to open a laundry at Felling. In Forest Hall, Santa Claus had a workshop and it was here I saw a beautiful pale blue wooden motor car. I asked Santa to bring it for Christmas. It disappeared from the shop and reappeared at my bedside on Christmas morning. I treasured that car for a long time.

I remember clearly the miners returning in the afternoons from their shift. Their faces, hands and clothes were black with coal dust as they trudged home, each carrying a miner's lamp. Where they changed their clothes and cleaned up, I know not, during summer may be in the back yard and in winter using the scullery or an outhouse. Allegedly, their homes were spotlessly clean.

My recollections of Newcastle are of Grays Monument, the Castle and a filthy black river Tyne, which we crossed by bridge when travelling by train. Jesmond Dene was a pleasant, and in those days unspoiled, leisure spot for picnics.

After about two years the laundry business failed and the laundry was closed. It took Father five years to repay creditors, which he did in full, out of future income from a dyeworks company, where he became manager.

Self at Whitkirk late 1918

He was fortunate to get this job, although it involved another move taking us in the summer of 1921 to Lydgate in the Todmorden-Burnley valley. It was at a time of depression and my parents lived in rented accommodation, which they shared with the owner's family. The owner was unemployed and as a child of five I enjoyed his friendly companionship. He kept poultry and I recall a particular incident when he called to Mother

Myself and Uncle Alec in the sea at Whitley Bay, 1919

in words to this effect. "E's gam Mrs. Udson." Mother misheard and thought he said he's gone. "Gone where?" she enquired in some concern. "No, no, not gone, your Douglas is gam, (meaning game) e's just 'elped me kill a fowl by wringing its neck. 'E pulled so 'ard on't rope it cut bird's 'ead off leaving't bird flapping all over't place with feathers flying."

The railway line crossed the main road between Lydgate and Cornholme at three places, the road being spanned by stone arched bridges. At the time these were built, it was not envisaged that high sided vehicles would travel on this road. In consequence, when an open top double-decker bus approached a bridge, the driver had to use the centre of the road and slow down considerably. The conductor would climb the steps and call out to passengers on the top deck as the bus approached a bridge, "Duck your 'eads and keep them down until't bus 'as passed through!" As a child I thought this great fun and I am not aware of any accidents.

Cornholme Board School 1924 includes (a) Bessie Whiteside, (b) Clifford Hodgson, (c) Charlie Holden, our teacher (d) Alice M Law and (e) myself

13

My parents and I, with friends Corson and Hilton, often travelled on a bus open top deck for weekend outings, journeying via Cornholme, Todmorden, Eastwood, Mytholm, Mytholmroyd to Hebden Bridge. We would then walk home from Mytholm over the moors to Portsmouth. In spite of the depression, a small café thrived in Mytholm, serving afternoon tea with superb cream cakes. It was not envisaged in the early nineteen-twenties that these small towns would become dormitories for cities like Manchester, Leeds and others. At the turn of the twenty-first century property prices would have rocketed to unimaginative levels. You would open the doors of many old stone built terraced houses and enter Aladdin's caves! At Haworth, a few miles north of Hebden Bridge, the Brontë country beckoned.

Later in the year we moved up the valley to Portsmouth near Cornholme, where my parents rented a house in the centre of a row of four, called Carr Field Villas. Immediately opposite was the Cornholme Board School (council school), where I started my school life at the age of six and a half years exactly, on 21st November 1922. The house had been built on ground covered in cinders, consequently it was infested with cockroaches, over which Keatings powder had little effect. The cockroaches got into my toy-box and other places. They terrified me. Mains gas was laid on for lighting, cooking and a boiler used for heating water on clothes' washday. The heating of general household water depended on the living room fire's back boiler. I went to bed by candle light, the flickering made shadows on the walls and ceiling, which also frightened me.

It was about this time Auntie Maud Calvert and my cousin Mollie came to stay. They brought a huge glass ally (playing-marble made of alabaster, or glass with coloured stripes), which Auntie dropped whilst leaving the Todmorden railway station. It bounced down the station stone steps, was retrieved safely and surprisingly suffered no damage. Mollie played with me at Carr Field Villas and remembers to this day, 16th November 2006, my toy steam roller and the sounds I made trundling it down the garden path. More about this later in the story.

I was a frail child and at the age of five my parents thought they would never rear me. The Doctor called three times on one day and explained to them that the only chance of my survival was to be moved out of the damp valley. Allegedly, I was suffering from a general constitutional weakness related to a rheumatoid condition. This prevented me from starting school earlier. I could neither read nor recite the alphabet, which I learned by phonetics, pronouncing letters b, c and d in a hard sound of bur, kur and dur. A year later I became the best reader in the class in spite of spending a lot of time away from school. The teaching syllabus was simple, mainly arithmetic and English, to which we referred as sums and spelling. When ill in bed, sitting up propped by pillows, I could watch the children in the playgrounds.

There were two playgrounds. The girls were separated from the boys except for organised drill, when the class performed exercises instructed by the teacher, of arms fling, knees bend, with hands on hips bend the trunk to the left, then forward, to the right and backwards. These would be followed by running on the spot, running around the playground and leap-frogging over each others' bended shoulders. No child was able to swim and there were no competitive games with other schools.

I was involved regularly in fights, twice with Charlie Holden, sometime called Charlie Greenwood. The different surnames puzzled me at the time. The fights were started generally by the older boys pushing younger boys together and then proclaiming "a fight" until all the boys in the school yard crowded round in a circle. They were not normally fights of animosity. When I was involved it upset Mother who could see and hear what was going on from the house. Twice she came out to separate us, bravely breaking through the circle of boys, some bigger than her, and telling the older ones they should be ashamed of encouraging little ones to fight.

To be like the other boys, I asked to have a patch on my trousers and wear clogs. I loved the clogs and had fun creating sparks by scraping the clogs along the pavement. Many children were poorly dressed, few carried handkerchiefs, their jerseys were filthy. My parents were often driven to distraction by the way I spoke and the expressions I used, not to be different. "Muther, what do they mean when they say, I'll porse thi orse?" (Meaning smack your bottom.)

Grandfather Pilley was a member of the Woodhall Golf Club at Calverley and gave me all his damaged golf balls. I gave many of these away to my poor friends, who really treasured them, whilst I enjoyed cutting other balls open to extract endless yards of varying thicknesses of elastic, revealing a small hard rubber ball, or a small bag containing a peculiar white paste. I have no idea what purpose this served. My friends and I made many dangerous catapults from the elastic!

I loved watching the goods trains and listening to the engines chugging, as they hauled their heavy loads up the line beyond the school. Sometimes there would be two engines in front pulling, at other times one engine in front pulling and an engine pushing at the rear. They were mostly goods trains comprised of coal trucks bearing the names of collieries such as - Bolsover, Manvers Main, Denaby Main, Ackton Hall, Frickley and others. It was nearly six years later before we moved out of that valley.

Mother was a strict disciplinarian and when she called I had to obey. I remember that twice, when in spite of my being frail, she thrashed me severely for misbehaviour. On one of these occasions she was mistaken. I was playing outside with other boys and did not hear when she called me to come indoors and ran off in the opposite direction. I was reprimanded immediately on arriving home. Mother would not believe that I had not heard her call. Over eighty years later, I recall her words as she bared my little backside for a thrashing with the flat leather sole of a slipper. "I would rather bury you than have you grow up to be a liar." I cried and sobbed until I was nearly ill, before going to sleep after being sent to bed. I had not lied.

I do not recall Father reprimanding me, yet ironically, I was closer to Mother than to him. She was a woman with rigid principles, a trait from her father Fred Pilley. They were not always right.

On Sunday mornings Father would take me to the dyehouse, where a skeleton shift ensured certain dyeing processes were maintained. I was always intrigued with the engine shed and admired the huge engine with its highly polished brass fittings. It was the responsibility of old man Abrahams, who always referred to Father as Hudson, to keep the engine working over the weekends, to ensure that power and steam were available for machines that had to be kept running.

Alongside the road between Portsmouth and Cornholme ran the river Calder, on the banks of which was another dyeworks. Effluent, including dye liquid, was discharged regularly into the river. When this occurred, we would watch fascinated, as the river rapidly became coloured, typically green, red, yellow, purple or brown.

During the six years we lived in the valley, two young men, Harry and Arthur, who were indebted to father for their technical jobs in the dyeworks, came to see us regularly. On their visits, Mother provided them with high tea. In return for this hospitality, every year without fail, a few days before 5th November fireworks night, which we called plot, they would buy a huge box of fireworks to the value of one pound. That was a lot of money in those days. There were a lot of fireworks, as you will understand, when small bangers called pom-pom cannon and little demons cost only a ha'penny each. How I looked forward to the arrival of those fireworks. What a delight it was for many neighbours' children, who did not have fireworks, to come and watch the display in our garden.

I got on well with Harry, who was a fount of information. When I was unwell he would sit at the side of my bed and tell intriguing stories about the war. Cartoonist Bruce Bairnsfather produced a magazine called The Bystander with clever drawings relating to the war. Some of these I tried to redraw, not very successfully. It is a pity we disposed of the magazines, they would be of great historic interest today. The cartoonist's main characters were two army private soldiers, Old Bill and I believe Bert. A cartoon I remember showed the pair, obviously trying to delouse, sitting in a shell-hole full of water up to their chins. Under the eye of a Belgian peasant woman holding the hand of a child, the expressions on their faces said it all. The caption read, "Tell 'er to 'op it Bert, I'm sittin' on a bit of shell or somethink." Another depicted a raven perched on the top of a tall chimney pot, under which a large hole had been made in the chimney breast by a passing German shell that continued unexploded on its way. The simple caption read, "Duds," quoth the raven! I didn't know what that meant.

Bairnsfather had his own inimitable style of depicting the dreadful detritus of no man's land. The pictures of the following remain clear to me. The first, of a brilliant full moonlit night in England and a young lady gazing towards the sky from her bedroom open window, saying, "To think, it is the same dear old moon shining down on him." The second, showed him in no man's land somewhere in Belgium, under that same moon, up to his ankles in mud, repairing barbed wire defences. Shells were shrieking overhead, there were explosions all over the sky and Verey lights illuminating bodies. Caption, "This blinkin' moon will be the death of us."

I started to read the Bystanders before I was eight and at the same time received my first annual called The Oojah Annual. Three verses from this annual, three simple verses, conveyed something to me as a child.

"Good natured Godfrey gives to his chums,
All his cakes and keeps only the crumbs."

"Painstaking Pansy is doing her best,
To teach every cuckoo to build its own nest."
Whilst:
"Terrible Thomas with sword and with gun,
Looks just as fierce as a regular Hun."

During the three weeks' school summer holiday in July 1923, workmen stripped the school roof of its old red brick tiles and replaced them with slates. The old brick tiles were used to resurface our road at the front, then crushed and partly flattened by a noisy "Dun duddle dun dun", (my abbreviated name for steamroller), which arrived on the scene to my great delight. The resultant surface was dreadful and took years to become really smooth.

Portsmouth (Cornholme) May Day 1923 includes myself, Father and Grandfather

The back kitchen window overlooked a narrow cinder pot holed road used by tradesmen's horse drawn carts. The milk cart was equipped with two large churnlike containers from which, farmer Greenwood, who called twice a day, filled a smaller open container. He carried this to the houses and with the options of a quarter pint, half pint or one pint ladle, dispensed milk according to housewives' requirements. Mr. Helliwell, the greengrocer, was a lame man who walked aided by a stick. He called most days with vegetables and fruit displayed from the cart. Mr.Widdup, the butcher, offered a similar service from a selection of meat joints. These could be chosen from the cart and cut and weighed to meet individual needs. The services from these tradesmen were excellent but often yielded small returns.

Without a cellar, and of course before the days of domestic refrigerators, it was difficult to preserve perishable food, milk in particular, during summer. Mother boiled it to prevent it curdling and going sour overnight. How I loathed the stuff and could only drink it in tea or cocoa.

Dustbins were emptied weekly. Each man lifted a heavy bin, laden almost entirely with cinders and ashes, from its place near the back door of every house and returned it empty to the same position. Every week there was a delivery of coal. Each sack of coal weighed a hundredweight and was carried on the back of a coalman who tipped it over his shoulder into the coalplace.

Lastly came the handcart of the rag and bone man. He heralded his arrival by ringing a large handbell and shouting, "Any rags, bones, bottles or jars?" Rags they were. There were no cleanly washed second-hand clothes. A donor was rewarded with a donkey stone - a small stone used to scour doorsteps.

The ugly view from the kitchen window over this narrow road was of the backs of a long row of stone, solidly built houses, with their drainpipes, downspouts, small yards and outbuildings. Immediately beyond towered a steep hill with craggy ravines, down which, when it rained, cascaded roaring torrents of water tumbling into the river Calder below, causing the river to rise dramatically. In winter late afternoons, the gloom was accentuated by black chimney smoke issuing from banked up house fires, on which wet kitchen waste rolled up tightly in newspaper, was left to smoulder. It created an eerie, almost foreboding atmosphere of satanic, awesome magnitude that will never go away. Rather like my fear of the dark, difficult to understand and explain.

The school caretaker, a crotchety, elderly man, lived in one of these houses. He was very lame and had a damaged hip, the outcome of having been kicked by a horse. He forbade us to play in the school ground after school when the gates were locked. This did not deter us from scaling the railings and dropping into the yard, where we could not be seen by him, to play cricket quietly. Unfortunately, one summer evening, my friend Alfred Whiteside accidentally drove the cricket ball through one of the school windows. Next day, all of us involved owned up voluntarily and accepted responsibility for the damage. In consequence we were not punished. The outcome, however, was an end to future cricket being played 'after hours'.

Real poverty was rife. Some families existed mainly on one pennyworth of chips each day. They could not afford the fish at twopence. On other occasions, many mothers, very creditably, baked superb meat and potato pies, with more potato than meat. Any child eating an apple would be stopped and asked by other children if they could have the core. The request would sound like this, "After you wit core." They would then argue with each other as to which of them should have it. "Go on with yu, I assked 'im, or 'er, first." No child suffered from obesity as a result of gastronomic excess.

The bobbin mill at Cornholme had been closed for several years and never reopened. In consequence Mr. Penny lost his job and he and his wife opened a fish and chip shop. It was a success in spite of the depression and enabled them to enjoy a simple early retirement, which was the acme of living in those days.

They became friendly and exchanged visits with my parents. Mrs. Penny was a small athletic lady who dressed always in black and wore narrow laced up boots. She took me for long walks on the moors, when often I would run ahead and clamber over rocky crags like a mountain goat. This, in spite of my frailness! She showed me a skylark's nest in the heather, but would not allow me to touch a single egg. I tried to locate this nest again to show my friends, but was unable to find it. Bilberries ripened in profusion on the moors in summer. We would gather these and having no bag or container would bring them home in our caps, which became terribly stained. I was never admonished for this and the resultant bilberry pies were a real delicacy.

Occasionally Mr. Penny would invite me to a bachelor's tea on a Saturday afternoon. I loved this. There was no tablecloth, just a well scrubbed, immaculately clean wooden table top. I really enjoyed the home baked meat and potato pie, served on a hot willow-pattern plate, and drinking strong sweetened tea from a large mug.

Bert Jowett, who lived with his wife and three sons diagonally opposite our house in Carr Field Villas, drove a light Buick lorry for the dyeworks company. The lorry's engine previously belonged to a thirty horsepower car. I was allowed to accompany him on some journeys, one of which was delivering dyed yarns to a mill at Greengates near Calverley. We would sit in the lorry cab, parked in the mill yard, and have lunch, which Bert provided wrapped in newspaper. Also wrapped in newspaper was a concoction of concentrated sweetened condensed milk and tea leaves. This mixture was transferred to a jug into which he poured boiling water, more like steam, from a tap in the mill yard. We drank the resultant brew from two huge pot mugs, delightful.

My real treat, at the age of eight, was to play billiards on their quarter size slate bed table. The billiard balls were of ivory and heavy. The two elder sons, Sam and Norman, always beat me of course. Upon leaving school at the age of fourteen they went into the haulage business and were employed by a small local firm. To my surprise, several years later, when living in the Midlands, I noticed on a number of occasions, in the Aston area of Birmingham, a colossal articulated lorry bearing the name JOWETT INTERNATIONAL.

Within fifty yards of our house was a weaving mill called Crabtree and Farrar. I shall never forget the rhythmic noise from that weaving shed when all the looms were working. Many operatives became completely deaf and used lip, or sign language, to communicate with each other in the shed. Often weavers were facially injured, some quite seriously, by flying shuttles, which after shooting from the

A shuttle which measures 14$\frac{1}{4}$ by 1$\frac{1}{2}$ inches

loom, would career across the weaving shed about head high. This was a recurring problem and to my knowledge was never resolved.

About six o-clock in the winter mornings a lamplighter came round the streets to turn up the light in the gas lamps. Another man, known as the knocker up, would follow and call out the time as he rapped on people's doors to waken them. Shortly afterwards one heard the sound of mill workers in clogs clattering off to work, the women all wearing the traditional black shawls. They would return for breakfast about an hour and a half later, then go back again to the mill.

Nellie, the eldest daughter of our next door neighbours, left school at the age of thirteen to enter the mill. Her father was a tackler (loom tuner and repairer) and earned good money. Her youngest brother, Corson, was my friend for all the years we lived there. His younger sister Bessie was a good sport, a real 'tomboy' and also my first girl friend at the age of seven. One could read, chalked on the nearby walls, 'BW goes with DH'. I played cricket with her elder brother Alfred, who was very patient and tutored me. We played all the year round, often on the 'rec' (recreation ground), which was a flattened cinder tip. We had no wicket keeper and had to do a lot of running to retrieve an errant ball.

Hilton, an older boy than me, was my carer and a very staunch friend. He was one of thirteen children and often would have gone without a meal had Mother not provided one. When I developed whooping cough, Hilton's mother was not in the slightest concerned that Hilton might catch it, if allowed to come round and play. She said simply, "Let him come round, if he's going to catch it he will." He did come round to play but never got whooping cough. I think many of the deprived children in those days became so hardened to living rough they developed a self immunisation. My parents knew that no harm would come to me with Hilton around. Later, Father got him a job in the dyehouse.

I was always fascinated by the huge steamrollers that were used to flatten the tarmac at the time of road repairing. I called them 'Dun duddle, dun duddle, dun, dun, dun', which to me was the sound they made as the heavy rollers trundled along the road. When I had whooping cough, Mother took me to Holme Chapel, where the road was being repaired. There was a 'Dun duddle' on site and a large device in which tar was made molten and which gave off very strong vapours, allegedly beneficial to sufferers of whooping cough. I was required to lean over this device and inhale the vapours. I received little, if any, benefit.

Hilton Leader Ingfield Terrace with Airdale dog, Bess and myself 1926

Towneley Hall Museum stood in beautiful grounds beyond Holme Chapel in the direction of Burnley. My grandfather, Fred Pilley, took me to this museum and during our visit the keeper showed us into a room not normally open to the public. It was here I saw a large and most comprehensive collection of birds' eggs. As a child I was most enthralled. Neatly catalogued, the selection

Myself and friends at Vale, 1926

and variety was unbelievable. A sight I shall never forget. Will that collection remain? I often wonder.

At the time of the general strike in 1926 we moved again, I have no idea why, to a house in Ingfield Terrace at Vale, down the valley towards Todmorden. Our next door neighbours had two boys, Vincent and Walter, who went to Vale school, to which I was transferred and thoroughly hated. Their father was out of work and to eke out a living, his wife, a charming lady and expert seamstress, carried out dressmaking at home. She made clothes for the family, turned garments, replaced collars and cuffs and stitched impeccably tears in trousers. Cricket was our favourite game, for which she made two splendid pairs of pads.

From the first floor landing of every house, a flight of stairs led to a large attic with a fireplace and dormer window. There was space for two double beds and bedroom furniture. Alternatively, it made an excellent playroom. Surprisingly, each Ingfield Terrace house, like those at Carr Field Villas, had two lavatories, one upstairs in the bathroom and the second in a small room downstairs, unusual in those days.

The family next door but one, like many others, was experiencing hard times. They had two children, a boy and a girl. Their son Arthur was older than the rest of us and although a good cricketer, did not take advantage of his superiority and would declare voluntarily, when it became difficult to bowl him out. We played a lot and benefited from Arthur's experience.

His sister Mildred was a delicate little girl, about my age, and spent a lot of time away from school. I visited her regularly and lent her toys to play with in her downstairs bed, where she rested during the daytime. She loved drawing and sketching but had few materials. I shall always remember the delight on her face, when I took her materials that Mother bought specially. They included a pack of crayons, some pencils, a pencil sharpener, a rubber, ruler and a thick wad of plain paper on which to write and draw. From these she derived endless pleasure during the weeks in bed. On recovery she played outside with the rest of us, enjoyed swinging the cricket bat and was a real tomboy like Bessie Whiteside. Simple pleasures were enjoyed by all children from few possessions.

Further along the track, in the direction of Lydgate, lived another family with whom we were friendly. Their garden, or should I say large plot, sloped towards the railway embankment at a point where the gradient was steep. The locomotives stuttered and shuddered and with a great clanking of buffers, the heavily loaded wagons almost came to a standstill before there was sufficient impetus to move ahead again. Bounty arrived for our friends when the locomotive fireman heaved one or two huge lumps of coal from the engine's tender. Conveniently, the coal rolled down the slope of the embankment to arrive on the householder's plot, sufficient, if used with a little slack, to keep a fire burning for a week.

Unemployed men stood idly on the streets or sat on their doorsteps, some chewing twist, which they would then expectorate on the pavement. A filthy habit, I thought, but from which apparently they derived some solace. It was probably cheaper than Woodbine cigarettes. Twist, resembled liquorice in appearance and was cut by the tobacconist from a small coil.

Every morning housewives swilled down the pavement in front of their house and washed their stone front doorstep. They would then use a donkey stone, whilst the step was wet, to whiten it, or colour it yellow. Woe betide anyone who trod on the step in dirty clogs, or boots, before it was dry. Lines of washing were hung from houses on both sides of the street.

Most families could not afford a holiday and children had few toys. Clifford Hodgson and I were the only two boys in the area with a scooter. These we shared with other boys, who probably had only a bowl and guider, an iron hoop with which they ran and steered using a short metal rod. No child had a bicycle.

Marbles were referred to as tors, a game we played by placing them in a circle. Using your own master marble, the object was to knock, and if successful, keep the opponent's tor. The game was conditional by stating before play, "No gobs, no mucks". I am sure translation is unnecessary. If you were asked to play a game it sounded something like this, "Arl lake thi at tors."

It had been easy to travel by train from Todmorden to Calverley, which I regarded as my second home. Visiting my grandparents, aunts, uncles and cousins was almost like going on holiday. We always spent Christmas at my grandparents' Pilley's house in Thornhill Street. It was there that Santa Claus came. The legend of Santa Claus, as I called him, rather than Father Christmas, was one in which I believed until I was over eight years old. It was wonderful.

From this age onwards I spent a lot of time at 'Hill Côte', where I enjoyed playing cricket with Mollie. We ruined parts of Uncle Harry's front lawn and to enable the grass to recover we graduated to the back. Mollie let me be Yorkshire or England and she would be Lancashire or Australia. We had to get each other out ten times, often twice, to complete a match. She was always kindly disposed to me until her older friend Mary Gray visited when they would lock me in the greenhouse to make me cry, which I never did. How I disliked Mary at that stage, but latterly I felt more kindly towards her. She never married and died in her late eighties after leading a rather sad spinster life. Strange how things work out.

I broke two windows playing cricket. One at 'Hill Côte', the other playing with my younger cousin Mary at her house in upper Thornhill Street. Neither Auntie Maud Calvert, nor Auntie Gladys, suggested that my pocket money of two pence a week should be stopped.

On one occasion my parents stayed at 'Hill Côte' whilst the Calverts were away. The Pilleys, Butlers and Calverts always kept a 'good table' and to conform with tradition my parents opened house for twelve guests for high tea. With everybody seated, it was suggested that the gateleg table required moving slightly. Father, who was sitting at the gateleg end, where all the cups and saucers were arranged, stood up to oblige. He performed the first part of his task satisfactorily, but on sitting down, a hook on his lace-up boot caught the fringe of Auntie Dorothy's beautifully crocheted tablecloth resulting in complete disaster. It created a costly, catastrophic, crockery calamity. It could be called Harold's costly mad tea party. I recall clearly Grandfather Pilley's bald head becoming spattered with tea leaves. Miraculously, he was not scalded and the broken crockery was replaced.

Auntie Maud Calvert took under her wing a charming little elderly spinster lady named Louisa. She worked faithfully for Auntie as cook and housekeeper in exchange for a home with the family. As children, we were never allowed to refer to her by her Christian name. Occasionally, my younger cousin Dorothy did it to annoy her. Dorothy was four years younger than me. She and I never got on well and rarely played together, she was petulant, sulky and terribly spoiled. Our relationship was to undergo a considerable change in later years.

My eldest cousin Eileen married Kenneth, a local kind and friendly young man, a grand fellow liked by everyone and at one time captain of Calverley football team. When the team reached a local final, I believe against Laisterdyke, Eileen, Mollie and I travelled with them to the match. Unfortunately Calverley lost and on the return journey in the bus, I remember one of the Calverley players commenting to the effect that although they had lost the cup, not to mind, there were plenty more at home on the dresser shelf.

Tragically, Kenneth was killed in a motorbike accident leaving Eileen a young widow after a short married life. When I bought a motorbike, soon after this accident, Grandfather Pilley was really angry. I was not allowed to leave the machine anywhere near his house and when visiting, had to park it elsewhere and remove all vestige of my motorbike clothing. This was long after our move to Skipton, which took place in 1927.

I was sorry to leave the Cornholme valley where I had grown up and accepted the squalor and poverty with which I had been surrounded, but to which I had not been directly subjected. It was the way of life for many. For me it had been different. As the son of my father, who transferred to Skipton and became dyehouse manager of a larger company, I was to be sent to Ermysted's Grammar School.

SKIPTON

At the time of the removal, and for a short period afterwards, I stayed with Auntie Maud Calvert's family at 'Hill Côte', near Calverley, about a half mile from the outskirts of the village. 'Hill Côte' was a lovely house, situated in a large garden with open unspoilt country views over the Roundhills. As mentioned earlier I enjoyed playing with my aunt's middle daughter Mollie (Margaret Evelyn), who was nearly three years older than me. She was my role model. In early February Auntie Maud took us both to my new home, an end stone built terrace house towards the bottom

Mother and Father at Hill Côte Calverley Circa 1928

of a steep hill. It had a back yard and small side and front garden, not ideally environmentally located. Newly built post war properties were not available.

The view from the front window was of a row of similar type houses and diagonally opposite, of a large weaving mill, which stretched some fifty yards to the bottom of the cobbled street. At the side, a wide unmade road led uphill, bordering a large sloping area of hen runs. These stretched towards a dirty beck, which flowed behind poorer houses in Newmarket Street, leading towards the centre of the town. Beyond a narrow cobbled back street was the Co-op Stores shop. It had a wide stone front forecourt and outbuildings at the rear.

The house was well proportioned, having large rooms, a bathroom with lavatory and a second lavatory in a small backyard complex. Lighting and heating were by gas. Electricity was never laid on during the time we lived there. I went to bed by candlelight and eerie shadows! There were still cockroaches, but not as many as at Ingfield Terrace and Carr Field Villas.

(Above) School House, Ermysted's Grammar School, Skipton, 1930. Douglas front row fourth from left.

Ted and Harold, sons of the spinning manager at Dewhursts, lived next door but one in Brougham Street. In autumn 1927 they joined me at Ermysted's as did Hughie Pritchard, a near neighbour. Ted and Hughie lost their lives in World War Two as did Ralph Rigby, a member of School House and the son of charming parents who farmed near Slaidburn. Geoffrey Holmes, another boy from Brougham Street, was a close friend and we became closely associated with the two Dorothys, Lancaster and Mawson, often referred to as Lanc and Mawson, or the two Dots. Seventy-five years on, I was interested to learn from ninety years old Ralf Hannam, an ex Ermysted's Grammar School boy living in Iceland, that he remembered my Dot Lancaster as a small, dark haired beauty. Ralph and I had similar recollections of School House, which, not quite a Dotheboys Hall, did not offer haute cuisine. Privacy was at a premium.

Hepworth's and Simpson's outfitters in Skipton were recognised suppliers of compulsory school uniform, including raincoat, white cricket flannels, games' shirts in the school colours, house caps and ties. I was very excited when Mother took me to buy these items and also excited at the prospect of starting at the grammar school.

The school was founded in 1492 by Peter Toller, re-founded in 1548 by William Ermysted and in 1719 Sylvester Petyt became benefactor. It has been described as a school of great antiquity, the endowment of the Foundation being mainly applied towards the reduction of fees, which in 1927 were £9 16s 6d a year including the cost of books. Boarding fees were an additional £63. I was the only new boy to arrive in early Lent term 1927 and became an easy candidate for bullying. This was routine initiation carried out by members of the first year's form and referred to as 'bumping and clumping'. It was unpleasant and sometimes even dangerous. Each boy was armed with a book and would lean against a wall to form an arch, under which I was forced to crawl and be struck by the books, as I made my way through. It was important not to blub, that would have made bullying worse. Worse still, would have been to 'tell', that is to inform a master. Fortunately, I coped well, withstood physical pain and never blubbed. On one occasion a gang from my form chained me to the railings of a pen in the cattle market off the high street, then ran off and left me. A surprised passer-by released me and asked why this happened. I told him it was just because I was the only new boy. He walked away looking more surprised. The new boy novelty soon wore off. I became accepted and settled down unmolested, to a normal, albeit tough school life. Ermysted's did not tolerate the faint hearted.

I was impressed by the cars, many of which were cabriolets, parked regularly in the High Street by the cattle market. There was the Trojan, a vehicle that had solid tyres. Others included the Bull Nose Morris Oxford and Morris Cowley, Model T Ford, Austin, Wolseley, Riley, Clyno, Singer, Buick, Citroen, Renault, Chevrolet, Chrysler, Dèlage, Donnet, Packard and Daimler. Perhaps their owners were professional businessmen, local mill owners or more likely wealthy farmers from the dales.

When I joined the school in 1927 the complement of boys was 280, of whom 30 were boarders. There were three houses, namely, Ermysted for local boys, Petyt for boys travelling from outlying districts and School House for boarders. Subsequently, Toller and Hartley increased the number of houses to five and pupils were rearranged. I retained the yellow badge of Ermysted.

Prayers were held every morning in Big School at 8.55, prior to which the Head Master announced, "Fall out the Roman Catholics." After general prayers they would be recalled to hear announcements.

The concept at Ermysted's was that strenuous physical exercise induced greater capacity for mental study, which required attendance at school on Saturday mornings as well as weekdays. Tuesday and Thursday afternoons, in autumn and Lent terms, were reserved for playing rugby and cross country running. Summer term activities were swimming and cricket. For the latter we had the benefit of an excellent large flat turfed ground called 'The Top', equipped with pavilion. It has been described in a prospectus as a large first-class ground, as fine as any school field in the north of England. Rugby pitches were also laid out on this ground, for use during the autumn and Lent terms. In addition it was used in early spring for the annual competitive house sports. The annual competitive cross-country runs started over rough farmland, where runners had to scale loose stone walls, then continue from the Craven Heifer down the main road and back to school, finishing at 'The Top'.

Games and sporting activities were compulsory unless a boy was physically incapacitated. In this eventuality, a written letter was required from a parent or guardian, requesting permanent leave off. For any short term incapacity, a letter had to be submitted requesting temporary leave off. Under these circumstances boys would normally undertake carefully planned walks accompanied by a master.

Boys were warned that in the event of truancy a heavy punishment would result, possibly expulsion. I am not aware of any such incident during the period I was at school.

I was a participator in all sporting activities, but never a winner. How I longed to win a silver spoon bearing the school crest. It was not to be, whereas my school work progressed favourably to the satisfaction of my parents.

I had one fight at Ermysted's and that was with a good friend and classmate, 'Bidger' Riley, a little chap about my size. I said something that annoyed him before afternoon school. "I'll see you after school in the locker room 'Soapy' (most Hudsons were nicknamed 'Soapy' at that time, after Hudson's Soap)." I thought he was joking, but he meant it and did see me after school in the locker

Father bowler hat and rolled up umbrella and myself, Ilkley Tarn 1928

room. We had a bare knuckle fight that was painful. I had a split lip beforehand, caused by the frost. It refused to heal and 'Bidger' played on this and made it worse. Also, he left me with a bloody nose and I arrived home in a sorry state to incur Mother's wrath. "You tell Riley tomorrow to meet you on the moors on Saturday and fight again. Next time you will win." We were the best of friends next day and his face was a 'right mess' with two black eyes to my one. After the removal of the blood, my face, although sore, did not look too bad. Our appearances did not go unnoticed by the gym master, who told us to see him firstly if anything like this should happen again. I expect he would have discouraged the fight, or made us wear gloves. The same afternoon, Riley came home with me from school. Mother took one look at him, said something to the effect of, "Don't be so silly again and forget about the moors on Saturday." Shortly afterwards Riley suffered a real setback with St. Vitus's dance, which required a lengthy time of recuperation.

During the school holidays I ran wild with the other boys. We roamed the moors and on one hot summer afternoon set fire to a gorse bush. The fire spread rapidly. We really panicked, took off our school jackets to beat the flaming bushes until finally succeeding in extinguishing the flames. The smoke could be seen for miles and we were congratulated on our return to town for putting out the spreading fire. We never let on that we started it.

Ermysted's had its own swimming bath, in which most boys learned to swim during their first year. I taught myself in the town public baths, where we spent a lot of our holiday time. I began with the dog paddle and progressed to the 'Soapy' special crawl. It never enabled me to win a silver spoon, just applause for style. The public baths were not in the town but located off a steep unmade road halfway towards the moors. In consequence they were generally poorly attended, effectively offering to me and my friends the facilities of a private club.

Auntie Hattie, Uncle Arthur's widow from Montreal, came to England during the summer of 1929. She stayed with us at Skipton for a while and with Mother and Auntie Dorothy was allowed to visit Ermysted's. They had permission to watch cricket matches from a

Back row: (l to r) Myself, Father, Cousin Eileen
Front row: Uncle Harry, Mother, Auntie Maud Calvert, Auntie Hattie, cousin Dorothy, cousin Mollie in Hill côte, 1929, note the hats and beads

seat by the pavilion on 'The Top'. Auntie Hattie was a lovely lady and enjoyed going to the local cinema. I asked if they had cinemas in Montreal to which she replied, "Douglas, if ever you visit Canada, I'll show you cinemas!"

As a young boy it was always a treat to be taken to The Majestic cinema in Leeds. I recall it as a large circular building of grandeur, dominating City Square. There were two other cinemas in the city, the Scala and Tower, to which I was taken by Grandfather Pilley to see silent films featuring such greats as Charlie Chaplin, Buster Keaton and Harold Lloyd, brilliant men who wrote, acted in and directed much of their material. Talented live pianists watched the films and played the piano without music, faster or slower as the film progressed.

This would be in the nineteen-twenties before the introduction of talking pictures, referred to as "Talkies". These were popularized by Al Jonson in the 'Singing Fool', which ran for several months. There were few coloured pictures before, during and for quite a time after the Second World War.

Towards the end of summer term 1929, I came home at lunch time with the good news that I had finished second in Form 2A. Father, who also came home for lunch, greeted this with stony silence. His news was not good. He had been given notice of dismissal and replaced by a younger man. I remember Mother saying, "Pray." Our prayers must have been answered. After his first application, Father was appointed dyehouse manager by a firm near Manchester and this involved another move. Not wishing to interrupt my schooling at Ermysted's, my parents arranged for me to be transferred to School House as a boarder.

Skipton schoolhouse Ermysted Boys 1930 - Including Front Row: Myself, Scott, Tyson, Rigby (Killed WW2) Back Row: George Hully (Killed Spanish Civil War), Thwaite, Arnold Blezzard

In early September 1929 they moved to a newly built semi-detached house at Worsley. A week later I returned to school.

On becoming a boarder after nearly three years at Ermysted's as a day boy, to my astonishment, I was treated as a new boy again with the attendant "bumping and clumping". I disliked communal living, there was no privacy and the food generally was poor.

Every Sunday it was compulsory to attend the Skipton Church of England, Parish Church, morning and evening. Junior boarders wore Eton jackets, referred to as bum starvers and we were marched to church crocodile fashion. Girls from the high school were subjected to a similar discipline and marched in crocodile fashion on the opposite pavement. There was much eye contact between boys and girls.

During autumn and Lent terms, it was obligatory for all boarders, unless ill, to be submerged in a cold bath every morning before breakfast. In the summer term we were allowed to use the swimming bath twice daily, before breakfast and the evening meal. It was our privilege to play cricket and sometimes rugby on 'The Top', in free time before meals, and after evening preparation, light permitting.

My class work deteriorated dreadfully and I dropped from second position to nearer twenty-second. In consequence, my parents arranged for me to be transferred to The Manchester Grammar School, where I was required to sit an entrance exam. Fortunately, I passed this exam and was invited to start school at the beginning of the autumn term 1930.

Sadly, my association with Ermysted's finished in unanticipated disappointment at the end of summer term. I said my farewells to many boys with whom I had endured and enjoyed stimulating competition. I recall the last words of 'Old Taylor' the gym master, for whom I had the greatest respect. I was leaving School House carrying a small bag of personal belongings and on my way to the station, when we met at the door. This huge man looked down and said, "Goodbye Soapy, you'll be all right again when you settle down at your new school."

G. L. Taylor, D.P.T. (Physical Training and Swimming) was a huge man, who had served as stoker in the navy during the war. He bellowed at the boys in his stentorian voice, was a strict disciplinarian but always fair. He encouraged boys to stand up for themselves, would not tolerate bullying and punished any swimmer who tried to intimidate a non swimmer in the school swimming bath.

There was a boxing booth at the annual fair, where a fairground heavyweight would challenge any onlooker to three rounds in the ring. He had it all worked out, with only one exception, no challenger won. Most gave in during the first round, but not 'Old Taylor'. He watched this fellow, got him weighed up and made the challenge on the last night to the delight of all the Ermysted's boys who had turned up. I missed the fight, which 'Old Taylor' won easily, knocking his opponent out. Next day he was summoned to 'Tosh' the headmaster and severely reprimanded for behaviour not in keeping with that of an Ermysted's ambassador.

HUDSON, MURRAY-HUDSON AND PILLEY FAMILIES.

I would describe my Grandmother Emily Pilley as a gentle, peaceable, kindly and friendly person, subservient to her husband Fred. He had a reputation for being difficult towards her and a strict parent. To me, his grandchild, he always behaved kindly and generously and showed an encouraging interest in many of my boyhood activities. I looked forward to his visits to Skipton with my Grandmother, when he would take me into town and buy extra parts for my Meccano set. He showed similar favours to my elder cousin, Mollie Calvert, not so apparently, to his children, in particular to the two elder offspring, Maud and Arthur.

He resented Maud's association with Harry Calvert, who was brought up in an orphanage. Nevertheless, she married him, they had three daughters and he bought a beautiful detached house. On one occasion, in an attempt to stop her going out with Harry, Maud was tied to a table leg by her father. A strange anomaly considering her father's marriage had to be arranged in haste, precipitated to preserve parochial proprieties.

His penchant for alcohol was known to cause occasional insobriety and distress to the family. Nevertheless, he was quick to admonish his eldest son Arthur for intemperate late night behaviour. Following a stern warning, the threat to bolt the door on his son was carried out. Arthur was forbidden to return home, left Calverley penniless and worked his passage from Liverpool to Montreal.

In desperation he applied unsuccessfully for many jobs until this incident arose. The owner of a wholesale clothing manufacturing firm threatened to throw him down the stairs for persistency, after telling him repeatedly there was no vacancy. Arthur, with discretion, made his own way down the stairs then turned to face the owner once again. "I'll do anything, sweep the floors, just give me a chance." He was given a chance. About twenty-five years later, as partner in this business and joint managing director, Arthur died unexpectedly in his early forties. He left a Canadian widow, my Auntie Hattie. I have no recollection of him re-visiting England. Grandmother Pilley was heartbroken, his death occurred at Christmas during our stay at Calverley.

His brother Walter served the hard way as an ordinary seaman in the navy and survived the war. Whilst living at home he would often get up early to gather mushrooms and blackberries. He could be selective, as mushrooms grew in profusion on the fields of the Roundhills and the hedgerows would be laden with blackberries in late summer. Auntie Dorothy would cook some mushrooms whole, starters for Grandfather's breakfast, and make a rich creamy soup of others. Grandfather Pilley always drank tea from a thin china pint mug, alleging that a second cup never tasted as good as the first. I would agree.

Walter, his wife Una and other Fenwicks in her family, entered into partnership with a Mr and Mrs Duncan, ironically to form a wholesale clothing manufacturing company in East Street, Leeds. They named the company Stylecraft and had a contract with the Yorkshire County Cricket Club to make and supply blazers and white flannel trousers for the players. As a boy I was thrilled to hear the names of famous players who called for measurements and fittings. One in particular was Herbert Sutcliffe, opening bat for Yorkshire with Percy Holmes.

Sutcliffe also opened for England with Jack Hobbs of Surrey. As a young child I remember incurring Mother's displeasure after noticing an advertisement for Jacobs biscuits on the back of a tram in City Square Leeds. The fact that the tram was on its way to Harehills and Crossgates is incidental. I called out loudly and pointed, "Look Mother, Jack Obbs."

Jack Hobbs presumably was a Wesleyan. When Surrey played Yorkshire at Headingley, he would stay in Calverley with Fred Pilley's brother Seth and attend the Wesleyan Chapel service on Sunday, which was always a cricket rest day. Mollie, who had the good fortune to meet Jack Hobbs, I was not so lucky, described him as a quiet kindly man.

Sunday was observed with much formality by many people. I remember when at 'Hill Côte' being allowed to stay up late one Saturday night and join in the whist playing with my elders. In the middle of a hand, to the surprise of everyone, Uncle Harry threw his cards down on the table face uppermost. When asked why, he pointed to his watch. The time was one minute after midnight, it was Sunday. Card playing was not permitted on the Sabbath.

For several years Fred Pilley and Harry Calvert were members of the Yorkshire County Cricket Club, with entitlements that permitted others in their families to attend matches. It was a great thrill for me to visit Bradford Park Avenue and Headingley to watch my favourite county team.

A private bus service operated in the Calverley area called the Hedna Bus Company, so named, because previously they 'ed na' (had no) buses. The buses would drop off or pick up passengers anywhere if signalled. 'Hill Côte' became a recognised stop. This all changed when West Yorkshire Road Car took over and put the reliable Hedna out of business.

Two independent taxi firms, Kirks and Pounds of Calverley and Greengates, could be relied upon to give a prompt service in impeccably maintained large, silent running and superbly upholstered Daimler cars. These were driven by the dignified owners in livery, or by polite liveried chauffeurs. Drives in these taxis were occasions to be remembered. Both firms were regularly patronaged by the Hudson and Pilley families.

Maud was the only daughter of Fred Pilley to receive education beyond that of the village school. She went on to teacher training college in Darlington.

Phyllis Pilley, who later became my mother, left school at the age of 13 to help domestically and look after the ailing young Ewart. It is tragic that she did not have the benefit of further academic education. She became self taught in good English, extremely well read and conversant with the Bible and the Works of Shakespeare. Her knowledge of the books of famous authors and poets, from which she could quote extensively, was quite exceptional.

Amongst her belongings I traced the following: Words I believe of Winston Churchill, which Mother wrote down when living next door but two to the house in which she was born in THORNHILL STREET, CALVERLEY, Nr. LEEDS.

"A sophistical rhetorician, inebriated with the exuberance of his own verbosity; and gifted with that egotistical imagination which can at all times command an interminable and inconsistent series of arguments with which to glorify himself and to malign his opponents."

Phyllis Pilley
Jan 22/14

Her sister Gladys's husband, Fred Butler, was a talented man who survived the trenches of the war to become a successful businessman with a textiles firm in Bradford. He had a Clyno car, in which he regularly brought his family to Skipton, when he and Father were experimenting with a chemical solution for waterproofing ladies' silk stockings. Although Uncle Fred patented the solution, the sales responses did not justify pursuing the project. Ladies' silk stockings were easy to wash and dried quickly.

Later he exchanged the Clyno for a Singer family saloon, in which he took us to several interesting places in north Yorkshire, including Buckden, to witness the total eclipse of the sun in the summer of 1928. Other places were Bolton Abbey, where we crossed the fast flowing river Wharfe by stepping stones. I was not allowed to jump the 'strid' further up river where it flowed dangerously and rapidly between rocks about a yard apart. I understand that Uncle Walter had jumped the 'strid' in both directions. Lives had been lost in these attempts.

The Clyno and Singer cars were classed as family saloons, each supported on a strong chassis well raised above the ground. The vehicles were equipped with running boards to facilitate entry, on one of which was mounted the huge spare wheel. A four wheel brakes red triangle warning sign was displayed clearly behind each car. Seated on two buffets, my cousin Mary and I travelled in the back facing the rear seat passengers.

Another accomplishment by Uncle Fred was the installation of electric lighting and heating in their terraced house, which had cellar and attic. Shortly afterwards, the Butler family moved to Chorlton-cum-Hardy, Manchester, where Uncle Fred contracted, what was irreverently referred to as galloping consumption, in those days, a killer illness. The majority of males did not reach the age when prostate cancer would be a problem. I believe that heart attacks were regarded as the outcome of old age. Uncle's body literally wasted away and he died in the family's country cottage at Hartwith. Auntie Gladys and my cousins Mary and Kenneth returned to Calverley.

Auntie Dorothy never left home and worked as housekeeper for my Grandfather and Grandmother Pilley. Each day of the week was reserved for specific activities.

Monday, being washday, Auntie would get up at five o'clock, light the cellar fire to heat water for the washtub, in which the clothes were 'peggied' and 'possed' manually. That is to say turned continuously and subjected to pressure. The 'peggy' was a heavy wooden affair with a long thick wooden handle, towards the bottom of which was an attachment with four short wooden legs for turning and twisting the clothes. After washing, the clothes were hung to dry in the back courtyard, or if raining, draped on a line in the cellar.

Tuesday would be reserved for ironing, airing of clothes and other minor household activities.

Wednesday was taken up with sewing, mending and general household duties. A charlady attended to blackleading and outside cleaning and sweeping.

Thursday was for baking, carried out by Grandmother and Auntie. These activities had to be witnessed to be understood. After kneading, the dough would be used for baking white loaves, brown loaves, plain and currant teacakes. These would be left in the hearth to rise before baking in ovens heated by the kitchen coal fire. Buns, cakes, tarts, pies and macaroons would follow. The smell of baking was mouth-watering and persisted.

Friday would be a day of general résumé, often including window cleaning by Auntie Dorothy, a dangerous practice when washing the outside upstairs windows. She would raise the sashes, sit on the outside stone sills facing indoors and with wash-leather in one hand, grasping the window frame with the other, she would proceed.

In the evening, Uncle Walter, who had a good baritone voice, would sing, accompanied on the piano by Auntie Dorothy. A game of whist would generally be in progress where I would often be invited to join in.

Relaxation was the order for Saturday although the usual fried breakfast, hot roast midday dinner and high tea would still be required. Auntie Dorothy spent most of her relaxing time crocheting or tatting, at both of which she was highly accomplished.

The Sabbath morning was reserved for worship at the Wesleyan Chapel. A family gathering often followed the service with the arrival of my three aunts and uncles. The menfolk, impeccably dressed in formal suits, always wore hats, carried or wore gloves and would not be seen without a walking stick to complete the genteel splendour. This was the time when Grandfather extended a little hospitality by offering whisky and cigars to his guests. This was also the time, during my visits to Calverley, when my young cousin Mary Butler and I disappeared to play for an hour before dinner.

Inconceivable that in nineteen-twenties middle class England there was no bathroom, nor flush lavatory in the house. Baths had to be taken in the cellar, where water was heated on a huge fire and then transferred to a zinc bathtub. A midden in the outside back courtyard served as a lavatory and was used for disposing of the contents from bedroom chamber pots. The midden provided so called amenities for the occupants of three houses. Each household had a key to its own small compartment in which a long wooden seat, with a large hole in the middle, was positioned over the midden. As clinical toilet rolls apparently were not available, newspapers cut into small squares were pierced, tied together to be torn off as required and used in lieu. In spite of these shortcomings, the cleanliness of the house and clothing of those who lived there was impeccable and conformed to a standard beyond reproach. It must have been endlessly difficult. As a child I was witness.

In the early nineteen-thirties this disgusting hygiene anomaly was remedied. A bathroom with bath, wash-hand basin and lavatory was built in the corner of a large bedroom over what was known as the entry. The entry led from the street to the back courtyard. It passed a side trap door to the coal place situated off the cellar, where a second lavatory and wash-hand basin had been installed. From a short passage between the kitchen and front living room was a door that opened inwards, revealing a steep and narrow flight of steps to the cellar. It was very dangerous and ridiculously conceived. Grandmother Pilley often asked me, "Just run down to the safe, lad," to take something, or fetch something, from the safe in the food cellar. It was the only place where perishable food could be kept.

Grandfather Pilley was head cashier at Lloyds main bank in Leeds. He was

My uncle Jim (James Weeding Hudson) Chestnut Grove courtyard circa 1920

smart, dressed immaculately and always wore a rose or carnation in the jacket lapel of his hand tailored expensive suits. One of the bank's customer accounts was Ackton Hall colliery, where money had to be taken every Friday for payment of the miners' wages. On one of these occasions Grandfather was invited by the colliery management to visit the coal face and see for himself the appalling conditions under which the miners worked. It made a deep impression on him. I shall never forget his words to me after this visit. "I'll tell you this lad, those miners earn their brass."

Early in the story I referred to the feud between the Hudson and Pilley families.

I visited Calverley with my parents so often I regarded it as my second home, the place in which to grow up. At one time or another, I stayed at the homes of all my relatives, but mostly at Grandmother Pilley's, where Auntie Dorothy lived. She had several opportunities of observing my growing up and commented regularly "You're a proper Hudson. You're getting to look more like the Hudsons every day. You're a real Hudson." Ad infinitum. I wondered, was there a stigma attached to being a Hudson?

'Chestnut Grove' in Calverley was a large stone built Georgian property divided into three dwellings. The back doors opened on to a pleasant, confined, walled, communal courtyard where the Hudsons had a glass hothouse with an established vine. At the front, a large garden was discretely divided for the use of each dwelling and as the name suggests, was enhanced by several chestnut trees. It was here that Auntie Maud Hudson started her own private school, where all my cousins received much of their education.

She was a highly talented academic lady and amongst other basic subjects, personally taught elementary Latin, French and German. Her Christian religion was not hypocritical and she attended regularly Calverley Parish Church. Before World War Two, with her friend Dorothy Cowling, she undertook the long journey of pilgrimage to see the Passion Play at Oberammergau, south west of Munich. She never discussed Wesleyan religion or religion at all, but in later life was very disturbed to learn that I had not been confirmed.

Cousin Mollie completed her full schooling with Auntie Maud, prior to attending business college. I believe the same applied to her elder sister Eileen, until she began work at Smiths crane manufacturers in Rodley. Their youngest sister, my cousin Dorothy and my youngest cousin Kenneth Butler, were schooled there until of grammar school entrance age and graduated to 'Salts' Saltaire Grammar School. Mary Butler completed her schooling with Auntie Maud and went on to business college.

To help Auntie Gladys, on her return to Calverley after the death of her husband, Auntie Maud accepted Mary and Kenneth, without charging fees.

The situations I have just described hardly suggest feud between all members of these families.

It was at 'Chestnut Grove' that I first met my cousin Marjorie from Berkhamsted. She spoke very differently from my Yorkshire cousins and called me, 'Daaglass.' The Calverley people thought her affected. She was not. It was her southern accent and she made no attempt to change it. We got on well together and several years later I attended her wedding in February 1939 at Berkhamsted, where she was married with David Blaxland.

It was here I met her much older brother, my cousin Lieutenant Colonel Gordon Murray Hudson and his wife Joan, née Joan Leslie Baines Conder. Joan was an aristocratic lady, who returned to live in Rhodesia and with whom I corresponded after Gordon's death. They had two sons named John Alan Conder Hudson and Hugh Henry Baines Hudson. I understand both were born in South Africa and I never met either, nor learned why they dropped the Murray from their surname. To digress a little, I should like to pursue a cameo of Gordon, which I consider forms an essential and interesting background to this domestic jigsaw.

After the First World War he adopted an army career as a married officer, rising to the rank of Lieutenant Colonel. He served in South Africa and India until the outbreak of World War Two, supported by Joan in the social capacities expected of officers' wives. He became a man of the Raj and believed in class and social distinction. A survivor of World War Two he never gained promotion and retired as Lieutenant Colonel, but of course was always referred to as Colonel. Ironically, his sister, my cousin with the beautiful maiden names, Marjorie Eileen Frances Murray Hudson voted for Clem Attlee at the first post war general election. Labour won the day!

Upon retirement Gordon took up farming on a large diversified scale in Rhodesia and became owner of an extensive area of land. He relied on native labour for all manual work. When speaking to me on a visit to England, he said, "Never give in to them, never thank, or praise them. It would be regarded as a sign of weakness. We rely on them, but give an inch and they will take a yard." Shortly afterwards the indigenous began making their voices heard. Gordon did not live to see the resultant takeover catastrophe that followed. Later, it became a tragedy for Joan from whom I received sad letters.

During the summer holidays, at a time called 'The Feast', a travelling fair visited Calverley and occupied the field immediately behind Uncle Fred's garden. They used this as a fairground where they pitched their vehicles and caravans. There were never any problems. Auntie Gladys often helped them out with drinking water. It was a great attraction to Mollie, Mary and me, and we became known to the fairground people. We loved the fair, especially the roundabout with cars driven by a magnificent steam engine. It was so colourful, made wonderful hissing sounds and activated gnomish characters. Music for the hit songs of the day, Bye Bye Blackbird, Keep Your Sunny Side Up, Show Me the Way to go Home and Ramona was played by automatic pianola.

About the late nineteen-twenties, Uncle Jim (James Weeding), Auntie Maud and Uncle Kem moved from 'Chestnut Grove' to a large stone built terraced house at the top of Thornhill Street. Auntie Maud continued with her small private school and Uncle Jim remained manager at Holly Park mule spinning mill. He always went to the mill first thing in the morning and returned home for breakfast ninety minutes later. I enjoyed accompanying him when staying at Thornhill Street and was fascinated by the mule spinning machinery. The carriages moved with a rhythmic elegance. Uncle Jim was endowed with an innate managerial capacity for motivation and was highly respected by the workpeople, to whom he extended tolerance and understanding. He knew them all by Christian name and would enquire solicitously of any known workperson's domestic problem.

Every weekday morning after breakfast, before the arrival of the pupils, Uncle Kem helped Auntie Maud to clear the breakfast table in preparation for the school books and requisite materials. All these had to be cleared before lunch and replaced again in time for afternoon school. My Aunt conducted her school activities with commendable expediency and acceptance of responsibility.

Uncle Harry Calvert, who had never driven a car before, bought a Bull Nose Morris Cowley, which he attempted to drive from 'Hill Côte' to Calverley village. He climbed into the vehicle, which suddenly shot up Carr Road out of control, to a nonplussed Uncle Harry. Finally, he managed to stop the car, climbed out and never attempted to drive again. The ultimate fate of the vehicle is unknown.

Auntie Dorothy inherited the property in Thornhill Street, Calverley, after the death of my Grandfather Fred Pilley on 22nd December 1942. In the later years of her occupancy, before moving into a retirement home, she befriended an elderly gentleman, to whom she referred as Mr Rennie, a friendly companion and paying guest for several years. He occupied the back bedroom and often referred to the countryside view across to Horsforth and Rawdon beyond. The spire of the church at Horsforth stood out as a landmark, which I remember back in my early childhood days. This friendly gentleman was uncle of the film star Michael Rennie.

I revisited Calverley in August 2005 and called on the present occupiers. When I explained my past connection with the house they kindly invited me inside to see the changes and improvements, which had taken place to modernise the interior. The view across to Horsforth and Rawdon was unchanged; just as I remembered it.

I also revisited 'Chestnut Grove'. The glass hothouse, which belonged to the Hudson family, had been removed and private garages for the residents had been built in the courtyard. Although some chestnut trees had been taken down in the large front garden and a new house erected, the immediate ambience had not been unduly affected.

MANCHESTER

Before starting at my new school I had six weeks in which to explore surroundings at Worsley and cycle in a traffic free area on the game preserve of the Bridgewater Estate. We called it the gamekeeper's parts and to avoid incurring his displeasure, we acquired a permit from the Eccles Council. Any conception of motorways would be mythical in those days. The environmental aspect was not unfriendly to the eye, more than could be said of the noxious chemical fumes to the nose, from the nearby Trafford Park industrial estate.

Our back garden bordered directly on a field. This stretched to a main line railway embankment, on the other side of which was Barton Airfield, used before the development of Ringway Airport. Beyond Barton Moss was a huge electricity power station, approached after crossing the Manchester Ship Canal by a suspension swing bridge at Patricroft. Traffic delays ensued when a ship passed through. There was little clearance between the larger vessels and the sides of the canal, when evil smelling disturbed water overlapped the towpath.

The Manchester Grammar School (MGS) was founded in 1515 by Hugh Oldham, Bishop of Exeter. At the 1931 Founder's Day service held in Manchester Cathedral, we learned he was motivated by Mancunian boys being pregnant with wit. This service was prior to the opening of the new school buildings at Fallowfield, south of the city, when it was stated, "The owl has opened its wings and flown to a fairer greener place."

Manchester Grammar School, 1931. Last year at Long Millgate Douglas: top of steps second from right. Form Master Mr J.P. Bowden MA.

I joined the school in September 1930 at Long Millgate in the city, before the owl had opened its wings. There would be 1250 to 1300 boys, more than four times the number at Ermysted's, where I knew them all. I found it impersonal and although again I started as the only new boy to the school in my form, there was no bullying. Classes were divided into modern, classical and science with separate maths forms, which would accommodate boys from any of these three

September 1931 First Day of arrival at new school

Manchester Grammar School, 1932, first year at new school Fallowfield. Douglas standing far right. Form Master Mr J.P. Bowden MA.

groups. They were all streamed. The modern group was streamed from A to E and I was in the third year B stream, which I found quite difficult. Those in the A stream were relative geniuses. The system provided for taking the matric exam in the fourth year, not the fifth year as was the case at Skipton and at most other grammar schools. Before morning prayers in the main assembly hall, the High Master would instruct all Roman Catholics and Jews to fall out.

John Clayton befriended me in what was the beginning of his third year at MGS. Previously, with Pete Brothers (later to become Air Commodore Peter M. Brothers CBE DSO DFC & Bar, ace Battle of Britain pilot), he attended North Manchester, the preparatory school for the main grammar school. Pete stayed at the preparatory school until joining the RAF.

The city was grimy. Statistics are available of the unbelievable weight of soot per square mile deposited over Greater Manchester in early pre-war years. Buildings were indescribably blackened and often eroded. The Grammar School in Long Millgate, the Cathedral off the city centre and the Town Hall in Albert Square were no exceptions. The sky in winter was black and the River Irwell flowed inky black, before, under and beyond Blackfriars Bridge, near Exchange and Victoria Stations. Winter smogs had to be experienced to be understood. Only the trams could run under extreme conditions. Motorists had been known to follow trams and finish up at the depot.

In spring 1931 John Clayton and I bought a small tent called the Guinea Tent, so named because that is what it cost - twenty-one shillings in old money. At the age of fifteen, during half-term in May, we set off for a ten days' cycling holiday. Financed with thirty shillings each, equipped with this tent, eiderdowns and groundsheets (in lieu of sleeping bags), rucksacks, two simple cooking stoves and a kettle, we were self sufficient. After leaving home I had no means of communicating with my parents. They were not on the telephone. The weather was horrible and serious flooding took place in the Doncaster and outlying areas. Soaked to the skin, we enjoyed it. We became responsible and independent.

Finally however, we were grateful for the help of a friendly farmer and his wife at Belper. We were allowed to live and sleep in their hay barn for a couple of days and nights, whilst they dried our tent and camping materials and clothing. They supplied bacon, eggs, milk,

Myself, ready on bicycle for camping holiday

butter and home baked bread without charging and permitted us to use our primitive little stoves in the barn. Sleeping in the hay was an experience, comfortable, extremely hot and itchy. We suffered no ill after-effects.

During the summer of 1931 we often visited the High Street swimming baths, which involved a tram journey to the Rusholme area of south Manchester. There were first class and second class large baths, housed in magnificent buildings. Prices of admission were four pence and two pence respectively. The buildings became listed. Seventy years later, under a scheme, from which they were awarded top priority, sums of money were granted for restoration. This was completed about the year 2003.

Later in 1931, John and I were privileged to join the Manchester Swimming Club situated in the Blackfriars area near Victoria Station. This was an exclusive club, patronised mainly by business men. To become members we had to be proposed and seconded. I believe it was John's uncle who proposed us and being Manchester Grammar School boys was sufficient to qualify for seconding. It was on the evening of a special swimming event that our Mothers, being invited as visitors, met and remained friendly until my Mother's death in November 1945. John's Mother, whose name was Alice, died just before her hundredth birthday.

Joan, 1933

Autumn term marked the start of studying for matric, which exam I sat in the following June. John Clayton was successful, I gained only School Certificate. I remember the words of his Aunt Gertrude when she gave us each two shillings holiday money. "Sorry about your matric. We can't all be clever, but enjoy your holiday."

It was my parents' intention to send me back to school for another year to try again. In August, father suffered a big reduction in salary and in consequence, it was decided I should leave school and seek a job. My grammar school days were over and in September 1932 I started applying for jobs advertised in the Manchester Guardian under the section Boys, Youths and Apprentices. I had no success during the next four months and in January 1933 I was still writing applications. In mid January I obtained a poorly paid job through an agency and immediately after acceptance received the offer of a better paid job as a result of my last written application. Typical 'Murphy's' Law!

During my last year at school I became friendly with Joan, a girl a year older than me, who attended Eccles Grammar School and lived next door but one. Her parents were strict and our families were friendly. We exchanged visits and regularly went to shows together at the Manchester Opera House. Joan's father had a responsible job at Barton Power Station. In consequence John and I were privileged to be shown round the station, when he explained the system and workings of the huge turbines. Joan left home to commence training as a nurse at Preston Royal Infirmary. Our relationship, mostly platonic, continued but was not really satisfactory for either of us. Courageously it was she who wisely wrote to break it off, whereby we both gained freedom and independence. We never saw each other again.

From now until the outbreak of war I lived at home with my parents. John Clayton and I remained friends and spent many cycling holidays and weekends together, travelling long distances to Wales and the Lake District the hard way, before graduating -*to the use of motorbikes in 1936. We both enjoyed female companionship and often took our girl friends, as pillion passengers, for weekend breaks and extended breaks at Bank Holiday periods.

I started work with a home trade company of textiles' merchant converters, a section of a larger company of textiles exporters. As I recall there were four directors, one of whom was French, two, father and son were German Jews and one Englishman, a Sir, whose name carried the initials W E T. He was known as the "Wet Knight."

Situated at the lower end of Princess Street, the firm occupied a large building with a deep basement for loading and packing. There were five floors above street level with offices and considerable warehouse accommodation for cotton and some artificial silk piece goods. Young people were not allowed to use the passenger lift operated by a semi disabled ex-serviceman, who would close the lift gates in my face with only three older staff members on board, if I tried to get in. If the German senior director arrived when the lift was about to ascend, any member of staff on board would get out hurriedly to give him sole occupancy to the first floor.

The Manchester Grammar School background helped me get this job but afterwards, initially, was not a passport to privilege. Most of my associates came from the poorer districts of Hulme and Ardwick and had no benefit of secondary education. I was ridiculed, sent for a long stand and left kicking my heels. When I asked what was a dhoti and nainsook, it was commented by my senior that I did not understand English, only spoke French and German. However, like school bullying, the novelty of ridicule soon wore off.

I never understood why my senior, who was a quiet unassuming man, resorted to occasional sarcasm. When he left to take up a better job, he was not replaced and I automatically took over for no financial reward, but I continued to gain experience. I worked from what had been his desk in the centre of a large pattern room where travellers' samples were prepared. Steve, a new rather supercilious man with some academic education, arrived. He was very tall, probably two or three years older than me and had a habit of flicking my ears when he passed behind my desk.

The day had come, to my surprise, and to the surprise of those who worked around me, which was to boost my status for the remainder of my short tenure. Steve approached my chair from behind and stopped. I, in anticipatory apprehension, put down my pen and placed my hands over both ears. "Oh, so we have got him worried. He doesn't know whether he's going to have his ears flicked, or not." He boomed to the men in the pattern room. It was his undoing. I got out of my chair quickly and with both fists clenched until my boney knuckles stood out, threw myself at this tall man and hit him hard with both fists, one to the jaw and the other in his face. In astonishment and pain he staggered backwards, lost his balance and fell into a large fent box, the top of which was about twelve inches below a solid wooden counter. It protruded a similar distance in front of the counter. In falling, he struck the back of his neck and head against the edge of the counter, was badly hurt and could not get out of the box. He pleaded to be helped and it took two men to lever him out. In some apprehension I stood at the ready with both fists clenched again, awaiting the reprisal which never came. He never flicked my ears again. With the passing of time we became good friends. This was the last occasion in which I became involved in a physical fight, although about three years later, a very serious situation in a tailor's shop was only just averted.

The spin off from The Manchester Grammar School had arrived. I was asked by two young men to word job applications for them or check their spelling and often asked how you tell the time in French, or say this or that. They would repeat the words phonetically, but hadn't a clue how to spell them. At lunch time we played cricket in a passage between the stillages in the huge warehouse using a soft tennis ball and a bolt of cloth for wicket. I worked overtime with them preparing samples for the travellers. (One week I earned sixteen shillings overtime, one and a half times my normal weekly take-home pay). To a man they supported Manchester City. They came from the poorer area of the city of Manchester. Old Trafford was a world away. They could walk to Maine Road.

In May 1934, just before my eighteenth birthday, I applied for another job with a firm that exported cheap cotton textiles in bulk to India, Ceylon and Burma. I got the job straight away at thirty shillings a week, a small fortune in those days. It was sadness and farewell handshakes all round when I left my first firm. Those young men

Myself in Delamere Forest, Cheshire circa 1934 cycling

with whom I had worked knew and lived in deprivation. What a difference sixteen months had made to our association. My wage with the second firm was increased to £2 per week when the buyer left and I was given his job. The firm closed a few months later and I got another job straight away at the same wage.

In October 1934, Mother went into a nursing home to undergo a serious operation for the removal of a cancer growth in her neck. I learned many years later it was then discovered there was inoperable cancer in other parts of her body. However at the time she required nursing attention at home for several weeks. After the arrival of 'Little Nurse' as Mother called her, I at the age of eighteen, experienced my first real romance with an experienced and lovely twenty-two years old woman. Life at home in the late evenings, after I returned from night school and at the weekends, was just beginning. I lived in a dream. On one occasion, after I had been a little over zealous in my attentions, I apologised. She told me not to worry, that I did not know how some doctors could behave!

'Little Nurse' Betty never neglected her responsibilities and when Mother's dressings had been completed, nurse and I were left alone. After she went away I never saw nor heard from her again. I knew her home in Egremont, Cumbria, but made no attempt to communicate. It would have deepened the hurt. At that age, time heals quickly. My other girl friends had not deserted me and my first motorbike had yet to arrive!

My work with the third firm was educational and fascinating. I assisted the warehouseman and physically handled (it was called humping) a variety of fabrics in heavy rolls, for export to South America. I left after twelve months and as Father had lost his job to a younger man, which was quite customary in those competitive days, we travelled together in his car, he as an agent selling soaps and chemicals to mills, I selling three brands of Pekoe tea from Ceylon to cafés and shops. These ventures did not work out, so I applied for another textiles exporting job in Manchester, which again I got straight away.

My Mother and myself, Worsley 1935

Father remained out of work for two and a half years. During this period he benefited from a legacy left by his aunt and earnings from part time evening lecturing at the Manchester College of Technology. After lectures he voluntarily stayed behind to answer students' questions. The English students always departed, only the Japanese and South Americans would stay to have their questions answered. This continued to the end of the last term prior to the outbreak of war.

I met Steve in September, when I enrolled at the Manchester College of Technology to embark on a three years' course - combined with the Manchester High School of Commerce - for a B Com. degree. Steve was in his third year and handed me reams of paper. He told me I should need these for taking down notes. He was right. After two years of extensive work, four nights a week and not arriving home until ten o'clock, I abandoned the course. It was extremely diverse and time consuming. Taking into consideration the depressed state of the textile trade, I believed that the course was insufficiently rewarding and less beneficial than the practical experience I gained at work. I was not a counting house man, nor particularly interested in drawing up trial company balance sheets and carrying out company audits.

The smaller exporting firms of cotton textiles rented offices and warehouse accommodation, for temporary storage of piece goods, in huge buildings owned by Lloyds Packing Warehouses. Lloyds provided packing facilities in their warehouses' basements, where the piece goods were cased and the cases banded, prior to being taken to the Manchester docks, generally on horse-drawn carts. The huge carthorses, with sparks flying from their hooves, struggled over the slippery cobbled setts and tramlines. Lloyds would raise the necessary bills of lading and payment was secured on sixty or ninety days drafts.

I was offered a new opportunity to return to my third firm, whose Managing Director, an Old Mancunian, had opened two tailors' shops in the city and a clothing manufacturing unit off Piccadilly managed by another Old Mancunian. It was my duty at the age of twenty, to supervise the running of these establishments and in particular exercise control over the financial side and cash flow. I was able to have four suits tailored from first class fine worsted materials, three for myself and one for Father at a cost of £3 per suit. Suits from these Keith and Henderson and Minty bunches would cost eight guineas, possibly more, from an outside quality tailor. I was able to buy top quality shirting poplins at manufacturers' prices for making up by Faulkner Shirt Company and enjoyed the added bonus of an association with their attractive young lady receptionist.

I now refer specifically to the tailor's establishment in Portland Street. The tailor and cutter, whose name I shall withhold, was most proficient at his job but an unpleasant person. One day, whilst checking the cash flow, I discovered overdue payments by clients, some of whom were friendly with him. Diplomatically, I drew his attention to this and was told immediately to f... off or be thrown out. Whereupon, as I refused to leave, he walked towards me brandishing a large open pair of shears and stated threateningly that he had used these before and would not hesitate to use them again. His brother-in-law, a pleasant man who worked in the shop, and a staunch Manchester City supporter, intervened, told him not to be a fool and prevented what could have been a serious assault. Later, I left the shop and never returned. Not surprisingly, it was closed down shortly afterwards.

In October 1937 I left the parent company, and through my friendly relationship with the townsman of a finishing firm, was introduced to Jaffés. This was a large, highly reputable firm of textiles exporters, with worldwide business connections. They appointed me immediately and I worked in their Scandinavian grey goods' department, as assistant to the buyer, until 1st September 1939, two days before the outbreak of World War Two.

Also in October 1937 we moved to a new semi-detached house at Kersal, overlooking the Manchester Rugby Football Club ground.

Shortly afterwards, Father got a full-time job at a nearby dyehouse, where he worked until my parents moved to Nelson whilst I was in North Africa.

I heard from John Clayton of Pete Brothers' experience in the RAF and sent away for pilots' short service commission application forms, to discover that junior officers may not be able to live on their pay! My cousin Gordon confirmed that it would be difficult without Father's support. It would have been pointless to proceed, so later, in June 1939, I joined the Manchester Royal Air Force Volunteer Reserve (RAFVR) as an air observer, subsequently to be known as navigator. I received some pay, which combined with the Jaffés' salary, enabled me to pay off the balance outstanding on my BSA motorbike. The only occasion I bought on hire purchase.

For about two years I had been seriously attracted to Hildred. She was a lovely girl and everybody except me, knew my feelings towards her were not reciprocated. In the longer term, this relationship would become hurtful. Hildred very wisely arranged the break-up before Christmas 1938. My other girl friends, who had seen the break-up coming, were very considerate. It was lovely to have friends. Thank you 'Fiery' Ann, Marian and Vera.

Ann was a real redhead. Well educated, she studied medicine and was charmingly philosophical and amorous. The moments we enjoyed together were infrequent and rather special. She lived with her Mother, who was housekeeper to an Indian Doctor and they occupied a large house, which included the surgery in Radcliffe, on the outskirts of Bury.

Harold and Ted Hole 1937 (Ted right as viewed) killed in Far East WW2

Marian's sister was Dorothy, John's girlfriend. She was petite, vivacious and amorous and often made up our motor-biking foursome.

My relationship with Vera was fun yet almost platonic. She was an accomplished ballroom dancer, an excellent partner at the Old Mancunians' dances and knocked spots off me at tennis.

Marian and Dorothy's mother was an experienced midwife. A kindly, sophisticated, buxom lady, she kept open house and often at weekends would cater for a mixed gathering of ten of us, or more. This was when the girl friends would get together. Everybody mixed and changed partners. On one such occasion an Indian girl, from a high social class, or perhaps caste, a niece of the Indian Doctor, joined the gathering. It was my good fortune to become her partner in some ridiculous game, when couples disappeared all over the house to hide with all the lights turned out. We chose the bed in a large bedroom and locked the door. This lovely Indian girl wore a beautiful and voluminous sari. The unveiling ceremony was pure tactile delight. It was wonderful to be young. The experience was worth its weight in rupees. Regrettably, later on, we had to join the others at tea. Nobody minded.

In February 1938 I bought my second motorbike a brand new 350 c.c.s overhead valve BSA. My popularity with the girls was assured. John acquired a brand new Triumph and the last holiday we had together was another tour of the Scottish Highlands, mostly in pouring rain during early August. My last motor-biking holiday was to the West Country, in glorious weather, with Mother as pillion passenger, in mid August 1939.

Ironically, Hildred was the only girl who wrote to me when I became a prisoner of war, other than my cousin Dorothy, with whom I had a serious relationship for two years leading up to the war. At this time, Cayo Torrealba, the nephew of Jaffés' agent Tejada Hermanos of Buenos Aires, was my protégé. He was a well educated, handsome young man with impeccable manners, a great attraction to the girls and had rapidly learned to speak English, primarily under my tutelage. (To gild the lily and ensure his fluency, he learned swear words from the warehousemen). He always

Hildred 1936

56

Vera 1937

called me Jaime Sabonoso, pronounced Hyeemay Habonoso, Spanish for Soapy James.

When he learned of my distress over the Hildred affair, he suggested we go out together and seek new pebbles. To do this we booked two front row centre seats in the dress circle of a Manchester theatre. The balcony, from which we had an excellent view of the chorus girls, virtually looked down on the front of the stage. Cayo caught the eye of two high stepping girls in the chorus front line and signed we would go back stage at the end of the show. We went to the stage door and were let in by the porter to await the arrival of the girls. On close quarters they did not appear quite as attractive as on stage and their first demand was a late supper at one of the expensive hotels, preferably The Midland. Neither Cayo, nor I thought this a very good idea and managed to get out of it.

On the outbreak of war Jaffés sent him back to the Argentine with utmost despatch. I never saw, nor heard from him again.

Other than Hildred and my cousin Dorothy, I never saw, nor heard from any of my pre-war girlfriends again.

This photo of four generations was taken in 1941 the year before Grandfather Pilley died. He is pictured with my cousin Mollie's eldest one year old son Andrew, now aged sixty six, on his knee. Mollie now in her ninety fourth year is standing behind with her Mother, my Auntie Maud Calvert now deceased. It was she who Grandfather tied to the table leg to prevent her consorting with Harry, the man she subsequently married.

OF FOOTBALL AND OTHER THINGS…

THE HOME OF LEEDS UNITED

When I was a young schoolboy, my grandfather took me to my first professional football match at Elland Road to watch Leeds United and Everton. Dixie Dean played for Everton and I remember a wonderful goal he scored for the away team. He received the ball deep in the Everton half, retained possession and then cleverly outwitted the Leeds defenders to beat the goalkeeper.

What impressed me most was the ease with which the players headed the heavy leather ball throughout the match, which Leeds won. I recall words spoken by a Leeds supporter to a friend, as he prepared to leave his seat in the stand. They sounded rather like these – "Ah well, tha'll be able to go 'ome an ate thi tay." Leeds must have won!

PARTLY CONCERNING MANCHESTER CITY IN EARLIER DAYS AT MAINE ROAD

In 1930, shortly after my parents moved from Skipton to Manchester, I began to follow the fortunes and misfortunes of Manchester City. Four years later they won the F. A. Cup against Portsmouth at Wembley.

The following year Father bought a Riley 9 Monaco Saloon car equipped with an open gate four speed non synchromesh gearbox. Gear changing in this vehicle was difficult for the experienced driver. For the novice it was almost impossible! Although I had no previous driving experience, I applied for a test straight away, under the belief that it could take several weeks to arrange. Several weeks turned out to be eleven days. Incredibly I passed first time, which was a terrific boost to my morale, as in those days very few young men of my age had the opportunity of learning to drive.

Occasionally, I was allowed to use the car to take Mother to Maine Road, where there was little difficulty in finding a place in the official car park by the ground. City became Division One League Champions in 1937, only to be relegated at the end of the following season. To compound my disappointment Father had sold the car.

Then I bought a motorbike, a second-hand two-stroke 225 c.c s

Royal Enfield, and with my Old Mancunian friend John Clayton ventured on a Scottish Highlands' touring holiday. John owned a second-hand 150 c.c.s. Francis Barnett two-stroke, on which he relied to make the journey. Both machines could be identified from great distances by the staccato, crisp machine-gun like noise, from their exhausts. Although we became separated occasionally, on those narrow winding Highland roads, we could never lose each other. Our friends told us, before we set off on this holiday, that we must be crazy to rely on two small ageing two-strokes to complete such a journey. The two-strokes won through, although the Francis Barnett did require a little coaxing on one occasion. This is no reflection on the maker of the machine. In today's terms it could be said it was past its sell by date.

The storm clouds of war were gathering over Europe in 1938, the year I exchanged my reliable little two-stroke 225 c.c.s Royal Enfield motorbike and became the proud possessor of a new 350 c.c.s. overhead valve BSA. (There is an incredibly ironical story concerning this motorbike, which I mention later in the book). Before its arrival I enjoyed the companionship of many young girl friends. Now it was as though I had carte blanche to an extended young female society. The attraction was the new motorbike of course, not my blond wavy hair!

The journey to the Lake District from my home in north Manchester, was relatively quick by motorbike. One of our favourite haunts was Torver near Coniston, close to the lake at the foot of Coniston Old Man. John and I would travel there regularly and could rely on very reasonably priced good food and accommodation at the local pub. The small field at the back of the pub was a useful place to teach young ladies the art of handling a motorbike, as can be seen from the photograph. It added a little extra interest to the weekend activities.

In August 1938 we spent our last holiday together in Scotland before the war. We stayed in a farmhouse at Spean Bridge near Fort William, close to Loch Lochy and overlooking the northern face of Ben Nevis. The approach to our destination, after a long day's travel, was on a warm dry evening with a magnificent sunset. We had an exhilarating motorbike ride over Rannoch Moor, down Glen Coe - The Vale of Weeping - and on to Ballachulish ferry. It was the only consistent dry spell of weather we encountered during the week's holiday!

BSA motorbike and girlfriend
Hildred at Torver

Royal Enfield

Most of the Highlands' roads were well surfaced, although winding, narrow and with enumerable passing places. We discovered one exception, the road to Mallaig from Fort William. In sympathy to our backsides and our machines, we had to *John Clayton on a Triumph* abandon this journey near Lochailort, with justification, as you will see from the photograph.

Mother was a frail lady, suffering from terminal cancer, of which she was unaware, when I took her, as pillion passenger, to watch Manchester City play Blackburn Rovers at Ewood Park in 1938. Both teams, surprisingly, were in the Second Division. It was the first time I had been to Ewood Park, but would not be the last. I had not seen Blackburn play in blue and white before, they always played in red jerseys when visiting Maine Road, which I believed was their normal strip. In those days supporters had far less information about other clubs and there were not the facilities for easy travel to away matches, which for most people was far too costly.

For some followers, particularly the unemployed, it was too costly to attend home matches. On one occasion at Maine Road, I was about to go through the turnstiles on the popular side, when seven shabbily dressed young men tried to enter the ground over the wall to the cheers of the crowds entering in the accepted manner. Their attempts to assist each other over the top, in spite of the broken glass which was firmly embedded in cement, were successful. Six of them managed. I got the impression that neither officials, nor the police, were in a hurry to intervene. It was not unusual, for unemployed supporters to crawl between one's legs at the turnstiles as they revolved, enter the ground that way, and avoid paying. I witnessed it on several occasions.

Road to Mallaig

I took Mother regularly to the City home matches. We had to travel early, normally by tram from Piccadilly in Manchester, direct to the ground, to ensure she got a seat on the stand. The tough football supporters showed great consideration and would help her get on, or off, the always moving trams going to, or returning from the ground. "Cum on, luv," they'd shout and give her a helping push. Travelling by tram was quick, uninterrupted, cheap, efficient and environmentally friendly.

Far from environmentally friendly was the industrial and domestic smoke, responsible for gross air pollution. The consequences of this were irretrievable impairment to health, and less consequentially, blackened buildings that suffered considerable erosion, and in many cases became dangerously damaged. Modern day weather forecasters give warnings of poor visibility when this is reduced to one hundred or two-hundred yards. In some of the pre-war Manchester smogs, I experienced extreme conditions, when visibility had been reduced to between one to two yards only. Younger readers may find this difficult to comprehend. It was so.

The greater part of the Manchester City football ground constituted uncovered, gradual sloping terraces. At one end of the main stand was a small enclosed section reserved for boys, youths and ladies, the first line of defence for their shell like ears, from the improper adult male language! On the days of extra large attendances, typical 70,000 and more, it was customary to roll the boys over the heads of the crowd and allow them to sit along the touch line. I recall the day when the England and Manchester City outside left, Eric Brook, scored the only goal in a cup match, directly from a corner kick, before a record crowd of around 84,000 at Maine Road.

A team sheet about that time, star studded with English and Scottish Internationals would have included the likes of:-

Frank Swift, goalkeeper, later to lose his life in the Munich air disaster, when travelling as a newspaper reporter with the Manchester United team. Barkas and Dale, full-backs. Matt Busby, seriously injured in the Munich disaster, later to become a Director of Manchester United and subsequently knighted for his services to football. Cowan, Bray, Toseland, Alec Herd, father of Manchester United's David Herd, Tilson, Marshall, and Brook.

Prior to every match, the gathering crowds were entertained by a military band. Often it would be the Beswick Prize Band, playing stirring military music. The instrumentalists marched around the pitch, preceded by their imposing and immaculate drum major, deftly twirling his mace. Skilful timing ensured that the band returned to its starting position, in front of the main stand, a few minutes before the teams were scheduled to appear. Over the entire ground an anticipatory hush ensued, to be followed by rising applause as the players emerged from the tunnel.

The last time Mother and I watched a match together at Maine Road was on Saturday 2nd September 1939. I had just returned briefly, from the RAFVR centre in Manchester, having been called up for service the previous evening.

War was declared the following morning.

It was inconceivable that I should live to celebrate my ninetieth birthday nearly sixty-seven years later. On 21st May 2006, looking back down the years, I marvelled how I had reached this milestone and intended to pass the day in quiet philosophy. My family thought otherwise and surreptitiously organised a party gathering of friendly neighbours.

I never learned the lesson and still follow the fortunes and misfortunes of Manchester City. In evidence, the wonderful ninetieth birthday cake is supportive.

Douglas walking down Oxford Street, Manchester in 1939…what lies ahead?

A Navigator's Story refers to my experiences with 101 Squadron and in more depth with 100 Squadron during the 1939/45 war when I served with both. My service period between the Squadrons was interspersed by two and a quarter years' captivity in North African prisoner-of-war camps. What follows is mainly a résumé of these combined experiences. It describes my association with wartime servicemen, the courage of whom was outstanding and set an exemplary standard for posterity. It was an honour and a privilege to serve with them. May the sacrifices of those who gave their lives for their country, or others who were subjected to extreme physical and mental sufferings yet survived, not have been in vain.

In the year 2001, my granddaughter, whilst at university read a draft of the Memoirs and afterwards made no attempt to disguise her emotional reactions. They opened the floodgates of reality to events she had learned through reading the history books. Not until she had read the Memoirs did she become fully aware of their impact.

The following chapter is a tribute to my wife Alice, who died unexpectedly on 30th May 2004 after nearly sixty years of our marriage. It describes her background and family history.

Alice was courteous, unassuming, deeply intelligent, of profound learning, yet never pretentious. Her radiant, natural smile was of aesthetic beauty. It was her hallmark to be remembered always.

She was a little lady with great strength of character. She had a deep Christian faith, which gave her a commendable understanding and tolerance to combat problems. Her greatest contribution to life was the impeccable manner in which she brought up, and with much wisdom, assured the good education and welfare of our two daughters, who are her priceless legacy.

The stories that follow present a saga, born and nurtured from the womb of enigmatic philosophy. A saga of palatable and unpalatable truths, they create a mélange of messages, from which all may reflect and draw their own conclusions.

THE ORMEROD FAMILY
and
BLACKBURN

The town derived its name from the burn Blake, on the banks of which a few dwellings stood many hundreds of years ago. At the turn of the century the population exceeded 100,000, composed mostly of cotton mill workers living in crowded back streets near their respective mills. Blackburn lay in a densely populated bowl. The better quality properties were built on the West End hillside, leading towards Preston New Road, Revidge then on to Mellor. This could be described as the gateway to the most spectacular countryside North East and North West. It led to such areas as Longridge

Isaac Ormerod (Circa 1905)

Fell, the Lake District, Forest of Bowland and Yorkshire Dales National Park and continued further north to the Scottish border.

Forebears of Thomas Ormerod, father of Isaac, (Alice's Grandfather) included one who was knighted for work he carried out on Greenwich Observatory. Thomas was foreman stonemason on the building of Blackburn Town Hall Library, and was noted for carved illustrations of the trade and industry of the town.

The father of Elizabeth Haydock, wife of Isaac Ormerod, owned a traction engine in the days when a person was required to walk in front waving a red flag. His sister married Richard Slater and they emigrated to the USA. After staking a claim on a plot of land, of which they were robbed, they trekked by covered wagon through South and North Dakota to Gladman, Saskatchewan, where Richard opened his own coal mine. His son married a Red Indian girl and brought her to Blackburn. It created quite a stir and no little interest in the town, when she arrived, dressed in full Red Indian costume!

Isobel Duckworth, a forebear of Elizabeth wife of Gilbert Ormerod (Alice's father), was educated at a convent in France and married Joseph Francis Miller, Director of Education for Brighton and Hove. His brother was a Cardinal at the Vatican.

Isaac Ormerod was a prominent figure in Blackburn and with other businessmen was involved at the time of the founding of Blackburn Rovers Football Club, in which he became a shareholder. This was before the club played its first League game in September 1888, after being invited to become a member of the newly formed Football League. The club moved in 1890 to what is still its present site at Ewood Park.

Isaac married Elizabeth, daughter of John and Elizabeth Duckworth, whose marriage had been arranged by special dispensation from the Pope, the Duckworths being a wealthy and influential catholic family.

He was a shrewd business man, the founder and Chairman of Directors of Cotton Brothers Co. Ltd. at Appleby Street Mill and later at Pump Street Mill in Blackburn. The responsibilities of running the mill were later assigned to his son Gilbert.

The St. John Ambulance Brigade in Blackburn owed much to the energetic leadership of Gilbert, who joined in 1908 and passed through the various NCO ranks in seven years to become officer in charge. On the outbreak of World War One he was one of the first men in uniform to leave Blackburn and qualified for duty to organise the running of a Field Military Hospital at Netley in Hampshire. Here, they received and tended wounded soldiers from the battlefields of France. Unfit for active service, Gilbert returned to Blackburn in 1915. Throughout the remainder of the war he assisted in training three hundred men for service with the medical units of the Army and Navy.

In recognition of valuable services rendered to the Order of St. John, he was appointed Honorary Serving Brother in 1920 and received the long-service medal in 1922. In 1924, he was commanded by the King to be present at a garden party at Buckingham Palace.

He went on to become a prominent Freemason, a member of United Brethren Lodge and the Knights Templar. He continued to carry out his mill duties with expertise as Chairman of Directors, until his untimely death in 1936 at the age of fifty-three. Gilbert's relationship and understanding with his loyal workers was beyond

Gilbert & Elizabeth Ormerod 1924 in Corporation Park Blackburn

Gilbert Ormerod in St John's uniform

reproach and earned their highest respect. He was a man of great magnanimity, who made personal financial sacrifices in times of depression to ensure the mill did not face closure.

The relationship with his Leicester friend Thomas Cook, the travel agent, enabled him to hire a coach every year and finance a brief holiday in Holland for his workers, quite an unprecedented gesture in those days. (Thomas Cook's Leicester home is now the Leicestershire and Rutland Branch Headquarters of the British Red Cross).

Gilbert's proposal of marriage to Elizabeth Duckworth, whose family was strong Roman Catholic, presented problems. He was a Congregationalist and to enable the marriage to take place, Elizabeth renounced her catholic commitments. Their three daughters, Elizabeth, Evalyn and Alice, were encouraged to attend the local Church of England church. This was the nearby St. Silas Church on Preston New Road, Blackburn, where subsequently all three daughters were married.

Elizabeth was a devout and gentle lady, who outlived her husband by sixteen years. He never enjoyed robust health and uncomplainingly, she nursed him for several years before his death.

She was a loving mother, wholeheartedly devoted to the interests and education of her three daughters, on whom she lavished love and kindness, but not to the exclusion of correction and discipline, when required.

Before joining Blackburn High School, Alice the youngest, like her sisters, was sent to Cross Hill kindergarten at an early age. One day, she came home in great distress. "It's mi shoes," she kept saying. Her mother examined the footwear and could find nothing wrong. "No, no, it's mi shoes, it's mi shoes." This bewildered her. Alice would not normally pronounce my as 'mi'. Finally the problem was resolved. A new teacher had been appointed in the kindergarten, a Miss Hughes, who had been cross!

A pall of industrial smoke hung heavily over the Lancashire cotton mill towns during at least fifty working weeks of the year. For one week the mills closed for the annual wakes (holiday). The boilers were shut down for cleaning and de-scaling, the smoke pall disappeared and Lancashire folk, who were not on holiday, could breathe fresh air. During this one week, Gilbert obtained some relief from his chronic asthma. The only other place locally, where he could breathe more easily was on Pendle Hill. He was unable to climb on his own, so his daughters helped him with the aid of a rope.

Just over nineteen hundred feet in height, Pendle Hill dominates the countryside around for several miles. It lies to the North West of Nelson and the North East of Blackburn and from either town is easily discernible. Its huge flat backbone constitutes an unmistakable landmark.

To say that each chimney, towering like a proud smoking sentinel over its mill, was a thing of beauty, might be granting the author an unqualifiable descriptive licence. Collectively, however, the chimneys formed an eye-catching landscape, to be found, most probably, nowhere else in England other than the industrial north. To withstand the rigours of all weathers, expert maintenance was undertaken by highly trained steeplejacks. Their courage and expertise was incomparable, as they scaled the face of these bricks and mortar swaying giants, to establish scaffolding, which offered little protection hundreds of feet above the ground. In her childhood days, Alice watched these men in awe and admiration.

When Alice was beginning to spell and write, she had been asked at school to compose a short story. Gilbert, by now, was suffering with serious asthma. It was the accepted duty of his daughters to clean and polish his boots each morning, then take them to his bedroom before he dressed. In her story, Alice misspelt the word boots. The sentence read "I take Father's 'boos' to his bedroom." This caused a few wry smiles. He was a total abstainer.

Whilst learning to count at kindergarten, one of the children struggled to ten, faltered and stopped. "What follows ten?" the teacher asked the class. "Jack, queen, king," came Alice's quick response, to the teacher's astonishment. Alice had been taught to play Patience at an early age, so that she could play quietly on her own, while her father, who was unwell, was resting.

Gilbert was a devoted father. In spite of his asthma, the welfare and education of his daughters were always uppermost in his mind. When Alice showed an interest in music at an early age, he did not ignore a possible pianoforte potential. He was delighted, when as a birthday present, an aunt bought her an Adams baby grand piano. A modification was required to enable her to reach the pedals and after this had been carried out, Alice began to practise. Gilbert's expectations were to be realised. From a child embryo, a lifelong pianist was born.

When her father was unwell, or resting, Alice would always seek his permission before practising. He rarely refused and would lie in bed listening, enjoying and gauging her progress. The sounds of her playing were almost therapeutic, as though they engendered a feeling of well being and contentment. They were the forerunners of achievement.

The photograph of Elizabeth and Gilbert was taken in 1924 at Corporation Park, created about the 1860 period onwards, at a time when the cotton industry was depressed. To carry out this project, which led to a house building development of good quality properties towards the Preston New Road area, the Corporation found employment for out of work mill operatives. The park, ten minutes walk from Alice's home, provided the family and local people with a quiet haven for relaxation. Its well cared for gardens, excellent collection of plants in the conservatory, tennis courts and bandstand provided splendid amenities.

Gilbert's responsibilities with the St. John Ambulance required his regular attendance at Ewood Park for Blackburn Rovers' home matches. Like his father Isaac, he was a shareholder in the club and was privileged to have a seat in the directors' box. The entire family were staunch supporters of the club, including a very young Alice. On match days she would stand at the gate of the house and with the wind in the right direction, could hear the cheers from the crowd at the ground. She became adept at predicting the number of goals scored by Rovers and would await eagerly the paper boy to seek confirmation from the stop press news.

In April 1928, approaching the age of twelve, she watched intrigued, as a young man in a neighbour's backyard raised a bucket above his head. Pretending the bucket was the F. A. Cup; the young man turned and brandished it aloft as if to face an imaginary crowd. This was practice, in the hope that he might be required to lift the real thing. Who was this young man? He was Harry Healess, the Blackburn Rovers captain, whose aspirations became fulfilled, when on 21st April 1928, Blackburn Rovers beat Huddersfield Town by three goals to one in the F. A. Cup Final at Wembley. On retirement from football, Harry ran a newsagent's business at Limefield - a short walk from Alice's home.

The Rovers team sheet for the 1928 Final read:-

Campbell, Rankin, Crawford, Hutton, Jones, Thornewell, Puddefoot, Roscamp, Healess, McLean, Rigby.

Douglas Shorrock was born in 1923, quite near to Alice's home, in Blackburn. He attended St. Silas' Elementary School, and later Queen Elizabeth's Grammar School. In 1933 his father enrolled him as a member of East Lancs Cricket Club, whose home was Alexandra Meadows. At this time, Gilbert Ormerod was a member of the club and took his youngest daughter Alice to watch many of the home games, played in this beautiful setting. Neither Douglas Shorrock, nor Alice Ormerod, imagined that seventy years later they would become closely acquainted. Douglas discovered in 2003 that my wife came from Blackburn. Later in correspondence, Alice mentioned that the game, which attracted the largest crowd at the Meadows was against Nelson, for whom the West Indian lawyer Leary Constantine played. He was a highly respected professional and probably the most accomplished slip fielder in the league.

In 1934 Gilbert Ormerod bought a Citroën car, in which his three daughters learned to drive. It was used as a family car, primarily for their father's benefit, to enable him to travel in comfort and avoid the smoky atmosphere of public transport. In January 1935 Alice received her full driving licence issued by Blackburn County Borough Council.

Four years earlier, Gilbert Ormerod had retired as Superintendent of the St. John Ambulance Brigade, a position he held for thirteen years. He was a public figure in Blackburn, held in high esteem for the services he rendered to the community. As mentioned earlier he was completely teetotal, that was until the day before he died. An anomalous situation was reached, when seriously ill in bed, he asked for a piece of Christmas cake and a glass of champagne. To the surprise of those present, he partook of this refreshment and died a few hours later.

A public funeral took place in early January 1936. It was an impressive ceremony. The "LAST POST" AND "REVEILLE" were played at the graveside.

His cap, belt and ambulance decorations, resting on a black velvet cushion, and the Ambulance Corps Flag, were placed on the coffin. A detachment of the Ambulance Brigade marched with the cortège, which included two open cars laden with flowers. The streets on the funeral route were lined with police and members of the St. John Ambulance Association Brigade. Masonic representatives attended and citizens turned out in large numbers to join them to pay their last respects at the passing of a loved friend.

For Elizabeth his widow, and her three daughters, Elizabeth, Evalyn and Alice, it was an unforgettable emotional experience.

After the funeral, a reporter said, "He died as he had lived, with everything in order. I can honestly say, I knew a man."

Alice continued as a student teacher of music at Blackburn High School for girls, where she had been educated. A friend and contemporary of her sister Evalyn, was Kathleen Ferrier, who became internationally famous as a singer with a deep contralto voice. Although Kathleen was four years older than Alice, their mutual interest in piano playing resulted in the development of a close association. Sadly Kathleen died of cancer in 1953 at the age of forty-one. One of her most popular songs 'Blow the Wind Southerly' was Alice's well remembered favourite, played movingly, at her own funeral.

At the age of twenty-one Alice left the High School to attend the Royal Academy of Music in London, where she gained two diplomas and became Alice Ormerod LRAM. ARCM.

She was appointed specialist teacher of pianoforte and elocution at the Prebendal High School for girls in Aylesbury, Buckinghamshire, where she taught throughout the Second World War. In the junior department of the school there were facilities for the tuition of little boys. One of these youngsters, to whom she taught elocution and music, was to become a well known personality in broadcasting. He was Richard Dimbleby's son David.

We must leave her at this point in the story, but please rejoin her later in the book, as the saga unfolds.

Alice

Chapter One

'THEY SHALL GROW NOT OLD
AS WE THAT ARE LEFT GROW OLD
AGE SHALL NOT WEARY THEM
NOR THE YEARS CONDEMN'

I recall a holiday Mother and I spent together touring Somerset and Devon during mid-August 1939. The weather was kind as were the West Country folk who catered for us in their spotlessly clean cottages. The memory of their hospitality and superb home cooking lingers on these sixty years. I shall never forget our discovering the charming village of Selworthy with its thatched cottages and kempt village green, away from noise and bustle, nestling at the foot of the hills in the Exmoor National Park. A true haven of peace, or so it seemed then.

We visited Weston-Super-Mare where I had my first air experience in a small aeroplane used for flying holiday makers on a sightseeing trip around the local area, about 1,000 feet above the town. Mother thoroughly enjoyed the trip and coped well. I felt most apprehensive having only two months previously signed Attestation Papers in the Royal Air Force Volunteer Reserve as Air Observer - soon to be known as Navigator - and had yet to become airborne in that capacity. How would I cope?

• • • • • •

The first Monday evening after my return to work in Manchester, I attended a scheduled class at the RAFVR centre, where the lecture was to be given by the talented Flight Lieutenant Dawson, a strict man, who demanded and expected respect, which we always accorded him. He knew his subject; his earlier lectures on navigation had been interesting and informative. He had always been prepared to stay behind after lectures to answer sensible questions. Tonight was going to be different.

He opened the proceedings by firing this question at one of the student observers.

"Describe a great circle."

The stammered response was not in accordance with Air Publication 1234 and prompted a quick rejoinder from the tutor - something to the effect of rubbish. Then turning towards me he snapped - "You."

My definition of a great circle was also at variance with the Air Publication and prompted an immediate rejoinder, this time also monosyllabic but unmistakable, "Balls!"

He turned to a third student. "You, tell them."

The student tried, but got it all wrong. The tutor, now almost apoplectic, screamed, "Abject balls!" He threw the book down on his desk and refused to continue either with questioning, or with the lecture scheduled to follow.

I do not forget his ensuing words.

"You will learn these fifty-eight definitions and woe betide any one of you who cannot quote them all verbatim at the next lecture in two weeks time. You will be off the course."

I took that publication home, took it to bed, to the office, to my girl friends' homes and asked all and sundry to question me on those wretched definitions until I knew them verbatim.

On Friday evening 1st September we heard on the wireless that all members of the Volunteer Reserves were required to report to their centres. War was declared two days later, only one day before our next scheduled lecture and as we had been called into service I never saw Flight Lieutenant Dawson again, but I had learned my definitions.

I firmly believe I owe my life to him. The lives of those crew members who subsequently flew with me may be owed also to this man who would not tolerate fools. His navigational knowledge was profound, and whilst I was in awe of him then, I now look back on him almost with reverence. It was he who taught me the importance of dedication, application, thoroughness and attention to fine details, essential ingredients if the navigator is to come to terms satisfactorily with this science.

A navigational launching pad had been established.

● ● ● ● ● ●

At 11 o'clock on Sunday morning 3rd September 1939 the British Prime Minister, Neville Chamberlain, stated over the wireless that our country was at war with Germany. Immediately after this announcement warning sirens sounded. People appeared at their doors and some looked towards the sky, others went straight to their air raid shelters. No air raid ensued. Was this a false alarm or done deliberately to test public responses? It marked the beginning of the phoney war.

Our small island stood alone, facing an implacable enemy, the ruthless strongly fortified Nazi Germany war-machine. Heroically brave young men, aged nineteen to twenty-three years, prepared to sacrifice their lives in defence of freedom. Supported by other dedicated men and women, they volunteered to fly and take the fight to the enemy. World War Two Bomber Command was created by necessity and nurtured by expediency.

Young men and women left their civilian occupations and entered extensive training in the Royal Air Force. Early in 1940 many volunteer reservists had qualified to combine with regular service personnel to fly operationally against the enemy. Volunteers from Australia, New Zealand, Canada, South Africa, India, Poland and Czechoslovakia, who had evaded the Nazis, together with Free Frenchmen and others from occupied Europe, swelled the increasing numbers in Bomber Command. A combined force, to be reckoned with by the enemy, was growing despite horrific losses.

AIR PUBLICATION 1234
(*Revised April*, 1935)
(*Reprinted April, 1938*)

DEFINITIONS

1. *Air navigation* is the art of conducting an aircraft from place to place by dead reckoning and fixing position by observations of terrestrial objects and celestial bodies. It includes the ability to maintain a given direction in or above clouds and mist, and by night.

2. *Air speed* is the speed of an aircraft relative to the air.

3. *Axis of the Earth* is that diameter about which it revolves.

4. *Azimuth.—See " Bearing ".*

5. *Bearing.*—(i) The *great circle bearing* of an object is the angle at the observer between the meridian passing through the observer and the great circle joining his position to the object. This may also be called the *azimuth*. The angle is measured clockwise from the meridian from 0° to 360°. (Fig. 1.)

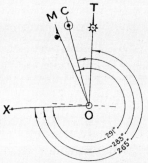

Fig. 1.—True Bearing = Angle T.O.X. = 265°.
  Magnetic Bearing = Angle M.O.X. = 291°.
  Compass Bearing = Angle C.O.X. = 283°.
  Variation = Angle T.O.M. = 26° W.
  Deviation = Angle M.O.C. = 8° E.
  Compass Error = Angle T.O.C. = 18° W.

(ii) Bearings are called *true* or *magnetic*, according to whether the angles are measured from the true meridian or the magnetic meridian.

(iii) In a *compass bearing* the angle is measured from the direction of a particular compass needle.

(iv) Bearings may be referred to the course of an aircraft, and are then measured from ahead through 180° to port and starboard, being termed respectively *red* and *green*. In Fig. 2 the bearing of A is Green 45°, and of B Red 120°.

(v) The *mercatorial bearing* is the angle at the observer between his meridian and a rhumb line joining him to the object.

6. *Cardinal points.*—The directions north, east, south and west. (Usually written N., E., S., W.)

7. *Compass error* is the algebraic sum of variation and deviation. (Figs. 1 and 3.)

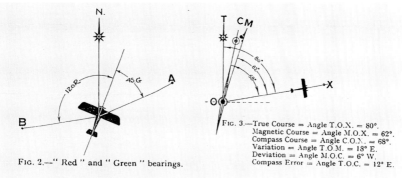

Fig. 2.—" Red " and " Green " bearings.

Fig. 3.—True Course = Angle T.O.X. = 80°.
Magnetic Course = Angle M.O.X. = 62°.
Compass Course = Angle C.O.X. = 68°.
Variation = Angle T.O.M. = 18° E.
Deviation = Angle M.O.C. = 6° W.
Compass Error = Angle T.O.C. = 12° E.

8. *Contour.*—The representation on a map of an imaginary line running along the surface of the ground at the same height above sea level throughout its length. A *form line* is an approximate contour.

9. *Conversion angle.*—The angle between the great circle and mercatorial bearings. (Fig. 4.)

10. *Couple.*—When two equal forces act on a body in opposite directions, they constitute a *couple*. The couple is the product of one of the forces and the perpendicular distance between them.

11. *Course.*—(i) The *true course* is the angle between the longitudinal axis of an aircraft and the true meridian. (Fig. 3.)

(ii) The *magnetic course* is the angle between the longitudinal axis of an aircraft and the magnetic meridian.

(iii) The *compass course* is the angle between the longitudinal axis of an aircraft and the direction of a particular compass needle.

12. *Dead reckoning* consists of calculating the track and ground speed of an aircraft. The *D.R. position* is the position arrived at by dead reckoning.

13. *Deviation* is the angle, measured in the horizontal plane, between the magnetic meridian and the direction of a particular compass needle influenced by a magnetic field not coincident with the earth's magnetic field. It is named E. (+) or W. (−), according to whether the north-seeking pole lies to the east or west of the magnetic meridian. (Figs. 1 and 3.)

14. *Dip* of a magnetic needle is the angle in the vertical plane between the horizontal and the direction of the earth's line of total magnetic force. Sometimes called *magnetic inclination.*

15. *Drift* is the angle between the longitudinal axis of an aircraft and the track : it is measured to port or starboard relative to the aircraft's head.

16. *Equator* of the Earth is the great circle of which the plane is at right angles to the axis. (W.E. in Fig. 4.)

17. *Fix.*—The position of an aircraft as determined on a map or chart, generally by the intersection of two or more position lines.

18. *Force.*—Any cause which tends to alter a body's state of rest or uniform motion in a straight line.

19. *Gradient.*—A rate of rise or fall, often expressed as a fraction. Thus 1/30 represents a rise or fall of 1 unit vertically in 30 units horizontally.

20. *Graticule.*—The network formed on a map by meridians and parallels of latitude.

21. *Grid.*—The representation on a map of a rectangular co-ordinate system.

22. *Great circle* is a circle on the surface of a sphere, the plane of which passes through the centre of the sphere and thus divides it into two equal parts. The shortest distance between any two points on the surface of a sphere is the arc of a great circle joining the points. (*See* Fig. 4.)

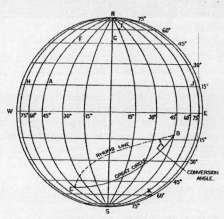

Fig. 4.—The Earth, showing latitude, longitude, great circle and rhumb line, etc.

23. *Ground speed* is the speed of an aircraft relative to the ground.

24. *Hachuring* is a conventional method of representing hill features on a map by shading in short disconnected lines, which are drawn in the direction of the steepest slopes.

25. *Horizontal equivalent.*—The distance in plan between two adjacent contours. (Written H.E.)

26. *Inertia.*—The tendency of a body to resist a change of motion.

27. *Isobar.*—A line drawn on a weather map, at all points on which the atmospheric pressure has the same value.

28. *Isoclinal.*—A line drawn on a map or chart, at all points on which the magnetic dip has the same value.

29. *Isogonal.*—A line drawn on a map or chart, at all points on which the magnetic variation has the same value. The *agonic line* is the line of no variation.

30. *Knot* is a unit of speed : it is a speed of one nautical mile an hour.

31. *Latitude* of a place is the arc of the meridian between the equator and the place and is named N. or S. according to whether the place is north or south of the equator. (In Fig. 4, Lat. of A = 15° N. ; Lat. of K = 60° S.)

A *parallel of latitude* is a small circle parallel to the equator. (HAJ in Fig. 4.)

Difference of latitude between two places is the arc of a meridian intercepted between the parallels of the places (written d. Lat.) ; d. Lat. from A to K = 75° S. (Fig. 4.)

32. *Layer tinting.*—A system of representing relief on maps by colouring the map between adjacent contours in a uniform shade, the shade chosen depending on the height.

33. *Longitude* of a place is the smaller arc of the equator intercepted between the prime meridian and the meridian of the place, and is named E. or W. according to whether the place is east or west of the prime meridian. (In Fig. 4, Long. of A = 45° W. ; Long. of K = 75° E.)

Difference of longitude between two places is the smaller arc of the equator intercepted between the meridians of the places (written d. Long.) ; d. Long. from K to A = 120° W. (Fig. 4.)

34. *Magnetic equator.*—An imaginary line on the surface of the earth joining all points where the earth's line of total magnetic force is horizontal, i.e. where the angle of dip is zero.

35. *Magnetic field.*—The region round a magnet in which its magnetism has effect.

36. *Magnetic meridian.*—The great circle on the earth at any place in the plane of which a magnetic needle would be, if freely suspended and influenced only by the earth's magnetic field.

37. *Magnetic poles* of the earth are the two positions on the earth's surface where the earth's line of total magnetic force is vertical, i.e. where the angle of dip is 90°.

38. *Meridian* is a semi-great circle passing through the poles of the earth (NAS, NKS, etc., in Fig. 4).

39. *Natural scale.*—See " *Representative fraction* ".

40. *Nautical mile* is the average length of a minute of latitude measured on any meridian. Its length is generally taken as 6,080 ft. (Symbol '.)

41. *Orienting* a map is the process of setting it so that the meridians on the map lie North and South.

42. *Poles* of the earth are the extremities of its axis of revolution. (N. and S. in Fig. 4.)

43. *Position error* is the error in the reading given by an air speed indicator due to the positioning of the pressure head.

44. *Position line* is a line obtained from observation of a terrestrial object or a celestial body, at some point on which line it is known that the aircraft must be.

45. *Projection* of a map or chart is any orderly system of representing meridians and parallels and the earth's surface on a plane.

46. *Quadrantal points.*—The directions north-east, south-east, south-west and north-west. (Usually written NE., SE., SW., NW.)

47. *Representative fraction* (written R.F.).—The ratio which the distance between two points on a map bears to the distance between the same two points on the ground. The ratio is always expressed as a fraction, of which the numerator is unity. It may also be called the *natural scale*.

48. *Rhumb line* is that curve on the earth's surface which cuts all the meridians it meets at the same angle. (*See* Fig. 4.)

49. *Run* is the direction and distance over the ground which an aircraft travels between two given instants.

50. *Small circle* is a circle on the surface of the sphere, the plane of which does not pass through the centre of the sphere.

51. *Spot height.*—The record on a map of the exact height above sea level of a particular point.

52. *Synoptic chart.*—*See* " *Weather map* ".

53. *Track* is the angle between a meridian and a line representing the actual path of an aircraft relative to the ground. It is measured from 0° to 360° clockwise from the meridian.

54. *Variation* (sometimes called *declination*) is the angle, measured in the horizontal plane, between the true meridian and the direction of a freely suspended magnetic needle influenced only by the earth's magnetic field. It is named E. (+) or W. (−) according to whether the north-seeking end of the needle lies to the east or west of the true meridian. (*See* Figs. 1 and 3.)

55. *Vector* is a straight line which, in both length and direction, represents a quantity such as a force or velocity.

56. *Velocity.*—The rate of change of position of a body in a given direction. Velocity therefore involves both speed and direction.

57. *Vertical interval.*—The difference in level between two adjacent contours. (Written V.I.)

58. *Weather map.*—An outline map on which are recorded meteorological observations made simultaneously at observing stations over a large area. The weather map is the basis of weather forecasting. (Also known as a *synoptic chart.*)

Chapter Two
PRESTWICK

For nine weeks from 1st September 1939, we had to report at regular intervals to the Manchester RAFVR Centre where we received procedural instructions pending posting to our flying instructional station.

On 11th November 1939 we travelled overnight by train from Manchester to Prestwick and with members of the Belfast and West Hartlepool Volunteer Reserves joined No.1 Air Observer Navigation School (No.1 AONS) where our flying training began. There would be about sixty of us altogether and we were divided alphabetically into two squads. In the following photograph of B Squad to which I was attached, it will be noticed that five of us had not yet been issued with service uniforms and were wearing the civilian clothes in which we had travelled.

We had the good fortune to be billeted on householders, a colleague and I sharing a house with three civilians, run by a charming and kindly middle-aged Scottish spinster, dear Joan Morton, who took very great care of us. One of her elderly guests owned a bakery in Prestwick! That was very useful. It was he, at the age of seventy-three, who proved to me conclusively how unwise it was to over indulge in the Scottish practice of drinking 'chasers'. To rub salt into the wound, sitting opposite me at breakfast next morning, he would rub his hands with glee and then add salt only to his huge steaming bowl of porridge. In spite of this, old Mr. Danks was a great guy.

Joan Morton kept in touch with my parents throughout the period I was in North Africa and it was a sad day when I learned of her death shortly after the war.

••••••

Our early flying training took place in two ex Dutch Airlines' large Fokker Aircraft Nos. G/AFZR and G/AFZP. Stripped of their civil flying embellishments, they were very suitable for the job. One of these aircraft served another very useful purpose in early January 1940, after heavy snowstorms had swept the region. Members of my squad and other personnel were detailed to help with the loading of emergency food supplies, to be flown to the aid of beleaguered soldiers, isolated in the hills and cut off by huge snowdrifts. This unexpected change of activity provided temporary relief from navigation.

Loading food supplies into a Fokker aircraft for dropping to soldiers marooned by snowdrifts in January 1940

Prestwick aerodrome was a training station for pilots and air observers during the period of late 1939 and early 1940. It had a huge grass airfield with no hard runways, thereby enabling landings and take-offs directly into wind, a procedure that could be accomplished satisfactorily by most trainee pilots who had gained a little experience. They trained initially in Tiger Moth aircraft, whilst observers' flying training took place in the two large Fokkers and reliable Avro Ansons. Little did we anticipate this aerodrome would develop to the extent we recognise it today and become a large international airport.

Observers were instructed by ex merchant navy navigators who had completed a special course in air navigation. They wore civilian clothes and were addressed as 'mister'. Their attitude towards us was friendly and I found them all helpful, patient and understanding. In consequence I thoroughly enjoyed my tuition and found navigation an exciting experience. I had fortuitously found my métier.

Most of the pilots with whom we flew on navigational cross-country exercises were regular RAF officers. The gulf in status between them and us leading aircraftmen observers under tuition extended to a chasm at times. I remember an occasion in late January 1940 when I had been detailed to fly with a certain Flight Lieutenant on a cross-country exercise. He had a reputation for being particularly difficult towards any pupil who did not show potential aptitude, so it was with some trepidation I climbed aboard the aircraft. I had been suitably warned what to expect by some of my colleagues who had experienced the acerbity of his tongue.

The weather conditions were most unsuitable for this sort of cross-country. There was maximum cloud cover, and as navigation had to be done by map reading, we had to fly just below cloud base, about 2,500 feet. Such conditions create extreme instability and our Anson aircraft was tossed about like a cork in rough water. On the flight from Prestwick to Stranraer I broke the points of three pencils, my navigational equipment slid from the table and shot all over the floor. It was difficult, but fortunately the exercise went very well.

On the return leg of the flight to Prestwick the pilot beckoned me up front. He said it was now too bumpy to attempt to keep a navigational chart and I could map read back to base. The turbulence got worse as he struggled with controls whilst chatting to me all the time. He wanted to know what I did in Civvy Street, tell him about it and asked if I had ever been airsick. I had never been airsick and he assured me that I never would be. After landing his endorsement of my uncompleted chart was very complimentary and he congratulated me for putting up a good show. It was an enormous boost to my confidence and I shall not forget that flight and its encouraging outcome. Neither shall I forget the 'difficult' pilot, with whom I was never to fly again. I wished there had been more like him.

One of our instructors, Flight Lieutenant Martin, had written a book on meteorology. He was an authority on this subject and emphasized the unpredictability of weather patterns and the unexpected changes that could take place. How right he was. These problems will be always compounded by the geographical situation of the British Isles which are subject to the influences of the Atlantic to the west, the European landmass to the east and vulnerability to cold polar airstreams; quite a combination of imponderables, a recipe for any forecaster's nightmare.

The weather pattern forms a very important part in all flying procedures. A high percentage of aircraft losses throughout the war could be attributed to the effects of rapid and unexpected synoptic changes, resulting in incorrect weather forecasting. There was the

human fallibility of many navigators, or perhaps I should say of most navigators at some time, or other. Inability to determine accurate wind speeds and directions could have disastrous effects. Many other hazards beyond their normal control, such as icing and poor visibility to mention only two, posed great threats. Cumulonimbus clouds (towering masses that formed in thunderstorms) were the arch-demons into which an aircraft could disappear and disintegrate.

We had been warned. Subsequent events proved this validity.

Self - at Prestwick N° 1 AONS prior to being issued with uniform - November 1939

Chapter Three
MARGARET IDE

Margaret Ide, who hailed from Bognor Regis, was born and bred in Sussex, a county of which she was proud. Billy Ide, her father, played cricket for the county and was well known for his left arm spin bowling. On the outbreak of World War Two, at the age of seventeen, Margaret had a job with a well known London store near High Holborn. Part time work with the W.V.S. was not sufficient for this young patriotic girl, who set her sights at service in the WAAF. Why wait? Adastral House was just round the corner, so off she went for an interview. As a result, her wish to join the WAAF was eventually granted on 20ᵗʰ March 1940.

The prompt reward for her enthusiasm was to be sent on a square-bashing course! This was followed by important radar training at Bawdsey, Suffolk, where she qualified as a radio operator.

Her work continued in this capacity at an Air Ministry Experimental Station (AMES) located at Dunkirk, Kent. Here she worked with other trained young contemporaries throughout the blitz of London and other cities, towns, villages. It was work of paramount and inestimable value to the war effort, at a time when the threat of Nazi invasion was a haunting and daunting spectre. Their duties required the locating by radar of the assembly of German Bombers, as they prepared to formate in preparation for their continued blitz of London and other targets in the UK.

Regrettably, due to shortage of aircraft and insufficient fuel to penetrate deep into Germany, we were unable to attack the assembling enemy planes from the air to prevent or hinder take-off. In consequence, this information was passed on to the plotters who gave advance warning to the British defences, the pilots of Fighter Command and anti aircraft batteries.

Margaret's next posting was to a similar AMES Station at Worth Matravers, Dorset. It was here, that whilst returning from the NAAFI with a Flight Sergeant, carrying a bag of buns for her colleagues, they were strafed by three low flying ME109 German Fighter aircraft. The Flight Sergeant promptly threw Margaret to the ground and protected her with his body. Fortunately, the only casualties were the buns. It was a narrow escape!

This was followed by a posting to another AMES Station, newly opened, at Cemaes Bay, Anglesey. They had an invasion problem here, but not by the Germans. This newly opened station was still relatively earthy on a site previously the habitat of snakes. The vipers, apparently resented the take over, and in their attempt to re-occupy, became responsible for disturbing invasions.

Her useful work continued, and upon discharge as a Technical Sergeant she was recommended for re-enrolment.

Here we must leave Margaret, who will reappear in later pages.

Margaret Ide

Chapter Four
EVANTON

Reality dawned on our next posting to Evanton Bombing and Gunnery School off Cromarty Firth. From the comforts of private billets we were herded into wooden huts sleeping thirty men. It was in one of these huts that a young Irishman, Julius Holland, aged only 19 years, recited after lights out, in a deep almost stentorian voice, bedtime stories, which literally lulled tough young flying aspirants to sleep. The bedtime stories, so well received by us and for which he got almost nightly encores, may not have received a similar reception by a nanny of a child's nursery.

Our gunnery and bombing flying training took place in such archaic aircraft as the Handley Page Harrow, Fairey Battle and the renowned two seater open cockpit Wallace. There is a photo of four of us suitably dressed 'Biggles' style for the latter aircraft, myself with

EVANTON 1940
Left to Right   Self   Harry Bowers   'Sticky' Leach and Alec Buckley

87

Fairey Battle

Handley Page Harrow

colleagues Harry Bowers, 'Sticky' Leach and Alec Buckley.

In spite of its relative obsolescence the Battle was manned by heroic aircrew who flew valiantly on operational sorties in 1939 and 1940 suffering terrible losses. The pilot and navigator of a Battle from 12 Squadron were awarded the Victoria Cross in May 1940 prior to the British Expeditionary Force evacuation from Dunkirk.

We learned to fire with the following .303 guns - Lewis, Vickers G.O. and Browning. The rate of fire of the Lewis was extremely slow, a sort of rat-a-tat. The Vickers was faster and the Browning fastest of the three and used operationally throughout the war. As well as firing practice from the Harrow at a towed drogue target (windsock) training took place on the ground firing range and without any protection for the ears. The noise was deafening and damaging.

Our instructors would deliberately, from time to time, remove small parts of the firing mechanism of these guns to test our proficiency. I remember one of these small parts was called a retainer keeper pawl, without which the gun would not fire. This created situations that were awkward enough to handle on the ground but extremely difficult in the air. We would come down with 'chunks' out of our hands and fingers from dismantling and reassembling the guns to the delight of our flight sergeant instructors. One instructor used to remark regularly, "The more blood and snot I see when you come down, the better!"

For bombing exercises, we dropped eleven pound practise bombs, generally from the Harrow at 6,000 feet, over nearby Tain Range north of Invergordon and Cromarty Firth. The range was fairly remote from dwellings, although on one occasion, as a result of a bomb hang up, a trainee succeeded in targeting a greenhouse. This created quite a furore back at the station; the owner was most displeased and did not hesitate to register his protests.

Two colleagues, like myself, were Old Mancunians (ex Manchester Grammar School boys). This tended to give us a common bond as we were near contemporaries. One of them, Don Chadwick had been put in charge of the hut, a job which carried an unenviable, thankless responsibility. I admired him for his philosophical approach to the task and for the manner in which he carried out his duties in the interests of maintaining hut discipline. Most men co-operated. A few could be difficult but Don handled them well.

The only free time we had at Evanton, other than evenings, was Saturday afternoon. Sunday was a full working day. Phil Massey, my other Mancunian colleague, was a quiet unassuming man and it was he who suggested one Saturday afternoon, that in the interests of physical fitness, I might like to join him on a cross-country run twice around the airfield. In a moment of recklessness I agreed. What folly!

We obtained permission to carry out the run provided we kept strictly to the outer perimeter of the airfield. After donning PT kit we set off, having grossly underestimated the airfield's dimensions. It was a relief to me when nearing the completion of the first circuit, a breathless Phil suggested that perhaps one circuit would suffice. How we ever reached the benison of the warm showers I know not. That night we slept more soundly than usual. Even the beds were comfortable.

Once every week we had the inevitable hut inspection, common practice on training stations. Sheets and blankets had to be folded in conformity with laid down regulations. The bed biscuits (in lieu of mattress) had to be stacked in a specified position on each bed and all toiletry requisites, shaving materials, hair brush and comb placed in a predetermined position and distance from each other on each airman's locker. The hut windows had to be spotlessly clean and footwear polished as mirrors. Not a vestige of dirt would be tolerated and each airman was required to stand to smart attention at his bedside in immaculate uniform with buttons gleaming like gold. It was Don's responsibility before each inspection to ensure that the minutest detail had been taken care of. Imagine the consternation therefore, when a few minutes before one inspection, members of the next hut with whom we were not on the best of terms, released a fire extinguisher through one of our windows. The ensuing mess was horrible and yet, miraculously we managed to get it cleaned immediately before the CO's arrival. Repercussions followed a week later directed at the hut next door.

We became a rebellious course and collectively behaved in a very anti way towards authority. This stemmed from the way we were treated, being regarded as the lowest form of animal life by many of the regular personnel. I could not quite understand this as we had all volunteered to be trained for a very dangerous occupation. Was it our rapid promotion potential as aircrew (entirely dependent on survival) of which they harboured an envy?

On one occasion a loveable and mischievous leading aircraftman Noel Hawthorne (see pic on page 24) from the Belfast RAFVR was put on a charge for some small misdemeanour. His punishment was to attend the firing range after duty and collect spent ammunition from the sand. As a man the whole course decided to join him and speed up the task. When the officer of the day passed the range during the course of his routine inspection, he found not one man, but thirty men searching in the sand for spent bullets. In consequence the whole lot of us were put on a charge. I, with a few others, was detailed for a week's 'spud bashing' (a lengthy period of peeling potatoes) in the cookhouse.

The climax was reached when 'Sticky' Leach, who had befriended a Waaf who worked in the orderly room, obtained a copy of our pending final examination paper. He passed it round the billet and we all had a wonderful preview of the questions. After the exam we were all called before the squadron leader in charge of the course who announced the results. "You have all done exceptionally well, above average." We were about to preen ourselves in satisfaction when he continued, "Now you will all remain where you are and sit the examination again. This time you will not have seen the paper beforehand!"

It was too late. We had the gist of the paper from the first exam. The second paper was a variation on a theme and we all passed.

A week earlier, a few of us regarded as being potential officer candidates, had been selected to attend an interview with the squadron leader. He was an autocratic man whose main interest in me was my civilian status and family background. He asked about my father's occupation and wanted to know which schools I had attended, had I been to boarding school and what had been my pre-war occupations? (How these prerequisites would change during the next year!) However, I felt the interview had been satisfactory and that a favourable proposal would accompany my records at the pending posting.

Immediately before this pending posting all members of the course were called together to be blessed and hear his farewell tirade! Obviously he had been displeased with our behaviour throughout and explained this in words of great satirical eloquence, concluding by telling us that those who had attended the commission interview could forget it, the reports had been destroyed. Finally he did bless us with a few simple words.

"When you leave here, God help the lot of you!"

But success had come to most of us; we departed as sergeant navigators.

Chapter Five

BICESTER

Our posting was to Bicester, where the adverse report from Evanton did not appear to have had any prejudicial effect; our attentions were never drawn to it and I wonder, if those in authority had reservations afterwards and withdrew the remarks. To condemn an entire course of thirty aircrew volunteers would not reflect favourably on the Evanton training establishment. Whilst I fully understood the necessity of enforced discipline, it must be administered without bias.

Harry Bowers and I bought a tandem bicycle, nicknamed 'Bogus'.

This photo of us with the tandem was taken outside married quarters at Bicester aerodrome where many of us were billeted.

By a later arrangement with Harry the tandem travelled with me to my first squadron and continued to be a very useful means of transport.

Bicester was our Operational Training Unit (OTU) where we graduated from the reliable Avro Anson to the then famous fighter-bomber the Bristol Blenheim. Tragically, during this period, the young Belfast RAFVR navigator, who had been put on a charge at Evanton, was killed on a training flight, when, in poor visibility, the plane flew into high ground.

Apart from the tragic death of the young Irishman and his crew the operational flying training at Bicester passed without undue incidents.

Noel Hawthorne

● ● ● ● ● ●

The Blenheim was a fast bomber aircraft capable of flying at speeds well in excess of 200 miles per hour (m.p.h.). On an average cross-country we would fly between 180/200 indicated m.p.h. compared with the Anson's speed of 120. This reduced the time available for the navigator to make his calculations.

We used to say an aircraft's instrument panel was a great liar. It gave so much 'duff' information a correction had to be made to most readings, including the altimeter.

There is a big difference between indicated and true airspeed, the latter being considerably greater, anything between 20 to 60 m.p.h., or even higher, depending on altitude and air temperature.

Course and airspeed are the direction and speed of the aircraft relative to the air, the medium through which it flies. Track and ground speed are the direction and speed at which the aircraft travels relative to the ground. The difference between the two is represented by the current wind speed and direction, which is calculated by the navigator.

This may sound complicated. The navigator's duty, his responsibility, was to understand these facets, interpret them correctly throughout the flight and promptly advise the pilot of any change in course required to keep on track. Some navigators were more adept than others and it was the luck of the draw which crews got the former.

Our flying training continued until the end of June and during the earlier part of this period the Germans had occupied northern France and the evacuation of Dunkirk had taken place. Blenheim aircraft, based in France before Dunkirk, had been taken over by the Germans who used them to their own advantage. We were convinced, as our OTU training drew to a close, that it would be only a short time before the invasion of our country took place.

The last of our restricted night flights was amusing and incorporated a turning point at Benson Beacon then changing course to Hullavington Beacon and flying back to Bicester on reciprocal tracks. I knew the pilot fairly well; he was a rather smug and autocratic flying officer who had given some stick to several pupil navigators. We had been flying about fifteen minutes when he asked peremptorily for our position. I had been looking ahead for Benson Beacon, of which there was no sign, although by now it should have been visible. I had to tell him I didn't know but that according to dead reckoning we should be nearing our first turning point. He then queried the course I had given him which turned out to be correct and this prompted a grunted "hmm" in response. I then had the temerity to ask him, most politely, what course he was steering. He had set his pilot's P4 compass incorrectly and instead of flying almost due south was flying on a reciprocal course almost due north. We were now twenty minutes flying time further away from Benson than when we started. For an experienced pilot he had, what we called, 'dropped a real clanger.' I wonder how he talked himself out of that one when he handed in his pilot's report.

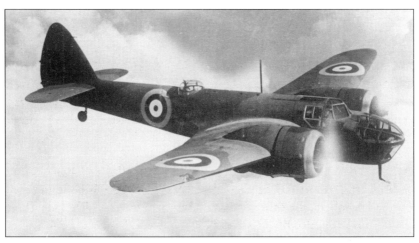

Blenheim

Chapter Six

101 SQUADRON WEST RAYNHAM

Although these months of training had been punctuated with inevitable flying problems, I arrived unscathed at West Raynham in early July 1940 with six other sergeant navigators from Manchester RAFVR who had completed training with me.

On the first morning after our arrival, we reported to flights for news of our final operational postings as it was unlikely 101 Squadron establishment would require us all. This coincided with the visit of Air Marshal Sir Charles Portal to carry out a station inspection and we never thought he would spare time to stop and speak to seven junior navigators. He told us to form a small circle and standing in the centre gave us a short pep talk and had an enquiring word with each of us in turn. He was a lean man, as I recall him, of cadaverous features. In his eyes I read a deep perceptiveness, that he could be kind, but hard and calculating, attributes required of a man to become Chief of the Air Staff.

I understood the squadron had been relatively quiet for a year and not required to go into action even when the Germans swept through the Low Countries and into France. About the time we arrived activities were stepped up and on 5th July the Commanding Officer, Wing Commander J.H. Hargroves and his crew lost their lives. Their aircraft had been one of three to take off individually, which was quite routine in those days.

Sergeant Parkinson and I were retained at West Raynham and became attached to 101 Squadron, navigating Bristol Blenheim twin-engined bombers, the other five were posted elsewhere. Two lost their lives by autumn, Alec Buckley and Harry Bowers. Sergeant Giblin, later awarded the DFM, was reported missing twice. One other, Gordon

Chadwick, later to become Flight Lieutenant, was awarded the DFC and survived the war.

Shortly after our arrival at West Raynham, a lone German bomber aircraft made a low level attack on the aerodrome. It would have been about 06.00 hours; most personnel were asleep and rudely awakened when a stick of bombs exploded damaging one hangar and missing the others. Had the aircraft attacked some fifty yards over to starboard, damage to barrack blocks and loss of personnel life would have been considerable. We all thought this was a foretaste of what was in store, yet, unbelievably, the aerodrome was never attacked again; at least during the period I was stationed there.

Parkinson's fate was tragic. It was on 25th July, his crew was on flying standby, whilst my crew was on stand down. Due to unfavourable meteorological conditions their flight had been delayed and would be cancelled if conditions did not improve by 16.00 hours, after which time Parkinson would be free to go on four days honeymoon leave. He and I were whiling away the time playing draughts in the sergeants' mess ante-room, the clock had got to 15.55, not time for another game and 'Parky' was preparing for leave when the tannoy suddenly blurted out that his crew was to report to flights immediately. They did not return, reported lost without trace.

The following day I was required, in the presence of the Station Adjutant, to go through his personal possessions. This was routine practice to avoid any possible incriminating correspondence being found that would embarrass family, wife, fiancée, or intimate friends. There was nothing. It marked the passing of a young man of impeccable integrity.

• • • • • •

During the weeks that followed we lived in a world of fantasy. Catering in the sergeants' mess was of a high standard and we were served at table by civilian waiters. Occasionally, after briefings for early morning take-offs, we would be put on standby pending favourable met reports and allowed to wander on the airfield to pick mushrooms that were well received by the mess catering staff, who served them as additional delicacies for breakfast. Accommodation was good, I shared a room with Tony Randall, my wireless operator, whilst John Riddick, our pilot, whenever possible, managed to live out with his wife who stayed at

Fakenham. The transport and communication liaison we established in case of an unexpected call was very creditable.

Fighter Command was now getting involved in the Battle of Britain and I think it fair comment to say the life style and off duty behaviour of Bomber Command aircrews was comparable with those of the Hurricane and Spitfire fighter pilots, at a time when losses in both Commands were very high.

• • • • • •

On joining the squadron I acquired a huge sheet of metal armour plating that with great difficulty I managed to get into the bomb-aiming compartment of the aircraft. It would offer some protection to vital parts of the lower anatomy in the event of an under belly attack by fighters. Alas, it was used only once for the flight to Gelsenkirchen before being stolen. I found it difficult to understand why any person would wish to remove such a heavy piece of protective gear and for what purpose? My pilot had a smaller sheet, which was more easily removable, fixed at the back of his scat offering protection to the head and shoulders. Fortunately, our aircraft was never hit, which was not the case with many other crews who returned quite remarkably uninjured in bullet-riddled aircraft.

All around us faces just disappeared, a situation we began to accept as inevitable. The losses of men and planes were quite disproportionate to the damage inflicted on the enemy with our meagre bomb load of one thousand pounds.

The losses inflicted did not apply to 101 Squadron alone. 18 Squadron was stationed also at West Raynham and crew members of both squadrons shared the same facilities. One learned to recognise most flying personnel but it was not always easy to discriminate and ascertain to which squadron they belonged with the ever changing faces.

Schipol airport, a regular target, along with the marshalling yards and manufacturing capacities of the Ruhr towns, appeared to be relatively unaffected by the attentions of the light bombers, whilst searches for enemy shipping often proved to be fruitless. My concern was the massing of enemy invasion barges, which I believed posed a real threat to our then vulnerable island. Fortunately, as events showed later, my fears were unfounded.

• • • • • •

The following incidents occurred within a period of only twelve hours but in my opinion were significant.

It was Saturday night in late July and four of us had hired a taxi to take us to Norwich. On arrival, by pure chance, I met Don Chadwick who had experienced a terrifying experience on a recent raid, whilst flying with a squadron leader pilot in the lead of a formation of Blenheims. Being in the lead aircraft was his salvation, as the formation was picked up quickly by enemy fighters after crossing the enemy coast. The fighters had a field day attacking relentlessly aircraft in the rear of the formation, until it was virtually decimated.

I left Don, after hearing this harrowing story and joined a Scottish navigator from West Raynham as we made our way to Samsons, a well-known dance hall with bars and attractive women.

We picked up two very charming young girls, one a Waaf on leave from Scampton and her friend, still a civilian waiting for call up. As the evening went by Jock got extremely drunk and it became my pleasure to see the young ladies home. Our wanderings through the city coincided with an air raid warning and there was no alternative other than to take shelter in a large shop doorway. I spent a very blissful half hour with my female companions and was rudely brought back to earth by the peremptory tone, in the voice of a stockily built middle-aged air raid warden, telling the girls to get off the street and go home. I told him that these young ladies were in my charge and were my responsibility, whereupon he assured me that one of them was his daughter!

There was no argument; no misunderstanding as he and I solemnly shook hands. He was a good father, doing a very important and often dangerous job outside his working hours and he knew that I was a young airman and where my real responsibilities lay. Thousands of other civilians, male and female, like this warden, were now making great contributions to a just cause. There were the parents, wives and other relatives at home, whose loved ones were away on service for their country, their lot was the most difficult and hardest to bear. The phoney war was over.

I made the taxi just as it was about to depart with Jock being carried aboard. He came round temporarily and began hurling snooker balls from the cab window muttering something about 'bombs away.' He had an endless supply in his tunic pockets, pinched from a nearby snooker club and when the supply was exhausted he passed out completely.

Back at the station he had problems to be compounded by a notice on the guardroom wall stating his crew had to report to flights at 04.00 hours. He had three hours to sober up - quite impossible.

Next day we were on routine 24 hours' standby and went in for breakfast at 08.00 hours. We then discovered Jock's crew had taken off at 06.00 hours with Jock on board. Unbelievable. During late morning, whilst we were still at flights, a solitary Blenheim came into view, then circled the airfield before coming in to a perfect landing. Jock and his crew climbed out of the aeroplane looking smug and self satisfied.

It turned out that a compassionate navigator worked out Jock's flight plan before take-off and gave a copy to his pilot with a series of quarter inch maps already ruled in chinagraph pencil, with tracks to the target and back. Quite feasible, as most navigation was done by map reading and compass bearings in those days. However, about thirty minutes after take-off and with 6,000 feet of altitude under his backside our delinquent regained his senses, his head cleared and he accomplished one of his most satisfactory trips.

Life was not always without a little humour. We were about to mourn the loss of a navigator, one Sergeant Gingell, a comedian and a card. He and his Blenheim had gone missing about 48 hours earlier and we were preparing to go through the rites with his personal possessions etc., when, suddenly, this jester of a man appeared at the end of the corridor and behaved as if nothing had happened. The sleeves of his tunic were up to his armpits and the trousers legs up to his knees. "Spent twelve hours in the drink when our kite was shot down," he explained. This was before being picked up by a Royal Navy motor torpedo boat (RN MTB) whose crew plied him with grog and dried his now extremely shrunken uniform.

We all agreed it was time for a drink and trooped off to the station guardroom en route to the nearest pub. Poor old Gingell was stopped by the Military Police (MPs) at the gate; they would not let him off the station for being improperly dressed!

This brave man and his pilot, Pilot Officer N. Bicknell, ditched again on 9th/10th September. Both received awards for their attempts in vain to save the wireless operator who went down with the aircraft.

A few days earlier two aircrew billeted in a room off the same corridor, handed letters for posting to their relatives to Tony and me, on our way to Fakenham. They had been briefed and were on call, standing by for an early morning take-off.

Next day their room was empty, their possessions had been gathered together including a bicycle they shared that had the name 'Willies' painted on the crossbar. That bicycle always attracted amused attention and I remember it well and the two brave chaps who used to ride it.

It was at this time I heard that Julius Holland's Blenheim had crashed into the sea just off the coast near Brighton.

• • • • • •

The tandem bicycle I brought from Bicester proved to be very useful. Whenever we were on stand-down, Tony, whose real name, incidentally, was also Douglas, and I, would cycle to the local village pubs, or to Fakenham, where we would join John Riddick and his wife. Using the tandem we were independent of an infrequent bus service and saved the cost of taxi fares.

Douglas, now always known as Tony, had earned this name as a result of his marriage to an Italian girl who had died before the outbreak of war. Whilst at West Raynham he met Heather, a loveable young lady to whom he became devoted. I was introduced to her friend Dulcie, she and I enjoyed a short, non-serious, almost platonic relationship. Dulcie was an accomplished pianist and entertained us regularly by playing in a local pub. It was she who introduced me to the game of bowls. The pub landlord kindly loaned us his personal set of woods and allowed us to practise on his pub's private bowling green. It was fun and light hearted, as was Dulcie. She was not troubled in the slightest when I told her I had a blind date arranged for our next stand-down, to meet Vera, a young girl who was serving in the Women's Royal Army Corps (WRAC).

Two evenings later Vera and I were introduced to each other by her WRAC Staff Sergeant. After the first drink we left the pub. Vera collected her bicycle from the pub yard and we sought the privacy of a quiet country lane where we spent the next two hours together, peacefully undisturbed. When we parted it was as though we had known each other for a lifetime and we pledged solemnly to see each other again, as soon as possible, and after that as often as possible.

It was at this time I understood a change in policy was scheduled to take place. Due to the heavy losses of sustained daylight bombing, particularly in 2 Group to which we belonged, operational flying would change to night bombing. Such a change in policy was quite understandable in view of the tragic losses already sustained in the Group. During the short period we were at West Raynham twenty Blenheims were lost from 18 and 101 Squadrons.

I quote two damning examples concerning 82 Squadron based at Watton.

17th May 1940. Twelve Blenheims were ordered to attack Gembloux. All twelve were lost.

13th August 1940. The same Squadron received orders for twelve Blenheims to attack Aalborg. On this occasion eleven aircraft failed to return.

Whether night bombing was brought into immediate effect I cannot recall, as two crews, my own and another to be flown by Pilot Officer D.K. Macdonald, received new orders and were taken off the squadron strength towards the end of August. Our new orders were: "Prepare to ferry a Blenheim to Heliopolis via Malta."

Next day our crew was ordered to remain on permanent standby and be available immediately to carry out fuel consumption test flights. We were confined to the station and never saw Vera nor Heather again.

The journey to Heliopolis would be in two stages, the first to Malta flying direct over Marseilles to the coast of North Africa and then east. We asked to fly to Malta via Gibraltar, land there to refuel and risk using the notorious short runway, but the authorities refused. They thought this presented a greater hazard than possible lack of fuel by taking the longer route and in spite of our pilot's strong protestation, the matter was taken out of his hands. Four special fuel consumption test flights later proved him to be right; nevertheless, we were ordered to go when the meteorological conditions were favourable. How the hell did they know in those days what the met conditions would be like in the southern Mediterranean?

We flew from West Raynham to Thorney Island on the morning of 26th August and were free to leave the station for a few hours, prior to briefing later that afternoon. I remember having a snack lunch in a pub in Emsworth whilst listening to the musical hits of the day on their jukebox, which automatically played a selection of the most popular recordings when a coin was inserted.

This was my last opportunity to write home before our departure and I scribbled a hasty note on the two sides of an inland telegram form obtained from a nearby post office. It read: -

This is a copy of the original form.

Emsworth. Hampshire.

Monday.

Arrived this place this morning. It is near Portsmouth and quite a pleasant spot. To-night at midnight I am off. Think of me tomorrow at breakfast time. The first stage of my journey should then be complete.

All my love, Douglas.

PTO

Would you kindly send 25/- of this to Sgt. H. Bowers. 4, Oak Road, Crumpsall. and say it is his share of the tandem spoils. Just a wee note to tell him I have gone away and he will understand. The remainder please put away for me. Thank you.

Douglas.

Unknown to me, Harry Bowers had been reported missing earlier during the month and would never receive his twenty-five shillings share.

Back at Thorney Island aerodrome, later that afternoon, we witnessed an amazing daylight raid on Portsmouth. Wave after wave of German aircraft bombed from tight formations and were continuously harassed and intercepted by our Battle of Britain fighters. The German bombers suffered heavy losses yet pressed on steadfastly and our fighters sustained losses in aerial combats that demonstrated great courage by both participants.

The airfield at Thorney Island had suffered from extensive German bombing raids. Bomb craters had been systematically filled (a similar situation to that prevailing at Schipol) and although the field was serviceable, landings and take-offs proved to be bumpy rides!

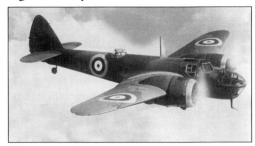

Chapter Seven
NORTH AFRICA

So, two Blenheims and crews, ex 101 Squadron, left Thorney Island at 00.05 hours on 27th August 1940 and lost sight of each other immediately after take-off.

We were under no illusions regarding the possible problems that could be created by fuel shortage. These problems became compounded when we discovered, immediately prior to take-off, that the aircraft had been loaded with Blenheim spare parts including heavy engine cowling. The well had been filled to capacity and the dingy stowed on top. Our remonstrations fell again on deaf ears.

Our flight was going well when we reached the French coast flying at 12,000 feet directly over Le Havre. We continued without any untoward incident for a further twenty minutes when the wireless operator sighted, what he identified as an ME 109 German fighter, well over to starboard. The German pilot had sighted us and began to close in rapidly, whereupon, John Riddick, our pilot decided we should make ourselves as conspicuous as possible and switched on the downward identification light together with the port and starboard red and green wing lights. Tony Randall, the wireless operator, fired off the colours of the day and flashed some quite unintelligible message on the Aldis lamp. I just stood looking out and, having turned up my navigation table anglepoise lamp to its brightest setting, hoped our stratagem would work. The German pilot must have become confused and 'buzzed' us (flew fast and close) three times after which, with a dipped wing salute, he flew off. During this procedure, John, showing little sign of anxiety, calmly continued to fly on a steady course and made no attempt to take evasive action. It was a remarkable escape, stemming no doubt from the German procedure, still in force, of flying captured Blenheims from occupied France. We were not intercepted again.

On reaching the critical point of our flight, i.e. the position at which a decision had to be taken whether it was safe to continue or safer to return to base, the gauges suggested we had adequate fuel to reach Malta, in fact sufficient for another fifteen minutes flying time! Jubilantly we pressed on.

We had flown over unoccupied France and looking down it seemed strange to see the lighted towns and villages. After crossing the coast near Marseilles we witnessed a magnificent sunrise heralding dawn over the Mediterranean. It was exciting with an air almost of mystique as we embarked on our journey to the apparently unknown, in reality Egypt, to fly in a desert war.

We passed the islands of Corsica and Sardinia, clearly visible on the port side. Our flight was proceeding within the limits of its tight schedule. Our confidence was buoyed.

I was able to keep Sardinia in sight for a long time and took a series of bearings with the useful hand held compass. This enabled me to take running fixes and verify our position until all signs of land disappeared. It was now everything started to go wrong.

Some distance ahead, near the North African coast, towering cumulonimbus clouds developed and we had to lose altitude, make a considerable detour and abandon our scheduled course. Our next sighting of land was Cap Bon in Tunisia and not Malta. Now, we were critically short of fuel and although we resumed the direct course for Malta, Tony had to break radio silence and transmit the international distress signal 'mayday' ironically, representing pronunciation of French (m'aidez 'help me') to alert Malta of our position. The crew of the other Blenheim, which left Thorney Island with us, was in a similar predicament. Tony overheard their 'mayday' transmission. A ditching seemed certain unless we turned back to Cap Bon. Should the latter eventuality arise we had been instructed at final briefing to destroy all evidence of our flight, including our flying logbooks but not the aircraft. There was no concrete evidence, although it was believed in the UK that the French in North Africa would be supportive!

Continuing to fly east we soon sighted the island of Pantellaria ahead and to port. Mount Etna in Sicily was clearly visible; we were bang on track for Malta, but it was too far with our fuel almost exhausted. John overruled an option to continue and quite rightly turned the aircraft round and flew a reciprocal course for the North African mainland. With one engine cut out he made an emergency landing on a stony field near Menzel Temime when damage was sustained to the undercarriage. It was now discovered that the spares and cowling had shifted during the course of the flight, no doubt at the time we encountered turbulence in the region of the cumulonimbus clouds. Had we ditched, it would have been totally impossible to extricate the dinghy which had become firmly wedged. It would require little intelligence from our captors to deduce from whence we came and whither we might be going with that load on board!

We learned from later information regarding the amount of fuel left in one tank only, had we continued, we would have ditched about fifty miles short of Malta. The other Blenheim was not seen again.

The experience of this flight was quite different from any earlier flights. It shaped our immediate destiny. Above all it clearly emphasized the wisdom of Flight Lieutenant Martin's words regarding the unpredictability of weather forecasting and weather patterns and changes.

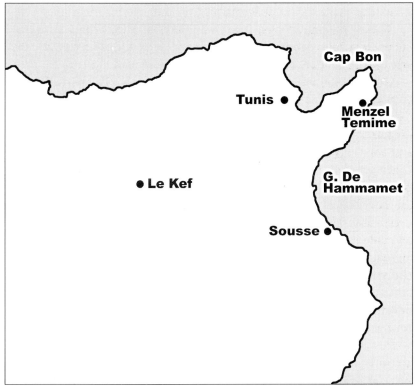

Blenheim crashed at Menzel Temime in North Africa

We climbed down from our unfortunate aircraft on to seasonally parched and arid stony land, not a vestige of greenery to be seen. Had there been any torrential rainfall in the nearby thunderstorms, it certainly had not reached Cap Bon.

The heat was becoming intense and we took off our heavy flying clothing before starting a huge fire of maps and papers that burned quickly. The smoke attracted local Arabs, who appeared suddenly, as if from nowhere. They were friendly but most intrigued and began a search of the aircraft, fortunately, not attempting to ransack it for souvenirs. We managed to communicate with one Arab in broken French and to his credit he made contact with authorities at the nearby village of Menzel Temime.

It was mid morning, the heat was now intense, as the sun shone from a cloudless sky, when a car arrived bringing a large pleasant looking man dressed immaculately in military uniform. He walked slowly across the uneven dusty field towards us and smiled cheerfully as he greeted us in fluent English.

"Good morning boys, how are you and what brings you here? Where is it you wish to go, Malta, Gibraltar and, by the way, are they still using the short runway there, or the UK?"

Ostensibly, it was the duty of this man, Capitaine Rubin de Cervans of the French Air Force to escort us and attend to our well-being for the next two days. He explained it would be necessary for our aircraft to be transported to El Alouina airfield near Tunis for repairs and this might take some time, so we should need some lightweight civilian clothes, much too dangerous to wander around Tunisia in RAF uniform, with all these Italians about.

He arranged for us to spend the night without guards at the French sous-officiers' mess (senior NCOs') in Menzel Temime, where we were fed and treated well. Next day de Cervans took us to a splendid store in Tunis where we were kitted out with colourful shirts, lightweight trousers, socks and shoes. Our presence attracted much attention, particularly from the young French female sales assistants, who had never met RAF flying men before, nor experienced the effects of wartime privations in this false paradise.

Sartorially kitted out, we were taken to the American Consulate in Tunis and had a long audience with Vice American Consul Springs. The discussions were vague, nothing positive was achieved, and he either could not, or would not answer our questions satisfactorily and seemed to be playing for time. He implied that our situation would be discussed in more detail at a Consulate dinner, to which we were all invited and where we were to meet other guests including his wife Marjorie, also a Russian Princess, a Spanish Baron and de Cervans and his wife. She was a charming petite French girl exuding guile and female attractiveness, but, allegedly with no knowledge of English. She was my attractive partner at dinner attended by a motley assembly to serve what purpose?

During and after an excellent dinner, accompanied by superb wines, the conversations became vacuous and purposeless. The atmosphere of protocol, combined with informality, engendered suspicion and we became very wary.

Later de Cervans drove us to El Alouina airport where we were to be billeted in sous-officiers' quarters, used by the French Air Force flying personnel. Apparently, we would stay here pending the arrival and restoration of our Blenheim, so everything was going to be all right until next morning we found the door of our room locked and outside were posted armed guards.

We quickly protested when de Cervans arrived later that morning.

"Don't worry boys, can't be too careful in the interests of your safety with all these Italians about. After coffee jump into the car and we'll take you to a chalet in the hills that will be your temporary home. Can't promise you white tablecloths every day but you will be comfortable up there whilst your Blenheim is being fixed."

"What about our Blenheim?"

The door closed as he left without replying. The outside bolts were rammed home and de Cervans had gone, not to be seen by us again.

• • • • • •

Under heavy guard and now in intolerable heat, we were driven on narrow, winding, uneven roads through precipitous and arid country, to a fortified military outpost in the hills at Le Kef where our chalet turned out to be a small stone built Arabs' barrack room in the confines of this military fortress. The room, with its strongly barred windows, was occupied already by two RAF senior NCOs, survivors of another Blenheim, Sergeant Ted Hart wireless operator and Flight Sergeant Stevens DFM BEM navigator who had gained these awards for service in France before Dunkirk. Both men had been separated from their

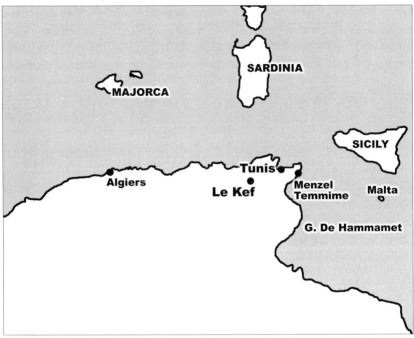

Route to imprisonment 27 August 1940

officer pilot who was incarcerated in another smaller room across a courtyard and our doors were locked from dusk every evening.

The Vichy French had no conception of decent hygiene and our sanitary facilities comprised a small zinc bath that was emptied every morning. Our fly infested food, referred to as 'la soupe', consisted of macaroni and sloppy dirty vegetables, the same as provided for the Arab soldiers.

Disillusionment and imprisonment had begun.

A few days later another RAF crew joined us, the survivors of a Hudson aircraft, shot down by a Royal Navy Fulmar, whose pilot perhaps with some justification, failed to identify the purpose of the Hudson's mission. Ironically, it had flown into a combat zone whilst on patrol search for us and the second Blenheim crew from Thorney Island, of which there had been no trace.

It was not until mid-December I heard from my parents that they had received the telegram letter posted from Thorney Island on 26th August and that two days afterwards, they received a more serious real telegram, officially reporting their son 755052 Sergeant Hudson missing!

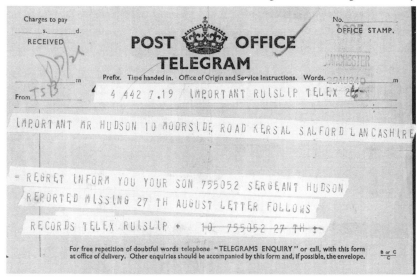

Early September 1940, I was lying on the bed in this evil room at Le Kef recovering from an early attack of dysentery and suffering a fit of deep depression. I was bruised mentally by the sudden enforced idleness and abrupt removal from flying participation in a war now gaining momentum and heavily loaded against the UK. Open bombing of the English cities by the Luftwaffe was beginning and our anxiety for those at home was acute.

It was as though I had landed in a pit of hopelessness, when a colleague handed me an English Country Life magazine sent from Tunis by the American Consul. When I opened it casually, a ray of sunshine revealed at that very page, a full plate coloured photograph of SELWORTHY village green and those charming thatched cottages.

Senior NCO prisoners did not receive any pay although the officers, of whom there were now four, did receive a small allowance, which would ultimately, become deductible from their pay. Through an Arab orderly they were able to buy a few fresh vegetables, a few eggs and occasionally a prized tin of condensed milk, before the village stocks of the latter ran out. The officers shared these most acceptable nutritional purchases very generously with us all. Unfortunately, the last unlabelled tin we opened of alleged condensed milk contained awful smelling parsnips!

During restricted hours in daylight we were allowed into the courtyard for exercise, always in the presence of armed guards, and under heavier guards were permitted 'promenades', walks outside the prison. These were beneficial, particularly in late autumn as the weather was much cooler and the exercise helped a little towards keeping a degree of fitness.

Although the civilian population in North Africa was beginning to experience the effects of food shortages, there was no difficulty in obtaining olive oil, which was used extensively for cooking purposes. Olives were grown in the region and the famed escargots (edible snails) were found in abundance in the olive growing areas. Not that we ate the latter, however the oil was useful and easily obtainable. Even in the small town of Le Kef there was a factory, where after harvesting, the olives were taken to be crushed and then put through a complicated processing plant to produce an excellent finished product. Once in lieu of a promenade, but still under heavy guard, we were taken to this factory to see the processing for ourselves. It was an unexpected diversion.

We were able to carry out limited cooking by burning charcoal. It was difficult to light but once started would burn fiercely and with little smoke. Ted Hart could fry excellent omelettes on the occasions when eggs were available. From time to time I was able to produce a vegetarian stew composed mainly of carrots, swedes, which the French called 'navets', haricots and lentils. We did not have any meat, but the occasional bone of doubtful origin, added a little to the nutritional value, or so we believed! The whole pottage was well boiled and was far more palatable than 'la soupe'.

On one of the more interesting promenades in a hilly off road area, we met an elderly nomadic Arab swathed in a multitude of garments. He stopped and spoke in Arabic to the French officer in charge of the promenade, asking if we would like to buy a chicken. He then produced from the nether regions of his robes, a large, live hen. The French officer enlightened us. If we bought the hen for a few francs, the Arab would wring the poor bird's neck, pluck and draw it, whilst we continued the promenade. He had nowhere to go so would be waiting with the bird all ready for the pot, when we returned. Christmas had arrived early; we had a one off treat for the evening meal!

An amusing incident occurred one morning whilst we were kicking a football about in the courtyard. A French 'adjudant chef,' rank similar to our sergeant major, appeared on the step outside his office and in a smug, pompous, supercilious attitude stood surveying the scene of prisoners relaxing. Ted Hart, an ex PT instructor before remustering to aircrew on the outbreak of war, casually lobbed the football, which described a perfect parabolic arc in the direction of this senior French sous-officer. With perfect timing and accuracy, observing the law of gravity, the football found its target and landed on top of the Frenchman's kepi (a tall military hat with a horizontal peak), flattening it and pinning it down over his eyes and face. He had to tug long and hard to release the battered headgear causing much humiliation to its wearer in front of the Arab guards and the British prisoners.

It was of course a perfect accident, and could not have been repeated with such accuracy no matter how hard Ted may have tried. We lost our football, at least temporarily. It was taken immediately into custody!

Ted was also an accomplished artist and adept at sketching. One morning, whilst idly browsing through a magazine, he came across a picture showing an English private soldier and French poilu (private soldier) standing together shaking hands on the battlefield. The caption below the picture read: - 'I believe our fathers fought together in 1914 to 1918.'

Ted cleverly redrew the picture and made a major alteration to show the French soldier stabbing the English soldier in the back. This was seen by a French adjudant chef named Aqua Viva who came from Corsica and was normally kindly disposed towards us. Not after this incident. It took a long time, with many reprisals, before a better relationship was re-established. Time is a healer and I am sure Aqua Viva began to understand why Ted had been so motivated.

Aqua Viva was quite a character, who spoke in very guttural tones exercising great economy with the use of words, preferring signs, grimaces and gesticulations to illustrate his dialogue. Flight Lieutenant Cooper told me one morning he had listened to him talking for twenty minutes during which time the man never said a word!

• • • • • •

The months in captivity unfolded; some of us still had not received any news from home when winter arrived. By then there were more prisoners and overcrowding added to our problems. In early December the weather became cold and wet, and under the cramped conditions in this small room bereft of amenities the stench was revolting. Relationships with fellow prisoners became very strained, sometimes dangerous, which I believe, under the circumstances, is the most simple and fairest way of summing up a worsening situation.

Could something be done to alleviate these problems?

Ted Hart and I believed there could. Escape! Difficult but worth a try. We made preparations hastily and planned to go on Sunday evening 8th December 1940. After discussing our proposals with Tony Randall, my wireless operator, it was agreed the three of us should attempt the escape together over the shithouse wall. That's what we called it and that is exactly what it was, although the French and the Arab guards referred to it as 'le cabinet'.

It was a filthy amenity, simply a round hole in the concrete floor with two raised steps on either side for the user to place his feet before squatting. The cavity below the surface would become filled with stinking human excrement and build up into a conical heap over the floor before our captors would clean up the mess. It had reached this state when I had a twenty-four hours attack of dysentery during which time I visited it seventeen times. During the night I had difficulty in getting the guard to unlock the door of our room and had to remonstrate with him through the bars of the window. After refusing my requests, to emphasise his petty authority, he lunged forward with his rifle penetrating the sleeve of my jacket with the bayonet. I had a lucky escape. Fortunately, a more intelligent Chef de Poste came to my rescue and arranged for the door to remain unlocked for the rest of the night.

Normal practice on visiting the cabinet was for prisoners to be accompanied by an armed guard but on the evening 8th December the weather conditions were atrocious with heavy snow falling. Nobody, not even the guards, would expect any prisoner to attempt an escape under these appalling conditions. Everything turned out to be in our favour. The evening meal was better than usual; there were potatoes, couscous, fresher vegetables and some real meat, not camel, in 'la soupe' and oranges to follow. Even the ration of crude red wine was quite palatable. Purely coincidental of course, it served as a useful send off.

After the meal we were ready, the guards did not attempt to accompany us to the cabinet and stood huddled together seeking shelter from the

Le Kef escape route

barrack room wall as they urged us to hurry.

Ted managed to scale the wall without difficulty by standing on Tony's shoulders, then, from the edge he gave me a final helping hand over the top. Tony was unfortunate and losing his grip at the top edge slipped and fell. In the course of his backward fall he collided with a large water cistern, the boom of the impact alerted the guards immediately and he was caught with no means of escape.

The alarm was really sounded. Lights appeared from all directions, inside and outside the caserne. Soldiers and guards emerged in frenzied panic as we ran up a steep hillside away from the Souk el Arba road. Ten minutes later, completely out of breath, we sought the shelter of a rocky outcrop looking down on to the caserne now fully illuminated. By luck we had got it right. The search, according to the flashing lights, was heading downhill towards the station and railway line to Tunis. There was not a light on the road to Souk el Arba, a small town and our destination some forty-eight kilometres away.

Fortunately, the snow ceased quite suddenly and the night

115

remained dry as we trudged along in quagmire conditions. It was incomprehensible how climatic and terrain situations could change so drastically from being hot and arid on our arrival four months earlier.

The road, almost a track, was deserted, but often we became disturbed by the noise of barking dogs. How sounds travel at night. It was disquieting and we became concerned lest the dogs' barking should raise an alert. Perhaps we had nothing to worry about; nevertheless we carried long sticks in case a dog should attack. Ted explained the importance of holding the stick almost horizontally, grasped tightly with hands and arms as far apart as possible. He said an attacking dog would leap and grab the stick in its mouth and hopefully not the person. Fortunately, the need to carry out this procedure did not arise.

After walking for several hours, we sighted a large river in the valley some distance away. The road crossed over the river by what appeared to be a suspension bridge. We decided to leave the road and approach the bridge by crossing a huge tract of open, steep sloping, boggy land, effectively, on the hypotenuse of a triangle, of which the road formed the two shorter sides. This reduced the distance but not the time, as conditions under foot were atrocious.

Wearily, we arrived at the unguarded bridge and crossed the river that turned out to be the Mellégue, as it flowed in spate from Algeria into Tunisia. It presented an awesome uninviting sight. I shuddered as we peered down from the bridge and looked into its swirling, dark, fast flowing waters.

We continued on the last leg of our journey by road and now, hampered by an increasing stiffness in our tired limbs, it became unwise to rest. Ted expressed concern that our muscles might become locked and seize completely, so we should continue to exercise them. It required determination and strong will power to keep going for the remaining few kilometres. How we made it I shall never know.

In a state of complete exhaustion, we reached Souk el Arba at 10 o'clock on the Monday morning wearing French army khaki trousers and to conceal our RAF tunics, khaki greatcoats issued previously by our captors. Their 'gifts', which were not intended for this purpose, kept us warm and acted as a disguise. To our relief we did not attract the slightest attention from the locals who obviously assumed we were French soldiers. With all the aplomb we could muster, we entered a small hotel and ordered two coffees. Those drinks served pleasantly and without hesitation, were absolute delectation and the prelude to our booking board and accommodation for the next three days.

Although my knowledge of the language was passable I could not keep up the pretence of being French and explained to our hosts that Ted and I were American graduates carrying out geological studies in liaison with the American and Vichy authorities. They asked to see our passports in evidence and thankfully accepted my explanation that they were lodged with the American Consul in Tunis for safe keeping. America was not yet involved in the war and we both signed the hotel register under pseudo names and addresses with no further questions being asked.

When our hostess left, after showing us to our twin bedded-room, we locked the door and moved a heavy piece of furniture towards it as a barricade in case of an emergency. We took stock of the surroundings outside our room at the back and noticed, that from the bedroom window, we could reach the flat roof of a low ground floor building and from there, drop to the ground.

I shall never forget those most comfortable beds. When our heads touched the pillows we became dead to the world until wakened for dinner at 6.30 pm. Should it have been necessary to attempt an emergency escape through the window, I would have failed miserably and I doubt if Ted could have made it either. Sitting up in bed I could scarcely move, being in the grip of extreme muscular tightness. Following gentle, painstaking, physical persuasion, the muscles were encouraged to slacken a little to enable us to negotiate the stairs, but only just. We entered the dining room very gingerly and with some trepidation.

Would word have got through from Le Kef? Might we be identified as the two British escapees? Happily, none of the diners took the slightest notice when we appeared. Could it all have been in our minds? I doubt it, but how important it had become to behave naturally.

Our charming French hostess never betrayed the slightest sign of suspicion regarding our identity, although Ted and I firmly believed she knew.

She was an excellent cuisinère and we enjoyed a superb meal comprising several individual courses all beautifully prepared. The meals we continued to enjoy during the remainder of our all too short stay were of a similar high standard.

Seated at a nearby table was a senior French police officer, who, apart from exchanging simple basic courtesies, such as "Bonsoir Messieurs, bon appétit," and later, when he left the room, "Bonne nuit, dormez vous bien," made no further attempt to enter into conversation. We could hardly believe our good fortune.

The following morning, without attracting any untoward attention, we walked through the town to the railway station to enquire about trains to Algeria and found there was no train to Souk Ahras for the next two days. We booked third-class tickets in advance and returned to our hotel where we spent the time relaxing, making the most of the hotel's catering and comfortable beds, our last luxuries for two years to come.

It was not until we boarded the train two days later we discovered that only the lower-class Arabs travelled third-class. This made us very conspicuous and we promptly moved into an unoccupied second-class compartment where we stayed undisturbed until the ticket inspector arrived. He accepted my explanation of our mistake and issued a supplementary ticket without any query. I still have this ticket, retained for nearly sixty years.

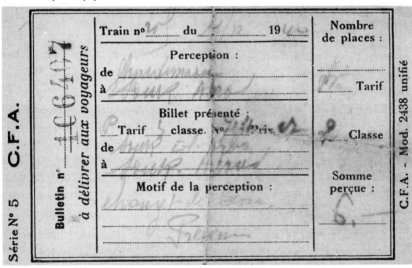

Supplementary rail ticket to Souk Ahras

Quietly, we relaxed, still undisturbed, taking in the changing aspects of a waterlogged countryside as the different scenes unfolded. We saw signs of how the poverty-stricken Arabs prepared to survive on meagre crops often grown on steep hill slopes bordering on forty-five degrees.

At this time of year the anticipated produce was not visible, the growing season would be extremely short. What other subsistence could they depend upon? Perhaps the proverbial couscous and macaroni?

On arrival at the Tunisian/Algerian frontier all passengers had to leave the train and queue on the platform for an identity check. We remained in our compartment, which was immediately opposite the spot where the official was carrying out his check and at the same time eyeing us with suspicion. Our problem became resolved quickly and unexpectedly when two French Military Policemen appeared in the corridor and opened the compartment door. One of them asked quite cheerfully, "Permission militaire?"

My simple reply in the affirmative satisfied him and wishing us both a good vacation he closed the door and the two departed. The official on the platform witnessed this and took no further interest in us. The passengers reboarded the train and by early evening we arrived with no further incident at Souk Ahras, only to find our connection had left five minutes earlier and there was no other train until next day.

Now short of money, we took to the road again, hoping we might find some sympathetic French civilian who would give us shelter. It was becoming dark when we made our first contact with a man who appeared to be well disposed when we spoke to him at his garden gate, in the light from a nearby street lamp. On hearing our plight he showed sympathy and was apologetic but unable to take any risk.

Shortly afterwards we were trapped, caught in the powerful headlights of two military vehicles carrying armed personnel who leaped out clicking back the bolts of their rifles and screaming for us to halt. We were frisked unceremoniously for weapons we did not possess and bundled into the nearest vehicle where we re-encountered, now in hastily donned uniform, the well disposed looking man from the garden gate. He was a French speaking Italian from the Deuxième Bureau, which collaborated on behalf of the Vichy French with the joint German Italian Commission, now in control of French North Africa. It was he who had reported us by phone to the authorities, and a few minutes later, back in captivity, we were locked in cells at the Souk Ahras military barracks.

Next morning we were taken to a military bureau and interrogated by a man of gross physical proportions who spoke fluent English. Employed by the Deuxième Bureau, his main interest was to discover how we had travelled from Le Kef to Souk Ahras. In spite of astute questioning he appeared satisfied that it was by train from Le Kef via Tunis and we made no attempt to disillusion him.

I asked if, as escapees having crossed the frontier from Tunisia into Algeria, we could stay in the caserne here at Souk Ahras. With no hesitation he answered simply, "ABSOLUMENT PAS," ("DEFINITELY NO,") and went on to explain in very good English that Le Kef was the belly button of the world to which we were attached inextricably by the umbilical cord, which would not be severed until the Allies were defeated. It should not take long!

"After that?" I asked.

He shrugged his shoulders, levered his huge frame laboriously out of the chair and left the room.

Q. "Qu'est-ce que nous pouvons faire?"
A. "ABSOLUMENT RIEN DU TOUT."
Q. "What can we do?"
A. "ABSOLUTELY NOTHING."

Surprisingly, we were not taken back to cells but to quite a large barrack room with heavily barred windows. Here we spent the next three days in relative comfort. The food was of a far higher standard than that at Le Kef and although locked in this room, we had permission, accompanied by guards, to go to the cabinet whenever necessary.

Our journey back began early on Saturday morning. It was to be in stages taking two days, firstly by train from Souk Ahras to Tunis and then to Le Kef under the escort of a French Army Lieutenant and two Arab guards who never left our compartment.

On arrival at Tunis on Saturday night the snow was falling quite heavily and the Lieutenant's orders were for us to spend the night in military cells. He assessed the appalling conditions and very generously, at great personal risk, as his family lived in occupied France, offered us an option. If we gave our verbal parole not to attempt an escape for ten hours, he would arrange our hotel accommodation for the night in a room adjoining his, but with an armed guard in the corridor by our bedroom door and another posted outside below our bedroom window. It was a magnificent gesture from a true Frenchman who had an invidious duty to carry out. No way would we have broken faith with this officer and gentleman, so far removed was he from those bastard 'Vichyites'.

After an excellent night's rest in clean and comfortable beds, we enjoyed a breakfast of coffee and croissants with him next morning, payment for these and the costs of our hotel accommodation were all settled out of his own pocket.

On leaving the hotel our paroles were withdrawn immediately and we were taken to a large military bureau in the city for completion of documentary formalities requiring the Lieutenant's attention. It was whilst waiting in this large bureau I set eyes on her. She looked so typically French; a slender graceful civilian girl, aged about nineteen, who left her desk and walked slowly towards me. We never took eyes off each other until she threw her arms around me in a tender, amorous embrace. There was a pause as she whispered her name, "Toussaint".' The few moments of idyllic bliss were shattered rudely by one of the guards as, with the butt-end of his rifle, he pushed me away, murmuring, "Défendu."

Toussaint was not to be thwarted and very deftly, using a sharp pair of scissors from her desk, snipped off an RAF button from my uniform tunic. She whispered, "Souvenir", as she kissed me and before we were finally bundled out of the bureau, surreptitiously pressed a small folded note into my hand again whispering, "Écris" ("Write to me").

It was a cold, long and tedious train journey from Tunis to Le Kef. The snow began to fall and the train stopped at every station. Many of the passengers were middle class Arabs travelling barefoot, mindless of the cold and the encrusted snow that melted on their feet in the relative warmth of the compartment. The women wore yashmaks, over which they peered at us in curiosity with those large brown eyes. Passengers seemed indifferent to our guards, who to their credit remained as inconspicuous as possible.

The weather was dreadful when we reached the station at Le Kef and we were taken quickly, under new guards, to a different section of the military caserne. It was here the Lieutenant left us, his sad mission completed. We never met him again.

Cells and dungeons formed a part of this caserne and for centuries they had served the purpose for which they had been intended. Ted and I were bustled unceremoniously towards the dungeons where we finished in solitary confinement. My dungeon stank and from the light of the guard's torch, before he slammed the heavy iron door closed, I noticed a filthy blanket on a large stone slab. My bed for the night! I remonstrated, "This is a horse blanket."

"The horse doesn't mind," he replied and with these words he slammed the door and I was in complete darkness. I had never experienced enduring complete darkness before, a condition to which my eyes did not become accustomed. I had to feel. There was no amenity so I urinated on the floor, as others had done before, then, from pure mental exhaustion, fell asleep on this cold damp stone slab under the cover of the stinking horse blanket. Poor Ted Hart in the next dungeon was experiencing exactly the same privations.

How low could these Vichy French bastards sink?

We remained in dungeons for two days. 'La soupe' was brought to us by armed guards and served in filthy army gamelles (mess tins). Fortunately we could not see the contents in the pitch-blackness and had no idea what we were consuming, although it tasted vile. However, we survived and on the third day were taken to a military bureau in the caserne where Flight Lieutenant Cooper, captain of the Hudson aircraft, now our British CO, was waiting.

We were paraded and stood to attention before a smug French Army Captain who, seated behind a large desk, was trying to put on an imposing presence. (It is surprising how a large desk creates a feeling of importance for those sitting behind it). Flight Lieutenant Cooper stood at our side facing him. He explained in French that we were not criminals but prisoners of war doing our duty in escaping and did not deserve the imprisonment in dungeons, to which we had been subjected. This made no impression on the man and by now, Ted and I were showing our feelings by body language expressing resentment, which did not escape his notice.

Captain Cooper, as we called him, quickly reminded me that the Frenchman did not like my attitude. "Tell him I don't like his," was my instinctive rejoinder.

"Watch it Hudson," Cooper replied, "I am trying to get you both out of those dungeons and he is perfectly capable of sending you back, where you could die in these conditions."

Our CO was right of course, so with reluctance, we behaved more correctly in front of this out and out Vichy bastard and were returned to our original quarters, where we were confined for fourteen days, with all so called 'privileges' withdrawn. That is how we spent Christmas 1940.

• • • • • •

Tunis le 2 11/40.

My dear friend,

I could receive your news. You are very. kind not to have forgotten me. I had thought that it would have been only an interview and no more. I thank you for all you wishes, you sent me. I also send you my wishes for the new year.

I hope that the year 1941 will bring the end of the war, and will permit you to go back to England, to find again you family and all the people you love. I hope also that all you wishes will be realized.

I hope that the christmas night has not been to much desagréable. and that you could have receive news from you parents.

I keep allways with plenty
care the button you gave me, and
I can assure you that I shall not
loose it. It has for me much more
value than you give to it.

Do you not forget when it
will be possible for you, to send
me your insign of the R.A.F.
I would be so happy.

You ask me a photo. It is
desagréable for me to send you it
now. You understand, that I
would prefer to wait that you are
in England, if you will think still
to me.

You can in the meantime
send me one of you photos with
great pleasure I would receive it.

The days might seem to be
long for you. I hope that my
thought (I think often to you) will
render those days not to much

des agreable.

I will not be angry if you do not write me often. I understand quite well.

I am late to reply you, please excuse me, but I will write you more in the future.

With much kindness.

T————e

Xxxxx.
xxxxx.

J'espère que vous me comprendrez. J'écris bien mal —

Letters from Toussaint who I met briefly in military bureau Tunis after recapture from Le Kef escape

Tunis le 18 Févri 1941

Cher camarade -

I am late to reply
to your letter, in order not
to change. I am lucky to
know that you are satisfaid -
the last news, which you recei=
ved from england have surely
brought to you all the satisfaction
you were waiting. I hope for
you that you will receive such
news very often., you must
learn to be patient and to
wait - you okay at le
Kef is not so disagréable - you
told me that you have passed
good evenings there.

the temperature must be
cold enough there, but you must
have the habit of it. you have
surely seen the snow, here we

never have seen it - the temperature
is a little bit better here now
happily for me, as I don't like
the winter - Do you take Wolla?
you will have soon the pleasure
to appreciate our nice sun

I thank you for the compliments
you give me. But I know surely
english much less than you know
french, you can be sure.

I regret that you have no
photos to hand me.

You will think to me, when
you will be back to england and
I hope it will be in short time -

I keeps allvays my dear
button in the meanetime, waiting
your insign of the Raf.

It is a little difficult to speak
of me: I fear allvays the control. there
in tunis, there are no distractions
since the war. but I hope that
better days will not be long to come
also for you - you are of my opinion,
indeed.?

127

will think to me, I hope also that you, if in other conditions
you can come back later in Tunisia.
Je vais terminer ma lettre en
français - Je n'ai d'ailleurs guère de
chose à vous dire - J'espère avoir très
bientôt de vos nouvelles - en attendant
je vous envoie toutes mes amitiés".

T -- T -- ne .

[+ x α x x
x x α x α x]

Tunis the 1st March 1941

The young girl, to whom you have written
some letters, asked me to write to you, in order
to ask you not to write her any more. She
has had some troubles in account of such
correspondence at home, and she can not
reply in the future to your letters. Please
do not write her any more, and excuse
her of such demand

A friend of her

This letter speaks for itself

128

Early in the New Year Toussaint and I began an exchange of letters, her letters to me were a comfort and great joy in those dark days. Then I received another letter from Tunis, written by a friend of her family at the request of her father, forbidding any further communication, or contact with his daughter and requesting me to destroy her letters. In view of the difficult situation in which decent French citizens were placed under the controlling German Italian Commission, understandably, he felt his family could become under suspicion and at risk. With sadness, I complied with his wishes. A precious and short relationship ended and I never heard from Toussaint again.

Letters from home began to arrive. I heard from my parents that on 23rd September 1940 they had received a telegram from RAF Records Office, Ruislip, informing them that I was safe in Tunisia.

The first Red Cross food and clothing parcels began to arrive and became our salvation. They were received with the utmost gratitude and appreciation by all prisoners and throughout my entire term of imprisonment continued to reach us. Words are almost inadequate to express the sincere thanks from all of us, to The International Red Cross and to all others, who in the cause of humanity, helped to alleviate our sufferings.

As overcrowding continued, our captors finally relented and opened up an extension to our existing barrack room that included three additional smaller rooms for use as sleeping quarters. We divided into three groups; friends stayed together, which contributed greatly to better 'domestic harmony' and toleration. John Riddick (my pilot) was an excellent Bridge player. He taught many of us the science and now we had better opportunities to improve our game. During the months of imprisonment to follow, Bridge playing became a wonderful therapy and contributed greatly to help preserve our sanity.

Although our captors had no conception of decent hygiene and medical facilities were at a premium, we were able to receive some dental treatment. This was only available in Tunis, so during March, Ted and I went there together and were accommodated in a small hospital annexe surrounded by very pleasant grounds. The dental officer, a decent Frenchman, was well disposed towards us and arranged for our treatment to be spun out a few days, enabling us to enjoy these luxury amenities, although we were closely guarded. The window of our ground floor room was heavily barred and an armed Arab soldier

Telephone No. : RUISLIP 3381 ;
and direct lines from Air Ministry.
Telegraphic Address :
RECORDS TELEX, RUISLIP.

Any communications on the
subject of this letter should
be addressed to :—
OFFICER i/c RECORDS,
ROYAL AIR FORCE,
RUISLIP, MIDDLESEX,
and the following number
quoted :-

RECORD OFFICE,

ROYAL AIR FORCE,

RUISLIP,

MIDDLESEX

Date 24th September 1940.

C7/755052

Dear Sir,

    In confirmation of my telegram
of yesterday's date, according to a telegram
from the American Consul at Tunis, transmitted
by the American Embassy, your son No.755052
Sergeant James Douglas HUDSON of No.101 Squadron,
Royal Air Force, previously reported as missing,
is now interned and safe in Tunisia.

    The actual place of internment
is not yet known, but will be communicated to you
as soon as received.

    I am,
     Dear Sir,
      Your obedient Servant,

       Squadron Leader,
     for Group Captain,
      Officer i/c Records,
      ROYAL AIR FORCE.

H.E.Hudson Esq.,
10 Moorside Road,
Kersal,
Salford.

was posted in the corridor outside.

We developed a friendly relationship with this guard, encouraged him to talk to us and gave him cups of coffee, a real luxury. It developed a trust, although behind it all was an ulterior motive.

A visiting clergyman, who was in touch with an organisation in regular communication with Malta, hoped to arrange an escape for us that depended of course on being able to immobilise the guard. It would then be easy to leave the hospital by a side exit, disappear into the shrubbery and scale an outside wall where a contact would be waiting. A date and time had been fixed and we became very excited.

Self   Wilbur Wright   Ted Hart

Le Kef February 1941

The clergyman was to provide us with a very strong powdered sedative, not a poison, which we would mix with the sugar and place in the guard's coffee. By now we had encouraged him to come into our room and sit inside to enjoy his drink. The plan couldn't fail!

You can certainly imagine our disappointment next day when the clergyman arrived without the sedative. Apparently the leader of the organisation had had second thoughts on the wisdom of the escape. He felt it could be traced too easily by the Deuxième Bureau and lead to the arrest of the clergyman and others involved. He also feared that it could prejudice an arrangement that had been kept secret, an arrangement with Malta that was vital and of greater importance than the repatriation of two young British airmen. It was a long and sad journey back to Le Kef.

• • • • • •

Due to the shortage of reading material in the camp we always looked forward to receiving books. These generally reached us via the American Consul in Tunis and were sent from the small British community, who although under constant surveillance still enjoyed living in freedom. One afternoon in early March we received a larger parcel than usual. It was brought into the camp and opened in our room under the strict supervision of a French officer, revealing a collection of books and a huge cake. What followed was most fortuitous.

Flight Lieutenant Cooper suggested it would be courteous to offer a piece of cake to the Frenchman, the least we could do as he had just staggered in with an extremely heavy gift parcel. We all agreed and this pleased the officer who graciously accepted the first slice, cut apparently with some difficulty, by 'Cap' Cooper who said, "The knife's a bit blunt and the cake crumbly, I'll cut the remainder later when I've found a sharper knife."

"Ça va, et merci," ("OK and thank you,") the Frenchman replied as he saluted our CO and left the room happily munching his cake.

The knife had not been blunt, nor the cake crumbly. 'Cap' Cooper's problem, when cutting the cake, was due to the knife coming into contact with a small metal file. Prior to baking the cake, the file had been concealed in the mixture by an elderly lady well-wisher in Tunis. It was fortunate that our CO, by his adroit manipulation of the knife, discovered the file before the Frenchman, otherwise the repercussions would have been serious for the elderly lady. Her punishment would have been severe, probably leading to imprisonment.

The back rooms of the officers' quarters, unlike those of the senior NCOs, faced directly outside the caserne. From all the heavily barred windows there was a considerable drop to the open ground below. Any possible escape would necessitate a descent by rope and it was estimated that four bed sheets knotted together would be required for this purpose.

Without delay, the officers put the file to good use. After two or three weeks they succeeded in filing almost through the top and bottom of two adjacent thick metal bars at one window, disguising their work by filling the gaps in the bars with a mixture of earth and black shoe polish. Although the filings were never discovered there were one or two narrow squeaks. Aqua Viva became a frequent visitor and would sit on this particular window ledge and rest his back by leaning against the bars. At first the officers believed he suspected and that this was a deliberate act. However, their worries were unfounded. His behaviour had been purely coincidental but later they took the precaution of converting the window ledge into a bookshelf!

The first escape plan provided for the senior NCOs to be invited to the officers' quarters, allegedly to celebrate an officer's birthday and join the party. Such an invitation would require permission from the French. As this could not be assured an alternative option would be needed, an option to which I refer in the next paragraph. On the eve of the escape, should number one plan be possible, we should create the usual diversionary noise whilst the final severance of the bars was carried out. Hopefully, undetected we should all get away! Unfortunately, the ensuing silence would soon arouse suspicion and would be promptly investigated leaving little time for us to move far before our absence would be detected.

In the meantime a second option was being prepared from the senior NCOs' quarters. The ceilings in these rooms were high and in the ceiling of our room there was a trapdoor leading to an unoccupied roof space that spanned the entire block. By climbing on to a supported chair placed on top of a table, one of the taller prisoners succeeded in forcing open the trapdoor, hoisting himself into the roof space and carrying out an inspection. It revealed a solid stone dividing wall, which blocked access completely to the end outer wall. From there we had intended to partially dislodge two or three roof apex tiles preparatory to their removal on the night of the escape. If successful, the only way to freedom would be through the gap created and then by rope descent. This rope would require at least seven sheets knotted together and secured to a rafter in the roof. The procedure would be dangerous and unpleasant for any prisoner who suffered from vertigo. However, this method presented the better option. Its timing could be coincided with the officer's independent escape, no diversionary noise would be needed and we hoped our absence would remain undetected until the next morning.

Firstly we had to deal with the barrier wall in the roof space. Two men worked industriously, as silently as possible, to dislodge two huge stones from the dividing wall and also completed the preparation for the removal of the roof tiles. By the end of April 1941 we were all set to make a total 'getaway'! We did, but not in the manner expected.

Ironically two excellent escape preparations had been accomplished but were never put into practice.

Chapter Eight

MÉDÉA

At the end of April 1941, quite unexpectedly, we received unbelievable news of good fortune. We were to be repatriated in
exchange for prisoners from a German submarine crew. Whilst
negotiations were taking place, we were taken by train from Le
Kef to Algiers and thence by road to Médéa, a pleasant small town
in the mountains south of Algiers. Here we met up with a small
number of army privates and senior NCOs who, after the fall of
Dunkirk, miraculously found their way to Marseilles and crossed the
Mediterranean to Algeria. Although it was still neutral, 'Maréchal'
(Marshal) Pétain had established his Vichy government and the poor
fellows found themselves behind prison bars.

Now they had been released and shared accommodation with us
in an hotel in the centre of the town. Although we slept crowded,
three in a single room with three beds, we were all free. There were
no guards and each day the hotel provided a light breakfast and two
main meals of a decent standard. As aircrew we received a small
monetary allowance enabling us to buy drinks in the local café bars.
It was here I met Daffy Watson, an army private of great physical and
mental stature. We became close friends after I offered to buy him a
drink when he had no money to repay. At first he refused, such was
his pride, but after further persuasion I prevailed upon the big fellow
to accept. More about him anon.

It was in one of the bars Ted Hart and I met two attractive young
French girls, Marcelle and Andrée, with whom we became friendly
and spent many pleasant evenings together. The girls' inability to
speak English presented no problems; sign language being universally
understood proved to be a useful substitute!

One evening they failed to arrive at the bar as was customary and
we were approached by an older woman who was quite upset when she
spoke to us. She carried a message from the girls' families forbidding

them to have any further relationship with us and for the same reasons as Toussaint's father. Below is my translation of the last letter I received from Marcelle in Médéa, dated 28th May 1941, a few days before we left for Aumale.

It is a sad letter, which tells its own story about a short, harmless and friendly relationship between two young French girls and two young English airmen. The girls were the charming daughters of two decent French families. In their hearts they bore no grudge towards the young Englishmen who fought with their French counterparts at the beginning of the war.

Dear Douglas,

You will now have returned from Algiers and will know something about the capital of Algeria. What do you think of it, that which we call White Algiers? There is a big difference between it and our little Médéa, they are not at all alike. Algiers is the large city, Médéa the big village with all its gossip and tittle-tattle, but in spite of all that it is not too bad. I have known it for fifteen years and like it a lot.

So, a little bird has told you my name, how indiscreet!

You feel you don't speak French very well, that's not my opinion. I say to you most sincerely you speak and write it correctly enough and that I will never be able to speak and write English so well. Perhaps that is not important.

Andrée is also sorry that your friend does not understand our language and that she is not able to speak English. Nevertheless, I expect they understand each other. In spite of all that you are there to interpret.

Didn't you have your daily walk today and go to Dormiette? I seem to think I saw you go by.

I will close for today and hope you are not as lazy as I when it comes to writing. In your next letter tell me a little about yourself and what you used to do in England.

All my love
Marcelle

I continue with my letter this evening since I saw you and you told me earlier you would be leaving on Saturday. It can only be a sad passing moment and I hope most sincerely everything will soon turn out all right.

I know only too well that life is not easy for you, but what can you do? Nobody can do anything. It makes one a little pessimistic but don't let it get you down, put aside depressing thoughts.

I hope we can write to each other if it isn't too much trouble for you. You

Miliana le 28 Mai 1941.

Cher Douglas.

Vous voilà revenu d'Alger
vous connaissez maintenant la capitale
de l'Algérie. Comment trouvez-vous
celle que l'on dénomme "Alger la
Blanche"? il y a n'est-ce pas une
bien grande différence entre elle et
notre petit Miliana; ce n'est pas du
tout la même chose Alger est
la grande ville, Miliana le gros village
avec tous ses commérages et ses
petites histoires, mais malgré tout
il n'est pas si déplaisant que
ça, j'y vis depuis 15 ans et je
l'aime bien.

Alors c'est un petit oiseau qui vous a donné mon nom quel indiscret !

Vous trouvez que vous ne parlez pas bien le français ? ce n'est pas mon avis, je puis vous dire en toute sincérité que vous le parlez et l'écrivez assez correctement, et que je ne serai jamais capable de parler et d'écrire l'anglais aussi bien ; mais cela n'est qu'un détail.

Andrée regrette elle aussi que votre ami ne connaisse notre langue et qu'elle ne puisse parler anglais, mais je suppose qu'ils se comprennent tout de même, et puis malgré tout vous êtes là pour faire l'interprète. N'avez-vous pas fait aujourd'hui votre promenade quotidienne, n'êtes vous pas allé à Damiette ? il me semble vous avoir vu passer.

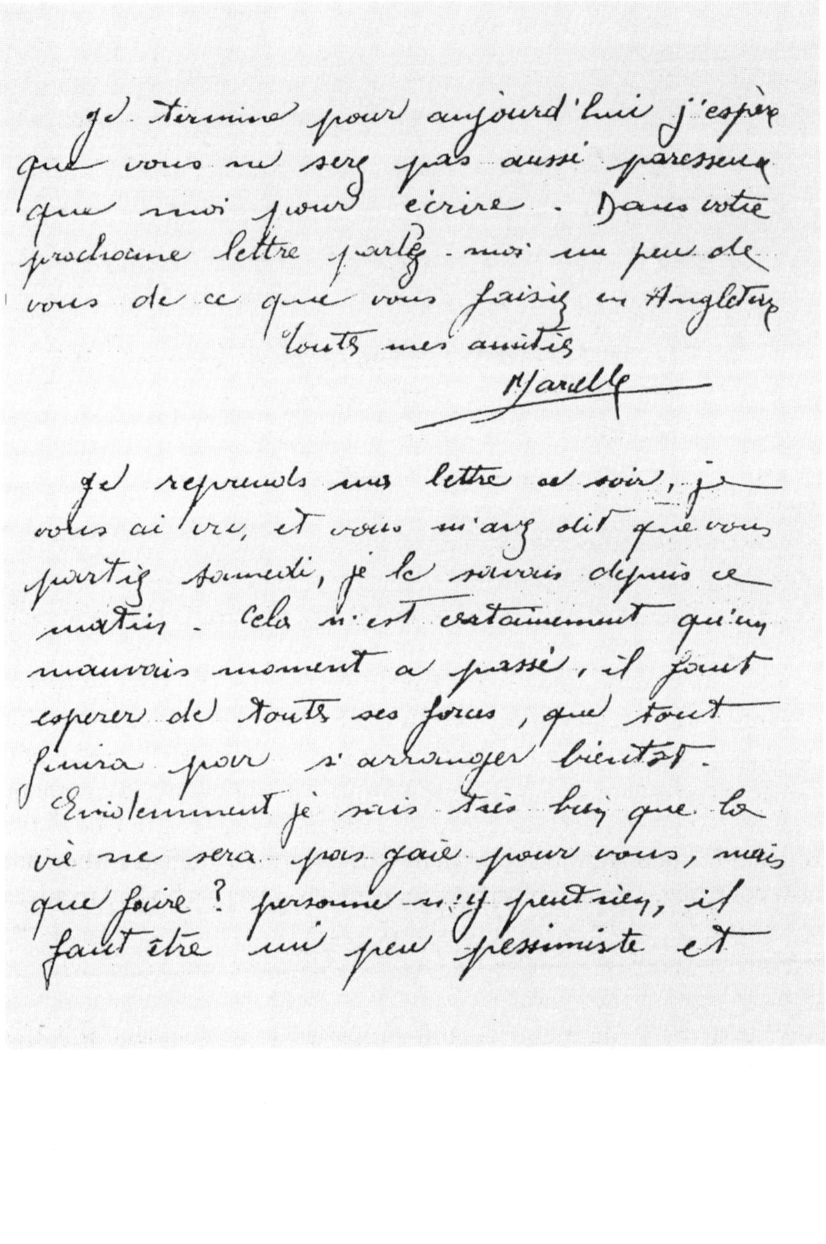

Je termine pour aujourd'hui j'espère que vous ne serez pas aussi paresseux que moi pour écrire. Dans votre prochaine lettre parlez-moi un peu de vous de ce que vous faisiez en Angleterre

Tous mes amitiés

Marcelle

Je reprends ma lettre ce soir, je vous ai vu, et vous m'avez dit que vous partiez samedi, je le savais depuis ce matin. Cela n'est certainement qu'un mauvais moment a passé, il faut espérer de toutes ses forces, que tout finira pour s'arranger bientôt. Évidemment je sais très bien que la vie ne sera pas gaie pour vous, mais que faire ? personne n'y peut rien, il faut être un peu pessimiste et

*ne pas se laisser abattre, chasser les
idées noires.*

*Toutes vous Douglas que nous nous
écririons si cela vous est possible, et si
cela ne vous ennuie pas trop, vous
m'écrire chez mes cousins ils veulent bien
recevoir mes lettres —*

*Voici leur adresse: Mons. et Mame Boche
Café Glacier. Médéa.*

Bonsoir Douglas et à demain donc

Marcelle

can write to me at my cousins' house, they will be only too pleased to receive my
letters.
Goodnight Douglas, until tomorrow.
Marcelle.

Tomorrow never came. We were unable to meet and never saw each
other again.

Maréchal Pétain and Pierre Laval had become clay in the hands
of General Huntziger and collaborators with the Germans. So, for
no fault of their own, these French people lived under the yoke of a
dangerous and hypocritical regime, members of the Vichy government
by whom they had been betrayed. They lived in fear of the Deuxième
Bureau that in turn, was subservient to the German/Italian authorities
now controlling French North Africa. French citizens who had relatives
in occupied or unoccupied France lived in permanent fear of reprisals,
lest inadvertently, they should act indiscreetly, or be considered to have
betrayed their Vichy masters.

Tunisia and Algeria were still supposed to be neutral and the
French became fearful of upsetting the Americans, not yet in the war.
Nevertheless, Vichy French collaboration allowed German and Italian
aircraft to take-off and land at El Alouina airfield. The situation of the
French civilians in French North Africa was getting more and more
precarious.

More allied airmen joined us and overcrowding in the hotel became acute. No decision had been reached about our repatriation exchange with the German submarine crew and tension was beginning to build between us and some of the local residents. Wisely, as we all believed, the authorities decided to move us to Aumale, where they explained, there would be more room and better accommodation.

Oasis street scene

Topical everyday scenes in Algeria at this time. The pictures were taken by a fellow prisoner. Camel train moving South.

Chapter Nine
AUMALE

Our transfer to Aumale, travelling in open army trucks without guards, began in early June 1941. When nearing the town we suddenly became aware of being followed by two military vehicles carrying armed soldiers. As our trucks entered the town we noticed the streets on either side were lined with fully armed soldiers and we were driven at high speed through a large entrance into a compound swarming with guards. It was a partly tree-lined compound in which a large two storey barn-like building with heavily barred windows on both floors faced the street. Once inside this compound, the huge gates closed formidably, we were trapped. The negotiations for our exchange with the German submarine crew had fallen through. Our British CO had been deceived and we were back behind bars in a new prison camp.

To what depth of duplicity could the Vichy French bastards sink? Lower than a snake's belly was our general verdict.

Aumale Prison Camp early July 1941

The number of prisoners now approached the sixty mark, still mostly RAF personnel. We were herded together on the first floor of the building in one large room divided by a partition to separate officers from the other ranks. Beneath us, on the ground floor, was an asylum housing pitiful female Arabs many of whom were incurably ill. Their haunting screams would often disturb us and echo throughout the night.

Don't be misled by the sylvan foreground façade.

In the left background can be seen the 'hell house' where all prisoners were incarcerated on the top floor. The opposite side of this building, with its heavily barred windows, faced the street.

This was a purpose built inferno during the heat of the summer months; a prison conceived by only the Devil incarnate, or by the Vichy French. It was created to guarantee absolute discomfort with a complete absence of hygienic facilities. The place was evil under the regime of a sadistic Vichy French swine of an officer. We ate, drank, played, quarrelled and suffered from dysentery under one roof in the same basic room.

Aumale: - Armed guards from immediate foreground to extreme background to ensure we did not escape when being transferred from barracks to cells

The climax was reached in July after a flight sergeant escaped. On hearing the noise of rifle firing we assumed he had been shot and we rioted. He had been shot at but not killed, nor wounded. This we did not know at the time. The rioting lasted throughout the night and the guards in the street below fired volley after volley through the bars of the windows. Bullets ricocheted around the room. Remarkably nobody was hurt.

Next morning we were all marched, under the heaviest guard yet, across the town to another barracks and placed in cells for sixteen days. I shared a cell with eight others in complete darkness. Most of us developed dysentery and had to make the best possible use in the darkness of one metal churn, emptied daily by two prisoners detailed for this privilege!

Food in the camp generally was vile. Twice a day containers of loathsome mess were dumped on the floor of the room for all prisoners. This description was no exaggeration. Again I cannot emphasise how indebted and grateful we were to The International Red Cross for their valuable food parcels.

• • • • • •

In mid-July, to the surprise of everyone, our captors proposed that the British prisoners should select a football team and play a match against the Arab soldiers. A proposition made no doubt, in the hope it might help to improve the relationship between captors and prisoners. If so, it was a forlorn hope, as the gulf between the British and the Vichy French became an ever-widening chasm that would not be breached. We bore no grudge towards the Arabs, nor towards the Arab soldiers who were compelled to obey the instructions of their masters. Consequently we selected a team of British stalwarts and an early evening match was arranged. At this time of day, although the sun would be low, the heat in mid-July would be stifling.

All prisoners not involved in the game turned up to watch. Guards were positioned around the entire periphery of the playing area; a hard and stony ground, most unsuitable for staging a football match and highly dangerous for all the players.

In a temperature of around 104 degrees Fahrenheit the game started. It became apparent that whilst the undernourished prisoners, wearing ill assorted types of footwear, were the more skilful players, their stamina was low and this led to them tiring more quickly in the heat. The Arabs however, although having the disadvantage of playing barefooted, were accustomed to the heat, tired less easily and were clearly the fitter.

The playing time of the match was reduced to twenty minutes each way by the British prisoner referee, quite rightly in view of the trying conditions. I cannot remember the outcome of the match; the result was unimportant in a game played competitively but in a friendly manner. The players on both sides were conscious of the dangers presented by the pitch and exercised restraint when tackling. There were no injuries, a credit to all participants. If a lesson was to be learned from this performance, then it was the Vichy French who should have attended the class!

On mid morning promenades at Aumale, we were always accompanied by a French officer and the column of prisoners was preceded by an armed cavalry soldier on horseback. Another similarly armed and mounted cavalry soldier followed at the rear of the column and several armed foot soldiers accompanied us on each side, lest we should be foolhardy enough to attempt to escape.

Aumale 'Promenade' July 1941
On this occasion guarded by four mounted French soldiers with a French Officer in charge. Arab foot soldiers were present but not in the picture

Unprovided, in broad daylight and in soaring temperatures, an attempted escape was unlikely, but it flattered our ego that we could cause them so much anxiety. It certainly tied up and kept occupied a large number of Vichy French military personnel, who could perhaps, have been deployed more usefully, in other directions. What must have been our cost to the taxpayers?

On one occasion we had reached the turning point of our promenade and the mid-morning heat was quite intense when we stopped to rest. The cavalry soldiers dismounted to stretch their legs. We were allowed to approach the temporarily riderless, friendly horses and demonstrate a little affection by caressing them in the manner of which animal lovers are capable. They were beautiful white Arab stallions and did not object to our attentions.

Leading Seaman Pickles had some experience of horsemanship and had always admired these animals, often expressing a wish to ride one. Quite out of the question of course, under existing circumstances, but not today. Standing near one of these magnificent stallions, he spoke to the French officer in charge of the promenade, and in perfectly good French, asked if he might be allowed to sit in the saddle. The officer was amazed at the temerity of this prisoner who had dared make the request. Pickles promised to give his word of temporary parole, which was endorsed by our CO, and to the surprise of us all the Frenchman agreed. Pickles jumped up into the saddle and encouraged, as the horse remained docile, asked if he might take it for a few strides. Surprisingly the Frenchman agreed again. We all stood around and I must admit were absolutely captivated.

Whether what ensued was by accident or design, I do not know. Pickles exerted a little knee pressure on the animal whereupon the horse was galvanised into immediate action. It positively took-off and careered down the stony track rapidly accelerating until it reached the parapet of an old stone walled bridge. Here it decided to dispose of its burden. The rider was thrown unceremoniously over the animal's head and disappeared from view.

The immediate concern of us all was for Pickles' safety and although he was bruised and shaken badly, he did not appear to have suffered any broken bones. In some respects it had created a rather amusing interlude. The guards appeared, if only temporarily, to have forgotten about their responsibility for the prisoners! A military ambulance was summoned to take our wounded hero to hospital where he remained for a few days before rejoining us, none the worse for his experience. No reprisals were taken against the British prisoners nor against the French and Arab guards.

Were our captors relenting? I doubt it. Preparations were under way already to move us south to the desert.

Petty Officer Wines, a Fleet Air Arm pilot, whilst undergoing all the privations of this hellish Aumale prison camp, always displayed an indomitable spirit. Like Daffy Watson, he was a man of great mental and physical stature. It was before the establishing of the Lieutenant Commander Lamb/Sergeant Hart's organised boxing school that this man alone, undertook to train prisoners who wished to practise boxing. He would stand and offer himself as a human punchbag, inviting prisoners of all weights to throw a punch at him. Never would he throw a retaliatory punch on target, although inevitably he received many blows from his pupils. At the end of a session he would stand there almost jubilant, bruised and bleeding. Whilst admiring the spirit of this man, our British CO discouraged the practice in the prisoner's own interests on the grounds of excessive physical demands.

● ● ● ● ● ●

The Vichy Commandant of the camp at Aumale, whose name now eludes me, was hated and despised by everyone. Certain prisoners swore that one day they would get the bastard. From what I read at a later date I understand that after liberation, following the American invasion of North Africa, one of them succeeded. If this were true, then justice had been done.

A later arrival to share with us the Vichy hospitality was a baby jackal. This little abandoned animal was rescued by a prisoner during a promenade and brought back to the camp as a companion for Raf, a little black and white short-haired terrier dog. For a week or so, they would play together, curl up and sleep side by side and waken us early in the mornings by scampering round and round the room under the prisoners' beds. They entered into a quite uncanny friendship.

The jackal is a wild doglike animal and lives in packs hunting and scavenging for food. Our little fellow grew up rapidly, thriving on a plentiful supply of our rejected obnoxious food and whilst never manifesting real signs of violence he could not discriminate between a gentle tweak and a playful bite that could be dangerous. With some reluctance we took him back to the wilds where, restored to his natural habitat, he was now quite capable of looking after himself. We missed the little chap, as did his companion Raf. By their little antics they had provided us with a lot of diversionary pleasure.

Whilst still at Aumale we heard of the German invasion of Russia on a very broad front, thereby, greatly extending their lines requiring reinforcements and communications. This news cheered us immensely and suggested they would become too heavily occupied on the Russian front to consider an invasion of the UK. It was a wonderful boost to morale.

I had been asked several questions during my sojourn in North Africa. I hoped that sojourn it would be. The dictionary definition is 'temporary stay'.

A middle-aged French lady in Médéa, who wanted to know why the English had burned Joan of Arc, posed the question to which I gave the most unsatisfactory reply. I had to think for a while before answering that one. When I said it was over five hundred years ago, and Joan of Arc was regarded as a heretic in those bygone days, I had trodden on a minefield. Alas, I was completely lost for reconciliatory words. It was Jeanne d'Arc Jour de Fête; the day the French reserved for commemoration of the Saint who was canonised in 1920.

The question, the response to which gave me the most satisfaction, was asked by a Vichy French Lieutenant who wanted to know why the Royal Navy bombarded and sank the French fleet when it was sheltering at Dakar in Senegal. The response that I could not resist was a question to his question. "Which ship was that?" I had trodden on another minefield, but it was worth it!

The Vichy French officers still smarted over the Oran incident, which occurred in July 1940, an incident about which they kept reminding us. It was then that the Allies, who believed the Germans might make use of captured French warships, after due warning, attacked French battleships at Oran and put them out of commission.

About this time the French General de Gaulle raised a legion of 'Free French', who were condemned by Pétain's French government, then established at Vichy. Frenchmen overseas, in Equatorial Africa, the Cameroons and as far afield as the Pacific colonies, rallied to the Allies' cause. Any mention of de Gaulle in North Africa was 'absolument' défendu (strictly forbidden). This inspired a satirical parody.

One of the prisoners composed a few lines written in the most appalling French but with quite a catchy accompanying tune. It was called "Oh! Vive de Gaulle." We would sing it lustily to annoy our captors and give it our wholehearted rendering when, dressed in rags and tatters, we marched through the streets of Aumale (and later of Laghouat) on our organised promenades. It showed the locals what we thought of their tyrannical Vichy masters.

This is how it went: -

> Oh! Vive de Gaulle, Oh! Vive de Gaulle
> Avec son armée Française
> Abas Darlan, lavez les mains
> Pas collaboration avec les Allemands
> Oh! Vive de Gaulle, Oh! Vive de Gaulle
> Avec son armée Française
> C'est la victoire pour vous
> Si vous joignez avec nous
> Darlan VOUS BÂTARD!

The last line was sung with a rising crescendo.

Again the problem of intolerable overcrowding grew and in October 1941 we left this 'Aumale Hell' and were moved to the famous, or infamous Laghouat in the Sahara desert about three hundred miles south of Algiers.

WELCOME TO LAGHOUAT...

...From The Room With A View

Chapter Ten
LAGHOUAT

Laghouat was a small oasis town on the outskirts of which was a large Foreign Legion Garrison. The town was basically a filthy Arab kasbah with a small French population and a Hotel Saharienne, used primarily for those French officers who were to run the prison camp. British prisoners occupied a section of a squalid barracks in a small compound that formed part of the garrison. This compound, encircled by a high triple fence of barbed wire, was surrounded by an even higher solid stone wall, encompassing the entire perimeter. Armed guards with machine guns were positioned strategically to ensure complete surveillance; their orders were to shoot any man who tried to escape.

The day after our arrival we were taken in small groups, heavily guarded and accompanied by a supercilious French officer, to the top of a minaret from the balcony of which we had a magnificent, uninterrupted, panoramic view of desert wilderness. Visibility extended in all directions for a hundred miles, or more.

Turning to the north this supercilious officer pointed and said:

"Regardez, au nord, le desert!"

Turning east he continued: -

"Regardez, a l'est, le desert!"

Then to the south: -

"Regardez, au sud, le desert!"

When lastly he turned to the west, we all chimed: -

"Yes, we know, a l'ouest, le desert!"

He had made his point.

One road passed through this oasis town, providing the only vehicular route north to Djelfa, the rail terminal from Algiers. To the south it became a winding, tortuous track leading to the small oases of Ghardaia and El Golea. Throughout all seasons the desert was an entirely hostile environment in which only the itinerant Arabs knew how to survive, so Laghouat provided the Vichy French with a 'tailor made' site for the incarceration of prisoners.

●●●●●●

I received sad news concerning the death of a close friend since Manchester Grammar school days. Lieutenant Louis Bingham Murray, aged 23, was a brilliant mathematician who graduated at Oxford University about the time of the outbreak of war. He had been killed serving in the Royal Artillery (RA) whilst flying on attachment with the RAF. His mission was to investigate and obtain a more accurate update on the effectiveness of the enemy's ground to air defences!

For the next few months living conditions in Laghouat were more congenial than Aumale. The weather was becoming cooler, the flies were dying off, we were less crowded and I shared a room with a new friend Jimmy Alexander, a six feet four inches beanpole of a man and a fellow navigator. Tony Randall moved into a small adjoining room, which he shared with a new aircrew arrival who had been subjected to extreme exposure, having spent several tortuous days and nights in a dinghy. The effects from the sun had caused severe skin blistering and dehydration. Other members of the crew perished.

Tony started work on a compilation to be called The Camp Echo of which he became editor. He had no difficulty in finding talented men in the camp eager to help with articles and illustrations, and for several months I was responsible for all the typewritten work. Our little publication was always awaited eagerly and contributors increased as the weeks went by. It created a rewarding diversionary pastime for many.

In the middle of December 1941 I developed a serious attack of dysentery, which persisted uninterruptedly, until Christmas Eve, when Flight Lieutenant Cooper and Flying Officer Davies, the pilots of the Hudson aircraft, knowing of my problem, sympathetically invited me along with some of the others to join them for drinks. They had acquired some rather special wines for the occasion and 'Cap' Cooper said, whilst pouring about a quarter litre of wine into my aluminium beaker, "Drink this Hudson, if it doesn't make you better it can't make you much worse!"

It was a good quality wine and created a soothing warmth to my tormented inside. The wine continued to flow until about midnight and we all enjoyed an evening of celebration. I felt very much better

Self - Typing the Camp Echo

Tony Randall - Editor of the Camp Echo (My Blenheim W/Op AG)

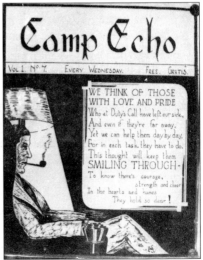

Mostly RAF personnel before the arrival of HMS Havock's Crew
Photograph taken in front of the Mark I latrine

and had the best night's sleep for weeks. In the morning I wakened without hangover, nor dysentery. The 'Cap's' medicine had done the trick.

It was unfortunate that an otherwise pleasant evening was marred by an unpleasant incident that occurred before we went to bed. A leading seaman mistakenly accused Tony of placing in his bed a large filthy besom brush, a brush that was used for cleaning out the three so called toilets. Tony was completely blameless and had nothing to do with this stupid behaviour; nevertheless he received a nasty head and facial gash by a blow from a broken bottle delivered by the sailor. A British officer intervened promptly and the guilty attacker was immediately handed over to the French military authorities who were more than capable of meting out punishment. This was an unprecedented action, normally the British CO would administer punishment for any prisoner's misdeed and although internal tensions often ran high, such an incident never occurred again.

● ● ● ● ● ●

During the next three months new prisoners arrived, initially, mostly aircrew and overcrowding did not present a problem. We worked happily on productions of The Camp Echo, whilst others, under the expert guidance of Flight Lieutenant Bertie Brain DFC and his capable assistants, were busily occupied in arranging camp concerts. The mass of talent they accumulated was quite incredible.

Under the direction of Lieutenant Commander Lamb DSO DSC and Sergeant Ted Hart, a well organised school of boxing was established that attracted many stalwarts anxious to improve their art in self defence. These activities coincided perhaps with the most important activity of all, digging the escape tunnel.

The weather in March was pleasant and although it was getting gradually hotter, we had not yet become plagued with flies and continued to enjoy the evenings improving our game of Bridge. The Red Cross food parcels arrived regularly and prison life was bearable. I do not wish to give the impression that Laghouat had become a leisure centre because it certainly had not.

Conditions would change for the worse.

Early April 1942 bore testimony to this with the arrival of the entire ship's company of HMS Havock, a Fleet destroyer, which had run aground off Cap Bon. At a stroke the camp became overcrowded, there was no extra accommodation for this sudden influx of prisoners and the three holes in the concrete floor of the heads, as the Navy called our toilets, were completely inadequate for a camp complement bordering on the five hundred mark.

Work had to commence immediately digging 'slit' trenches whilst the French also hurriedly opened up new rooms in a barrack's extension. These rooms, used previously to accommodate twenty-four Arab soldiers, were required now to house fifty British prisoners of war. Our captors worked in a frenzy to increase the barbed wire fortifications.

All aircrew NCOs were moved from their relatively comfortable accommodation to make way for the new Royal Navy officers. I had to share, what previously had been a French sous-officier's single room, with six other men for the duration of my imprisonment. Under these cramped conditions I found it difficult to continue with my typewriting task for the Camp Echo, a responsibility I handed over with reluctance to Tony Randall.

Many of the younger Royal Navy officers objected to being confined in the same camp as the ratings. Ratings! I ask you? Many of us old timers, having nearly completed our second year of imprisonment, were actually by now warrant officers first class, fully qualified flying

A selection of camp concert photos

Prince & Princess Charming

Lt (RN) Robertson's Rocket

King and 'Ladies' in waiting

Blessing the Witches' Brew

Sartorially well kitted out

Sparring partners

Keeping fit in Laghouat

Also well kitted out

Laghouat chorus girls

Laghouat boxing team

personnel with operational experience. Unfortunately, our NCO promotions had not been promulgated during our absence from the UK, a promotion situation that did not apply to officers. There were instances of officers with the rank of pilot officer on arrival becoming Flight Lieutenants before repatriation. During this period the opportunity to apply for commissioned rank had been denied the NCOs.

I, and others in the same position, found this unforgivable and inconceivable. We were regarded and treated as subordinate to men

Relief or occupational therapy under the surveillance of an armed guard

allegedly, but not in reality, of higher rank. We became subjected to the demeanour of taking their orders, yes taking orders from new arrivals who were civilians when we became prisoners. It may seem trivial now, but it was damned important then.

Young new naval officer arrivals continued to moan, complaining their treatment was contrary to the Geneva Convention! They were not too pleased having to share with us the same slit trench facilities under public gaze. As one wag rating put it - "They even think their shit doesn't stink but, they'll know it does when they get dysentery, that is no discriminator of rank."

Without any doubt the most important new arrival was Commander R.F. Jessel DSO, previously captain of HMS Legion. He sustained a broken leg when his ship was bombed at Malta and was on passage home aboard the Havock when it ran aground. This senior Royal Navy officer stood out head and shoulders above any officer I had met previously.

A brave man of fortitude with enormous strength of character, Commander Jessel was a true leader who commanded the respect of every prisoner in Laghouat and of whom our captors were in awe. When he was in charge at 'appel' (roll-call) the discipline of the parade was impeccable and the response to his orders, issued in a stentorian voice, was instant. We behaved like this for him and to support our British CO. By this demonstration in front of the French, they knew they would have a force of British prisoners, with which to reckon, if matters really got out of hand. Oh yes, our captors feared this man, who regrettably, was soon taken from us for hospital treatment. In his temporary absence, Lieutenant Commander Watkins, captain of the Havock, a kind man whom I would describe as a gentleman and an officer, assumed the responsibility of British CO.

• • • • • •

Since he joined us at Le Kef I had been friendly with Sergeant 'Wilbur' Wright, the young wireless operator who sustained serious leg injuries when the Royal Navy Fulmar shot down his plane, the Hudson, in August 1940. He had spent several weeks in hospital receiving extensive treatment for his wounds and on arrival at Le Kef one leg bore severe scar tissue from knee joint to ankle. He was a stoical little chap who exercised and made a remarkable recovery, never complaining, nor betraying any signs of animosity towards the pilot responsible for his injuries.

Tony Randall became interested when he learned that Wilbur and I were going to box, and with other prisoners of different weights, help to provide entertainment for pending visiting dignitaries from

Algiers. I explained to Tony that I had no previous boxing experience, whereupon, he, as an ex-recreational light heavyweight, proffered advice and suggested we might go to the courtyard and practise. What a wonderful opportunity.

He explained the importance of the left arm jab. "Get your opponent on the defence with his head back and poke several short jabs at his face. This should be followed by a straight left, aimed directly at the opponent's face. He will have his guard up now, so, aim below into the plexus region. This will bring the opponent's guard down and present an opportunity to land a well-timed hook to the point of his jaw." A knockout would be guaranteed. Poor Wilbur wasn't going to stand a chance and I began to feel sorry for him.

Down to the courtyard we went and donned the boxing gloves. "Are you ready?" asked Tony, and before I had a chance to reply he let fly with a well timed straight left to the point of my jaw. My next recollection was of lying flat out on my back on the ground, my head was swimming and I experienced an awful feeling of nausea. A very concerned Tony was bending over my prostrate body vigorously waving a towel in an attempt to revive me. For the first time in my life I had been knocked out. Slowly, I began to recover from a very positive and practical lesson, a lesson I should never forget. Wilbur, most certainly, would not stand a chance now! Tony was more upset than I. "I thought you were ready, I thought you were ready," he kept repeating. I did not enlighten him. I had been ready!

Twice Wilbur and I did engage each other in three rounds of boxing and, with other prisoners of different weights, did entertain the visiting dignitaries from Algiers. They had come to check on our well-being and ensure we were being treated properly! That was the beginning and end of my boxing career. Wilbur beat me on points on both occasions and I am sure broke my nose in the second fight. His enthusiasm for boxing endured and whilst at Laghouat he joined the boxing school where he received expert tuition from Lieutenant Commander Lamb, a Royal Navy Services' champion. Wilbur never lost a fight at Laghouat and if my information is correct, after repatriation, continued to box and became featherweight champion of the RAF.

He was perhaps better known in the Laghouat prison camp for his talented music playing by ear on an old honky-tonk piano, a piano that possessed more damaged than undamaged strings. We enjoyed regular sing-songs to his marvellous accompaniment and he was invaluable at the camp concerts. Whenever newcomers arrived from England he would ask them to hum, sing, or whistle the tunes from current song hits, which he would strum out on the piano and commit to memory. We all learned these tunes at his sing-song evenings and on repatriation arrived home fully au fait with the latest hits.

• • • • • •

Conditions at Laghouat worsened. As summer wore on, temperatures soared above 50 degrees Centigrade, in other words reaching the higher 120 degrees Fahrenheit. In the filth and squalor of the overcrowded camp, swarming flies did not discriminate between the contents of the slit trenches and the dirty tins carrying our basic means of survival, the evil 'la soupe'. They journeyed from the former to the latter creating a dysentery epidemic that rose to new high levels. Nevertheless, in the early mornings and the late afternoons Daffy Watson and I would exercise, gently wandering round the periphery of the compound trying to put the trials of imprisonment to rest. Although Daffy was not a scholar of literature his use of suitable expletives

Jimmy Alexander, self, Daffy Watson   *Self, John Riddick, Tony Randall*

would paint a descriptive picture deserving of an Academy Award.

In addition to being a tower of physical and mental strength, he had an almost prodigious capacity for versatility. Temporarily, he held the title of heavyweight boxing champion at Laghouat and at the same time developed a wonderful new characteristic. At the camp concerts he became one of Bertie Brain's attractive young ladies in the front line of the chorus.

It was understood by all prisoners that when exercising in the compound a discretionary distance should be maintained from the barbed wire barricade. Never attempt to approach it in a nonchalant manner! Such apparent indifference could be misinterpreted immediately by a trigger-happy guard who could be capable of shooting first and counting afterwards. In the course of a game, never attempt to rescue an errant ball should it roll underneath the wire. Always draw the attention of the guard and ask for supervised assistance. This was not an act of weakness; it was an act of plain common sense.

The possibility of developing a symptom referred to as 'barbed wire fever' could not be ignored. Normally, even under the existing difficult circumstances, prisoners behaved rationally. If a man became emotionally distressed, caution and sometimes physical restraint had to be exercised to prevent him from behaving irrationally and threatening to 'storm the wire' in desperation to escape.

I mentioned earlier the importance to us of the game of Bridge. After his return from hospital, Commander Jessel joined Lieutenant Commander Watkins as Bridge partner in the officers' team drawn to play against the NCOs in an organised competition. Jimmy Alexander and I were drawn to play against this formidable pair in a three rubbers'

Mostly RAF aircrew and three army escapees from Dunkirk!

161

tournament that we approached with some trepidation. We were invited to play in the Commander's quarters where we were received with the utmost courtesy. He shared a good bottle of wine between us and it developed into a wonderful evening. Jimmy and I had the unexpected good fortune of winning the game in the last rubber, our hosts accepted defeat gracefully and we returned in exuberant mood to our quarters.

• • • • • •

In the Laghouat camp we were guarded by two regiments at alternating periods, namely the Premier Spahis and Tirailleurs. The Premier Spahis was a crack cavalry regiment under Commandant Jeunechamp, a veteran French soldier who had lost an arm in the First World War. He had an unenviable task to carry out that he did with as much consideration for our well-being as possible under the circumstances. For this he earned our respect.

Not so another French officer Lieutenant Martin who earlier, had seen service with the Tirailleurs in Syria where he had been bombarded by the Havock. Not surprisingly, he was not too kindly disposed towards this ship's captain and its crew and never lost his vindictiveness. This was made evident one day after the arrival of Red Cross parcels, which he ordered to be stacked on the outside of the barbed wire barricade. Later, when they had been left in the heat of the sun for several hours, he ordered the Tirailleurs' guards to pierce the tins with their bayonets so the food could not be stored and used later for possible escape purposes.

For anyone who has not experienced the effects of malnutrition it is difficult to understand the value of one tin of corned beef that has to be rationed between four men, all of whom are close friends. To avoid dissatisfaction, with its attendant arguments, we always cut cards to decide, firstly, who should divide the meat into four pieces, secondly, cut the cards again to determine the order in which these pieces should be taken. I have witnessed men coming to blows in disputes of allocation, fortunately not in our immediate circle.

Malnutrition affected prisoners in different ways. A few, gauging by their physical appearance, ostensibly, were unaffected. The majority lost weight and their bodies became emaciated, a symptom reflected in their sunken eyes and facial expressions. In my case it was different. From

Time on my hands in Laghouat, March 1942

being naturally of extremely slim build, I became flabby, considerably overweight and developed a distended stomach.

My comrades teased me regularly and could not resist giving a pat to the offending part of my anatomy as they passed. They would make solicitous enquiries, asking when was it due, was I expecting twins, or perhaps triplets. It was all in fun, of course, and I took it in good part. Nevertheless, it was a physical condition that caused me concern.

• • • • • •

Valuable items received from the Red Cross were tea, dried milk, prunes, butter and soap; all unobtainable elsewhere. We soaked the prunes in water; this caused them to swell and create a very pleasant juice to which we would add reconstituted dried milk. The latter was called Klim and came from the Canadian Red Cross.

Tea was most acceptable but we had to find a method to boil the water. In the height of summer, whenever tea was available, we would fill a tall enamel jug and place it, raised from the ground on two stones, outside in the compound, for heating up by the sun. At mid-afternoon, with the application of a little extra heat from of a few carefully rolled paper firelighters, the water could be brought to the boil. The system was simple; it worked and was used by many other prisoners, who generally combined in syndicates of four to six men for this purpose. As there were seven men in our small room we worked as a seven-man syndicate for the purpose of Red Cross food distribution.

It was a fascinating sight to see all the containers of varying shapes and sizes dotted about the compound, unattended, for three or four hours. Never, did any prisoner attempt to tamper with these ingenious little stoves. Whilst supplies lasted, our stove helped to provide each of us with a daily one quarter-litre beaker of tea, for which we were extremely grateful.

• • • • • •

It could take several weeks for letters to and from home to be received. Nevertheless, we were fortunate in being able to communicate with those at home, who were now able to send small, restricted parcels to us, containing a few essential articles. Soap was my number one priority request, and, occasionally, I received a bar of Crossfields carbolic soap from my parents.

'Dhobiing' was a word used by the navy prisoners for washing clothes. I took advantage of my precious carbolic soap to carry out this procedure, paying particular attention to shorts and trousers in the interests of hygiene, whenever the restricted water supply permitted. During mid-summer the heat of the late morning sun was so intense that the clothes drying process was instantaneous. The first item of wet clothing would be dry and hard as a board before the next item had been washed.

There was a simple golden rule. Never leave your soap behind when you leave the washing trough; it will not be there when you return to retrieve it. This happened to me on one occasion, my whole new bar of precious carbolic soap had disappeared within a few minutes of being left unattended. I was upset and cursed man's inhumanity to man. Imagine my surprise, therefore, when an hour later, a sailor from the Havock came to our room carrying a bar of soap and asked, "Has any one of you lost this?" He was a very honest man and when I asked if he had any soap, he answered, "No, I don't have any but I thought it must be yours, you're the only chap with carbolic soap." I was deeply moved by this man's honesty and integrity and cut my precious soap into two halves. "You have some soap now and damn well deserve it," I said, handing him one of the halves. At first he refused to accept it. "No, that's yours, keep it," Finally, I persuaded the chap to take it. He was extremely grateful. I was chastened.

I shall never forget the incident of the scorpion. It arose after a sailor, horrified to discover a scorpion in his room, by some incredible piece of luck managed to catch this lethal arachnid and confine it in a bell jar. How he managed this I do not know, nor from what source the bell jar was forthcoming! We were soon to become fascinatingly enlightened by what was to follow.

The sailor explained that the scorpion used its jointed tail, bent over, to inflict a poisonous sting on its prey. If, however, the scorpion itself became cornered, it would literally commit suicide by a self-inflicted sting. He hoped to be able to prove this.

Later that afternoon he dug a shallow trench outside in the sand, forming the circumference of a circle two feet in diameter. He proceeded to fill the trench with a combustible mixture of small sticks and paper impregnated with paraffin. After setting it alight, the resultant flames completely enveloped the circle, in the centre of which, he gingerly released the scorpion from the bell jar. It was trapped and encountered a small wall of fire, no matter in which direction it ran. After repeated unsuccessful attempts to escape, it accepted the inevitable, bent its tail and committed suicide.

The bell jar was used again for another demonstration after a prisoner cornered an invading snake in his room. He succeeded in placing the snake in the jar where, coiled in its cramped position, the reptile endured a few days of solitary captivity. Later, it was joined by a small lizard, captured by another prisoner. By this time the snake had worked up quite an appetite and as the relationship between the two reptiles was most incompatible, decided it was time for dinner. After stinging the unfortunate lizard into a stupor the snake slowly and systematically began to swallow its prey. Starting with the head, it continued until the whole body and tail of the lizard had been engulfed. After these exertions the snake appeared to be exhausted and fell asleep. The outline of the lizard was clearly noticeable inside the snake's body until the intestinal juices completed the slow process of digestion.

One prisoner remarked after witnessing this second demonstration, "Thank goodness we are not imprisoned in the African jungle!"

We had one small, friendly visitor, a member of the lizard family, our likeable chameleon. Endowed with a grasping tail, long tongue and protruding eyes, it was also capable of changing colour, which could create unbelievable camouflage. It was indeed a likeable little creature, befriended by one prisoner who wandered round the camp with his little companion happily at home grasping his chest under his open necked shirt. He loaned it to us one afternoon and it stayed on the shoulder of one man almost throughout a Bridge session. It had a voracious appetite and was most adept at catching flies with its long tongue, which it would flick out instantly and with deadly accuracy after sighting its prey. I never saw it miss. It never went hungry.

• • • • • •

Shortly after our arrival at Laghouat one of the prisoners rescued from further maltreatment an abandoned smooth-haired brown and white mongrel dog, which he called Wimpey. This young animal was a companion for Raf whom Wilbur had brought from Aumale and the two became inseparable. A bond of friendship developed between them, they played together and spent hours running around the camp, which was their playground. During the heat of the summer late mornings and early afternoons they would sleep, lying fully stretched, until it was cool enough to resume wanderings. Remarkably, as if by instinct, they never strayed into the no man's land beyond the barbed wire enclosure. They were well groomed and kept spotlessly clean by their masters, more than can be said of many prisoners, and were the friends of every man in the camp. Feeding presented no problems, their palates were not as discerning as ours and there was plenty of gash 'la soupe' to keep them alive, until one day during Lieutenant Martin's tenure, they were shot dead for no justifiable reason.

It came as a great blow to everyone. This thoughtless action saddened all prisoners and Wilbur Wright was openly heartbroken. He had ceaselessly looked after Raf whom he discovered on a promenade at Aumale and rescued from maltreatment at the hands of a local Arab.

During the heat of summer 1942, prisoners occupying one of the larger rooms in the caserne suspected there was a cavity under the flagstone floor and decided to investigate. With difficulty, they managed to lever a flagstone, which revealed, not a cellar as beneath Captain Montgomery's room, but a series of water filled compartments. Discreet enquiries confirmed that these had been purposely constructed to ensure The Foreign Legion of a water supply in the event of siege and we were able to establish that this water was not being used currently for drinking. Heaven sent facilities for bathing were unexpectedly made available for a small section of privileged prisoners, of which I, as a veteran, was included. It was inky dark in this subterranean swimming pool. Although the water was extremely cold, it was very refreshing and the ledges of the compartments provided useful resting places. Occasionally, the guards would make a routine patrol of the prison quarters when the flagstone would be quickly put back in place. These were quite terrifying interludes, but happily, we were never abandoned to a watery demise.

Laghouat - December 1941

The latrines

Ted Clayton's successful search for lost property in the latrine!

Prison Camp section of Laghouat Garrison

Chapter Eleven

THE TUNNEL

Shortly after our arrival in Laghouat, Captain Montgomery suspected there was a cavity under the floor of the room he shared with a fellow officer, Lieutenant Robairre, a French speaking French Canadian, whose fluency in two languages was extremely useful. They decided to investigate. With the help of other officers, a huge flagstone was levered up to reveal a large empty cellar, an ideal place from which to start a tunnel and store the excavated sand. The officers did not divulge their find until they had succeeded in removing foundation stones from a wall at the cellar base and creating a gap sufficiently large for a man to crawl through to start digging. It was now 'Monty' approached a selected number of NCOs, myself included, explaining the officers' intentions and asking if we wished to help. He spoke to us outside in small groups, outlining the hazards of claustrophobia, the likelihood of roof collapses and problems of breathing that might be encountered in the confined space of a tunnel they calculated would be sixty-eight yards long. Nobody refused to volunteer. However there was no absolute guarantee everyone would be allowed to escape if the project were successful.

After very careful calculations had been made it was estimated the cellar was sufficiently spacious to accommodate the excavated sand although there was little latitude for error. The problem of lack of ventilation could not be ignored when the cellar storage space approached capacity. How providential there should be a cellar at all. It was an invaluable asset that reduced the likelihood of sand having to be transported outside and dumped in full view of the guards.

The importance of concealing the tunnel's entrance from our captors cannot be over emphasized. We had to be on permanent alert as they were capable of springing a sudden search without any prior warning. Although their suspicions must have been roused they never succeeded in discovering our well-kept secret. Occasionally, prisoners working underground would be sealed below during an unexpected search. This was an unpleasant experience but fortunately never resulted in any casualties. We had to ensure that tunnel digging and attendant procedures ceased in good time before appels. Resumption of such operations always had to be withheld immediately after the roll-calls to allow our captors time to leave the prison compound. Often they would delay their departure, which in our opinion was deliberate.

Sometimes when a search took place, all prisoners were ordered to leave their rooms and assemble outside on the compound whilst their rooms were searched thoroughly. At other times prisoners were allowed to remain. On these occasions we could not resist preparing a few 'red herrings' in the form of misleading clues, or creating distractions that were not necessary. One favourite was to glance at a picture on the wall, or shuffle uneasily over a flagstone from which surface cement had been removed deliberately. On removing the picture, our captors would find nothing hidden behind. On one occasion they went to considerable trouble to lever up a flagstone under which nothing was revealed other than a quite remarkable colony of ants. Meaningless half prepared maps leading to nowhere would be left casually on a table with an odd quite ridiculously forged identity paper. There were many others.

Digging began earnestly in January by about forty volunteers. Not all of these intended to escape and risk the hazards of exposure in the Sahara wilderness but they showed their true mettle by being prepared to risk the hazards of the tunnel to help others.

We were fortunate in having at our disposal the skills of Squadron Leader Brickell, in Civvy Street an engineering and building contractor. He had been on his way to somewhere in the Middle East to supervise the construction of airfield runways, when his plane crashed in transit and consequently he had the misfortune of joining the rest of us in Laghouat. Although he did not take part in the actual digging he probably spent more time down there than anyone else, checking the progress and advising when alterations in procedure had to be made. He explained that the tendency when burrowing underground was to go upwards. If the result of this tendency had not been checked frequently we should have reached the surface prematurely. Sometimes we would veer to the right, at other times edge towards the left. This man knew and corrected us accordingly. His advice became invaluable.

Normally we worked in pairs, one man digging at the face, the other stacking the sand into containers called crachoirs (metal containers, literally French word for spittoons!) about six inches in depth and in width slightly less than that of the tunnel. They held a large quantity of sand and by an ingenious system of ropes were dragged to the tunnel entrance, emptied and their contents stacked in the cellar. Being a small person I spent a lot of time digging at the face, working three or four watches every week.

As the tunnel progressed the air became so foul our home-made candles, burning rancid fat and with wicks of pyjama trouser cords, would flicker and die. After progressing thirty yards it looked as if the tunnel would have to be abandoned, but no. Thanks to Squadron Leader Brickell and other talented officers, an ingenious ventilation tube was constructed from empty cans with their bases cut out. When attached together they formed a flexible tube like an elephant's trunk and were carefully inserted from the roof of the tunnel through a decoy slit trench at the surface.

With our backs to the armed guards on the prison roof we made pretence of using these amenities, each time adding stones and sand very carefully until the trench was filled. The ventilating effect in the tunnel exceeded expectations. Instead of flickering and dying, the candles blew out, but we could breathe fresh air.

Ingenuity knew no bounds. Experts succeeded in tapping into the camp electricity wiring system and by attaching together any bits and pieces that would conduct electricity, created a most efficient lighting system in the tunnel.

One night, working down there alone completely naked and crawling towards the face on hands and knees, my backside accidentally made contact with an exposed section of wiring. I was subjected to a sudden sharp shock from some two hundred volts and this not only plunged the tunnel into complete darkness, but the whole prison section of the camp. This caused panic among the French who thought it was the prelude to a mass escape and they were quick to locate the fault caused by the main fuse having blown. It was replaced promptly and from groping in absolute darkness, I became dazzled by blazing light. The French never discovered the source of the problem and normal tunnel services resumed without further interruptions.

Ostensbly digging the 'Amenity slit trench' in reality the tunnel's ventilation shaft

Raf and Wimpey our little dogs who were shot by the Vichy French

Outside wall at extreme left of picture was where the escape tunnel came up (the prison camp occupied part of this Caserne and was 'Barbed Wired Off')

The object of the tunnel was to create an opportunity for a general escape and although other individual attempts did take place they all ended in failure. I recall two such attempts. There was another, the outcome of which I am not sure.

Sergeant navigator Claude Belcher, a hefty swarthy New Zealander with a magnificent black beard, made his solo bid in the guise of an Arab. His negotiation of the barbed wire at a restricted blind spot was nothing short of miraculous. To my knowledge, no other prisoner succeeded in avoiding detection by the guards and emulating this performance.

After eight days of freedom, making steady progress north of Djelfa, Claude took refuge under a bridge, where, to rest his swollen feet he removed his boots and fell asleep. On wakening he found his boots had been stolen! One of the great attempts to escape had been thwarted.

An American Sergeant Pilot, attached to the RAF, saw his chance in Laghouat one evening after appel when a large French 'camion' (lorry), carrying wooden sectional parts of a building, drove into the garrison and was admitted into the prisoners' compound. He joined a working party of prisoners detailed to unload the camion of its wooden sectional parts, required for the building of a hut to house an overflow of midshipmen and junior Royal Navy officers. Undetected, the sergeant climbed into the vehicle's large, unlocked spare wheels' compartment, in which he was to hide and endure a very bumpy ride seventy miles north to the Djelfa rail terminal.

At appel the following morning a cover up aroused the suspicions of a new French officer in charge who demanded two more counts before being satisfied. The ironic comedy arising from this was his courteous apology to our British CO with the added comments, "Honi soit qui mal y pense." This caused a few wry smiles! Our escapee's absence remained undetected.

The young pilot was caught three days later in the Djelfa railway sidings whilst trying to board a goods wagon as the train moved off for Algiers. Another very good attempt to escape had been thwarted but his absence had still not been discovered back in Laghouat. Our cover up boys had done a wonderful job.

The next solo attempt was something of a mystery involving a new prisoner who arrived dressed in civilian clothing but was referred to as

Captain. A few of us were told by a senior British officer it was important this man should escape, presumably he had an outside contact.

The attempt would be made during a fixed promenade. In order to reduce the number of guards for this specific activity, the French introduced a new system. Prisoners who wished to enjoy the privilege were required to hand in beforehand a card printed in French, stating the prisoner named would not attempt to escape during that promenade. The card was handed back to the prisoner immediately afterwards. Effectively he was on temporary parole, a doubtful agreement condoned by our officers of which many of us took advantage.

The day for the prefixed promenade dawned with a larger turnout than usual, so was this 'officer' about to break parole? We set off on the road north to Djelfa, stopped for the usual break after about a half hour, far enough in the heat, and at this point, unnoticed by the small number of guards, the escapee disappeared into an area of dense shrub. We returned without him and he was never seen again. Unsubstantiated hearsay implied dreadful events had taken place from torture to successful evasion. I have no corroborated facts and make no further comment.

Commandant Jeunechamp was on duty when we returned and I had never seen this decent veteran French soldier so angry. After discovering a prisoner had broken faith his wrath became uncontrollable and as he raged, two guards left the compound carrying away our radio, the first reprisal.

As the parole cards had been printed in French it required a very small alteration to change completely the meaning of the most important sentence. Simply eradicate the word 'ne' and the sentence read, 'The prisoner would attempt to escape.' The captain's card had been amended accordingly which was pointed out afterwards to the Commandant, who, quite rightly in my opinion and many others, regarded it as an act of duplicity. Were we justified in adopting this method of support for the escapee? Beforehand we had been in favour; afterwards we were not convinced.

• • • • • •

Twenty-one years later a lady who knew about Laghouat and that I had been a prisoner there gave a letter to me. She had been engaged to an aircrew prisoner, with whom I was well acquainted, and who was killed after returning to England. This letter had been written to the navigator's mother in July 1946 by (I shall call him Captain X) from North London. I quote the following sentences, extracts from his letter.

"I was with your son as a prisoner in Laghouat but was surrendered to the Germans by the French."

"I am sorry to say that very many of the old boys have fallen and needless to say, I was very sorry indeed to hear the bad news re your son."

As far as I am aware, the Vichy French in Laghouat did not surrender, directly from the camp, any prisoner to the Germans. Could this Captain have been the mysterious escapee?

• • • • • •

Working in the tunnel was hard, enjoyable, positively occupational and a great reliever of tension. Towards the end of May we had reached the foundation of the outside wall having completed some sixty-six yards of digging which proceeded about a yard beyond the wall then continued slightly upwards. Extreme caution was now needed lest we breached the surface, or caused a roof collapse from the outside.

I was asked by Monty to carry out a task that would be the most exciting I had undertaken, to dig a pilot hole upwards and determine the depth of sand and earth from the tunnel roof to the outside surface. I felt very privileged to be entrusted with this important delicate operation to be undertaken alone and in complete darkness. It seemed an age crawling along those sixty-six yards of tunnel on hands and knees in complete obscurity. On reaching the wall I managed to turn over and lie on my back, my stomach just clearing the base of the wall foundation. I hoped most fervently the damn wall would not collapse. From this position, with my eyes tightly closed and using an old kitchen knife, I worked upwards against the outside wall, the sand and earth showering down on my face. I had to be careful not to create too large a hole and was about to give up, having arrived at the limit of my reach, when suddenly resistance ceased and there was a narrow beam of blinding light. I had broken through to the surface and to my relief upon hastily withdrawing the knife I was plunged again into total darkness.

Monty was delighted and called in the experts to complete the final digging procedures and establish a solid wooden trap door within a few inches of the surface.

• • • • • •

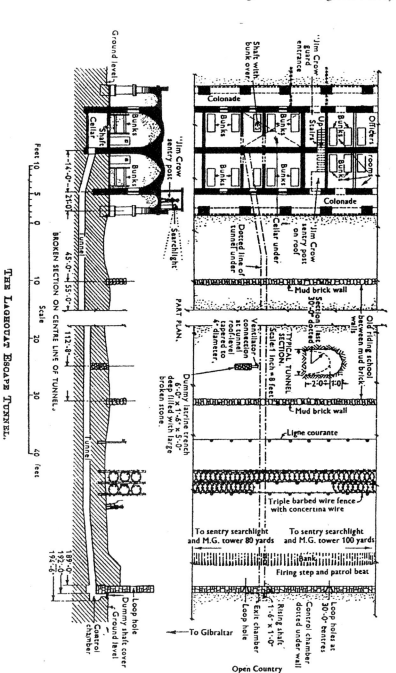

This sketch was prepared by Sqdn Ldr Richard Brickell, the tunnel architect, and shown to the Institute of Civil Engineers after his repatriation in November 1942.

THE LAGHOUAT ESCAPE TUNNEL.

The tunnel was completed after seven months hard toil.

Once opened it could not be closed for use again. It would not be possible to conceal its existence from the outside. The likelihood of it being discovered by chance could not be ruled out, so the escape committee had a difficult task. Not surprisingly there was much dissension amongst the officers, sometimes resulting in physical violence. Such was the diversity of opinions that quarrels and arguments ensued over the decision as to when the tunnel should be used and by whom. NCOs had no say in these matters. It came to a head one night when a Royal Navy officer, who had expressed his opinion that the opening of the tunnel should be delayed, received such a going over from fellow officers he could not appear on appel.

Army Captain Montgomery held the Vichy French officers in utmost contempt and showed no signs of hiding this contempt by his behaviour at appel. He was a tall man and would stand on parade in a nonchalant attitude with his battered filthy trilby hat pulled down well over his eyes in complete disdain. When his name was called out, should another British prisoner succeed in producing a loud belch, Monty's impassive expression implied that it had escaped his hearing. How it riled our captors! He was also capable of manifesting contempt towards any prisoner with whom he was not on the best of terms. There were very few, albeit one man in particular.

At appel, prisoners were required to line up closely to facilitate the taking of the roll. When the tunnel had been completed, Monty distanced himself by a yard from an officer who had raised specific objections to an early opening. An obvious gap was created between them that did not go unnoticed by prisoners on the appel. After two days Monty had made his point and a decision was reached to open the tunnel in early June.

• • • • • •

Twenty-nine men were chosen to attempt an escape. Tony Randall, Jimmy Alexander, I and a few other NCOs were included. Before our departure Commander Jessel spoke to us all extending his good wishes and adding, "If any one of you succeeds in reaching Gibraltar give this message to (he named an Admiral) saying Commander Jessel has a plan to take Laghouat." This brave man was in possession of intelligence of which we had no information, but as events turned out his plan was not put into action.

None of the escapees underestimated the potential dangers and problems that lay ahead. Temperatures in early June were beginning to soar and dehydration presented the most serious hazard. After escaping, we must avoid the Djelfa road, rely on finding an artesian well and use the pathless desert tracts for the first few days. We had mapped the locations of the wells on a carefully prepared chart, copied from a special map to which we had access at the camp. The nomadic Arabs relied on these wonderfully conceived deep wells that, from a considerable depth, provided beautifully cool fresh water of outstanding clarity, perfectly safe to drink. The water was obtained by winching up a bucket from the bottom of the well to the surface. After emptying, the accepted courtesy was to return the bucket by winch to the depths below, thereby, ensuring it remained clean and available for the next traveller. It was a practice, I understand, all travellers observed. A rule of the desert.

The day for our planned departure was getting close and I had not resolved my footwear problem. One friendly RAF Sergeant Gibbins who had accepted the responsibility of becoming camp postman noticed this. His duties were to collect prisoners' outgoing letters, then, under guard, take them to the French Bureau outside the prison section of the camp, where they were censored. He would collect any incoming mail, which he would distribute to the prisoners on his return. It was on such an occasion he visited our room whilst I was trying to come to terms with an offending pair of escape footwear. 'Gibby', who was not one of the escapees, just said, "You can't escape in those Doug, take these," and promptly took off his own well soled and heeled pair of boots. The more I demurred, the more he insisted and left the room barefooted. Perhaps it was fortunate that the boots were too large. I did obtain a more suitable pair of correct size through the escape committee and returned the other boots. It had been a wonderful gesture on his behalf. He was that sort of a man.

Our plan was to travel by night under the guise of Arabs by draping Arab style, large off-white sheets over our heads and shoulders. From a distance, at night, we should not be readily identifiable by a chance wanderer. We planned to rest by day, if possible in a scrub area, then use the sheets as tents and protection from the sun.

Water was our priority and we were fortunate in acquiring three

Mae Wests (inflatable life jackets worn by aircrew as a precaution in case of ditching). We filled these with water, each could hold over a gallon, possibly sufficient to ward off serious dehydration for four days by which time we hoped to reach the Djelfa area. They could be worn like a jacket under our sheets, thereby distributing the weight. For emergency rations we each took a kilo of compressed, stoned, dry dates. I had a bottle of rough brandy called eau-de-vie (French literally 'water of life'), to be used of course, for medicinal purposes only!

Equipped with genuine identity papers in case of recapture and an issue of French francs, in notes supplied by the escape committee, we were prepared! The money was hidden carefully in the seams of our clothing, between the soles of our boots and inside rolled up cigarette papers with tobacco pressed in each end. It was never discovered.

The night of the escape in early June arrived. The positions in the tunnel for Tony, Jimmy and me were numbers nine, ten and eleven so we could not complain. These were minutes of tension and apprehension, the time when our bid for freedom had arrived. I crawled along the tunnel with my two colleagues in absolute silence, laboriously pushing my rolled up sheet and scant provisions ahead along the tunnel floor. The water filled Mae West literally weighed heavily on my shoulders and, as I was the smallest, my colleagues allowed me to go in front. My mouth had become parched already and I bit into a date stone hoping to create more saliva. I carried a small precautionary supply of these.

After what seemed an eternity, we reached the tunnel exit and climbed to the surface to gaze up into a sky of magnificent splendour with myriad stars. The pole star, our celestial compass, was visible to guide us north, the direction we wished to travel to freedom. I breathed in deeply the late evening air. It was like breathing in the elixir of life. We had broken the chains of captivity. A welcome drink of water, proffered by a naval officer who was carrying out a fantastic job of marshalling outside the tunnel exit, eased my parched throat.

All twenty-nine men got away undetected.

Beneath the canopy of a star embroidered firmamental tapestry, guided by the celestial shepherd, we trekked north throughout the remaining hours of darkness. At the rising of the sun our shepherd in Ursa Minor, also called Little Bear, abandoned the celestial compass and disappeared. We knew this navigator's friend would reappear by nightfall.

In the early light of dawn, after covering a distance of fifteen miles, we found a suitable spot to pitch our improvised tent, well concealed, as we believed, in a small area of scrub. We had not allowed, however, for the presence of swarming ants that caused us considerable discomfort, a discomfort to become compounded by the rapid rise in temperature. The heat quickly became unbearable.

These hardships had not to be endured much longer. In the distance we saw and heard mounted Arab soldiers riding rapidly towards us in fan shape formation. We were captured, with no chance of evasion, by eight armed Premier Spahis cavalrymen who encircled us on those marvellous Arab stallions. They hurled abuse in Arabic as they galloped round and round raising an almighty dust and brandishing their loaded rifles. What an incredible display of horsemanship. Just when we thought our number was up they stopped, three of the soldiers jumped down from their mounts and offered us water, then, in simple French, ordered us on to the backs of their horses. They remounted, threw their rifles across to three other soldiers, who then rode back carrying two rifles apiece.

We were still wearing the water filled Mae Wests from which, as yet, we had not taken a drink, having previously quenched our thirsts from water carried in a spare bottle. With difficulty, I managed to fill my aluminium cup, after which I felt ill immediately. The contents were loathsome. The water was absolutely teeming with wriggling creatures. The water in Jimmy's and Tony's Mae Wests was similarly contaminated. We ditched the lot.

I made a grab for my bottle of eau-de-vie and took several long swigs of the potent liquor. The soldiers noticed our predicament and to their credit, slowed down, enabling me to pass the litre bottle to my colleagues. Between us we drank about a third of the contents.

Riding bareback on the rear of an Arab stallion, whilst holding on for dear life to its rider, as his mount galloped rapidly across the desert under a blazing June sun, was an exhilarating yet painful experience not to be emulated. Our backsides became red raw and took weeks to heal. However, we made much better time on the return journey than on the way out!

We had a further brief respite when the soldiers rode up to a well, stopped and allowed us to dismount. It was our first experience of drinking cool, fresh, uncontaminated well water that lived up to its reputation. What a wonderful provider nature can be.

This was an opportunity, still under a blazing sun, to take further swigs of eau-de-vie before remounting. By now the contents of the bottle had been reduced to a third.

On the approach to Laghouat we were ordered to dismount and complete the last part of the journey on foot.

Entering the outskirts of the town, we made a final attempt to sing the masterpiece "Oh! Vive de Gaulle." as we passed to each other the almost drained bottle of eau-de-vie. Sweating, dehydrated and caked in sand we presented a pitiful sight in our filthy bloodstained ragged clothing, as we trudged wearily back to imprisonment, surrounded by eight mounted Arab horsemen guards.

We walked within a few yards of the house of a middle-aged French lady who heard our singing as she stood at the front door. She watched as we passed by and when our eyes met, buried her head in both hands, burst into tears and turned back into the house sobbing uncontrollably.

••••••

Alas, within twenty-four hours after departure, all twenty-nine prisoners had failed to evade recapture.

No heroes' welcome awaited us on return to camp, neither was there a mug of fresh tea, nor an inviting bath, instead we were taken to a colonnade awaiting the next move. When I asked the Arab guard for permission to visit the cabinet he refused and in a gruff voice said, "Il n'y a pas." Which translated literally means, "There isn't any." I tried again, quite politely. Came the snarled response, "Défendu."

With venom in my voice I told him to take a running jump and get ****ed, whereupon, he strode towards me and with the butt end of his rifle knocked me flat on the flagstone floor of the colonnade. Tony Randall bravely went for the man, had it not been for the prompt intervention of a more civilised Arab Chef de Poste, he would have been shot, most assuredly. "Vas-y!" ("Go!") With those words, the Chef de Poste ushered me courteously to a nearby soldier's filthy, stinking cabinet. Then we were split up and marched to cells in another part of the garrison.

Here, I joined 'Digger' Latter, an Australian with whom I shared a single cell for the next sixteen days. We were locked in throughout this period only being allowed out into a high walled courtyard to use the communal churn, shared by other escapees, which two of us took in turns to empty. Usual cells' procedure! Fortunately, neither Digger, nor I had dysentery, a complaint to which I was readily prone. On this occasion such a disaster did not arise perhaps in my case, thanks to eau-de-vie, which as I have said before, had been taken for medicinal purposes!

Now we had sixteen days in which to talk and swap opinions. He was a sort of dry philosopher, not easy to understand and although we differed in our political persuasions we had one common determination, make it as difficult as possible for these Vichy French bastards. Digger was perfectly justified, having arrived at Laghouat after spending seven days and nights with others of his crew, afloat in a dinghy in the Mediterranean.

Whilst in cells we received an unexpected visitor, a French General, veteran of the First World War. He enquired, through the medium of a junior officer, if we had any complaints. I was not sure how to take this. Could he be serious talking to us in our present environment and asking if we had any complaints? I could have given him a string of them, but reserved my reply to make one complaint only. This surprised him and he became more surprised when, speaking in French, I answered him directly, not through the junior officer. I tried to accord him the courtesy his rank demanded and stood politely to attention, not subserviently, explaining that permission had been withdrawn for us to write letters home and our letters from England were being withheld. His response was immediate and positive. He instructed his aide to ensure our rights, as prisoners would be restored without delay.

I was still standing to attention, we never took eyes off each other, and in his face I peered into the open pages of a book. I don't know for whom the sadness was the greater. He was an elderly, true and genuine Frenchman, a victim under Nazi and Vichy suppression, who faced a young true Englishman, similarly suppressed under similar regimes. Within an hour we received pencils, writing material and envelopes. The General had honoured his word.

It would be churlish not to pay tribute to those eight young Premier Spahis Arab cavalrymen, who had held us at their mercy in the desert, with no senior officer present to control them. They had acted, using their own judgement and could have shot us dead on the pretext that we resisted arrest. No questions would have been asked. In a matter of days our bodies would have been picked to skeletal remains and quickly reduced to powder and disappeared. An organic fertilizer would have been wasted on a fruitless desert. Instead, these young men had offered us water and given us a free ride back to an imprisonment that provided shelter from an inhospitable desert. They had certainly saved our lives. May they be eternally blessed.

On the morning after the escape we had not been present, of course, to witness the chaotic events at appel. We learned to our delight that although Commandant Jeunechamp was in charge, it was Lieutenant Martin who was duty officer and had been on duty all night. He took the roll-call count three times, after which the French searched the camp hoping to find the missing twenty-nine men hiding as a practical joke. This was not reality; twenty-nine men had escaped and Martin was last seen as he left the outside colonnade, leaning against a wall in despair with head in hands. He would almost certainly face a court martial.

The desert, during my imprisonment years, ALWAYS claimed its victims. The escape, condoned by the majority, was criticised by some as being irresponsible and a waste of time. This I deny. It was not a wasted effort and caused considerable consternation for the Vichy French who were left under no illusions. They had a powerful force of British prisoners to control and restrain.

They were forced to rethink. Their logistics had been thrown into complete disarray causing upset to their disposition of military personnel. Troops had to be redrafted and ravitaillement (revictualling) became disrupted due to added transport difficulties. Senior officers were charged by the Vichy French hierarchy with gross ineptitude and threats of reductions in rank. Alas, the Garrison Commander, known to us as 'The Slug', did not sever his jugular!

Prior to appel on Sunday mornings, the French officers and sous-officiers appeared before the parade dressed in their best uniforms, called by us their 'ponce' uniforms. The trousers were very wide with broad stripes down the sides. Our captors' appearance on these occasions encouraged us to practise using our vocal cords and to the tune of the song 'Bless 'em All' we would chant in unison as they stood before us,

"Here they are
In their ****ing great trousers with stripes down the sides,
With ****ing great pockets and **** all inside
To the bastards we're saying 'goodbye'." Etc.

Then we would change the words and sing to another familiar tune,
"This is our story, this is our song,
We've been in Laghouat too ****ing long,
So roll on the Rodney, the Nelson, the Hood,
For this ****ing prison camp is no ****ing good!"
(Regrettably the Hood was sunk on 24th May 1941 in action against the Bismarck.)

In some respects, although our singing might have appeared to be pointless, it acted as a form of relief, we got something off our chests and our captors were left under no illusions regarding our feelings towards them.

Petty Officer Wines back behind the wire under armed guard surveillance

Chapter Twelve

HELLISH CONDITIONS

During the entire period of imprisonment Tony had written
to his girlfriend Heather and in return he received regular
comforting letters. For some months, however, she had not been well
but bore her illness bravely and remained faithful to him throughout.
As she never complained, Tony did not imagine her illness to be
serious and looked forward to the day of his repatriation and return
to England when they hoped to get married. Tragedy struck when
he received a letter from England, addressed in a handwriting he did
not recognise. Hastily he tore open the envelope to read the dreadful
contents, which informed him Heather had died after a short brave
fight against insuperable odds.

Still grasping the letter, Tony paced up and down the room, beating
the wall with tightly clenched fists his distress almost turned to rage,
"Why, oh why, does it happen to me? Why do women die on me?"
he shouted.

I was lost for suitable words of consolation. Only the passing of time
would help him now.

He faced up well to his sorrow and entered more wholeheartedly
than ever into his editorial responsibilities towards The Camp Echo.
Later, after careful preparation, he delivered two excellent lectures and
creditably regained composure in spite of the trying elements of prison
life.

• • • • • •

The hellish conditions in Laghouat became compounded in mid-August
with the arrival of half the ship's company of HMS cruiser Manchester,
torpedoed in the Mediterranean. The number of prisoners doubled
overnight to reach a total of a thousand, resulting in at least one hundred
British prisoners being crowded into rooms originally intended to house

only twenty-four Arab soldiers.

By this time the Royal Naval officers had taken over entirely the running of the camp, which the aircrew chaps now called 'HMS Laghouat', the ship that ran aground in the Sahara! The Royal Navy was the senior service and let us know it. A petty officer was always regarded as senior to an RAF sergeant, a chief petty officer senior to a flight sergeant, whilst a midshipman was senior to a pilot officer and so on up the ranking scale.

We pleaded with our senior officers for RAF personnel to be allowed to run our own affairs, but in vain. It would not be possible. There was a possibility however, of the French transferring the RAF prisoners to an open camp at El Golea, two hundred miles south, a possibility we welcomed, which never materialized.

• • • • • •

Perhaps this is a time to indulge in a little philosophical introspection. It should not be difficult to reflect less critically on adversity and seek more rewarding attributes, such as the characteristic qualities ascribed to persons. Contemplate their positive and generous contributions from which, at some time or other, we had all benefited during imprisonment. Must we always dwell on man's inhumanity to fellow man?

Let us consider all the camp activities, the splendidly organised camp concerts, boxing tournaments, gymnastic displays, lectures and debates, the library with its dog-eared books, supervised by willing enthusiasts. All these helped lighten the burden of inactivity, the malaise that breeds ennui and lassitude, the destroyer of a man's spirit and his determination to withstand the trials with which he is beset.

Interesting lectures, delivered by prisoners well versed in their subjects, varied from banking and finance, accountancy, the British Press, parliamentary affairs, plumbing, the theatre and life in a circus to poaching. An army private, an escapee from Dunkirk, delivered the last talk. He had relied on his subject, poaching, to augment regular income in Civvy Street. I suppose it could be said that in this field he was an accomplished professional. Bill's talk was delivered simply and graphically. We all accompanied him as we evaded the gamekeeper, sometimes on the moors, sometimes wading in fast flowing rivers or walking along their banks seeking evasive plump trout and salmon. It was simpler snaring rabbits and trapping the almost defenceless pheasants. Bill may have been an adept provider for his family at home but he could do little in Laghouat to appease our hunger.

The last entertainment was provided by a conjuror who captivated us with his feats of legerdemain. Not until the inevitable wag asked him to produce a rabbit or two from his hat, or a few plump pigeons from the nether regions of his blouse, did he manifest signs of embarrassment. Although the conjuror took it in good part, the show ended sooner than had been scheduled.

• • • • • •

Before closing the North African saga there are a few incidents I should like to mention, not necessarily in chronological order.

One terrible incident occurred in the summer. It concerned a very young naval stoker from the Manchester who became trapped in the barbed wire whilst trying to bribe a guard to whom he was handing his watch. He had become helplessly entangled in the wire and his attempt to extricate himself must have been misinterpreted as determination to escape. The guard opened fire from point blank range and killed the young sailor.

This started a riot. Every NCO prisoner, myself included, and every lower deck sailor of this boy's ship, stormed the wire barricade. Commander Jessel was in the garrison hospital at the time and unfortunately was unable to take action. We were completely out of control; our officers could do nothing about it. We began chanting in unison at the top of our voices, "WE WANT JESSEL, WE WANT JESSEL, WE WANT JESSEL," continuing until the great man appeared, under heavy guard, on the other side of the barricade. He was extremely lame; yet he stood upright holding up his hand to quieten us. Silence fell like magic at this unspoken command. Then the great man addressed us in his stentorian voice ordering us to return to our quarters and promising the incident would be fully investigated. The riot was over but the memory of that little limp body straddled across the barbed wire lingers on.

For a short while we benefited from the valuable services of HMS HAVOCK'S Medical Officer who, with the most restricted medical supplies, administered with praiseworthy diligence to the needs of invalid prisoners. How he obtained smallpox vaccine from the French I shall never know, probably because of their dread of the spread of an epidemic. I was one of the lucky ones he vaccinated.

Shortly afterwards, in pursuit of his duties, he himself fell victim to polio and was sent away with others into isolation but never recovered.

It is said that tragedy often strikes three times. It is known that deprivation, hunger and malnutrition combined with filthy hygiene and squalid living conditions can seriously affect a man's will to live. This is what happened to one man in Laghouat, a chief petty officer who had served with service distinction before arriving only a few days earlier at this dreadful camp and on whom the conditions I referred to above had not escaped notice.

This new arrival, with justification, criticised the behaviour of our captors as being downright criminal from bastards not at war. He had become mentally very upset and went off to sleep in this dreadful state of mind. He did not wake up.

With the daily arrival of 'la soupe', a prisoner would call, - "COME AND GET IT," in a voice that would reverberate around the compound at the arrival of what appeared to be the garbage cart pulled by an emaciated donkey. The distressed animal would be enveloped in a horde of buzzing flies that did not cause any concern to the shabbily dressed Arab driver. It was not the garbage cart; it was the prisoners' evening meal. The flies encompassing the donkey, paled into insignificance, compared with the horde surrounding the unappetising contents of the cart. The sweet course, a large deposit of evil smelling, fermenting, sand laden, fly blown grapes, whose juicy contents left their liquid trail on the ground, contributed to the problems of dysentery, already rife. Wine, a potion of purple sludge, arrived in old kerosene barrels and when poured, a film of oil would rise to the surface. Ironically, this was less lethal for drinking than the water!

A notice on the door of one room, housing one hundred men and intended for only twenty-four Arab soldiers, read, "ABANDON HOPE ALL YE THAT ENTER HERE". A notice on another door read, "ROLL ON DEATH", whilst on a third it asked, "DEATH WHERE IS THY STING?"

Contrary to these implications the morale of the prisoners was high. In spite of moments of depression, hope, if not patience, found sanctuary in our hearts.

The entire prison camp accommodation was bug infested, our room and the double tier wooden bunk I shared with 'Pincher' Martin being no exception. It was agreed our bed should be stripped down and the bug problem investigated. This attracted an interested bunch of spectators including French officer cadet Rossignol whose presence under the circumstances was extremely useful. The outcome of the dismantling was a revelation, exposing hundreds of these vermin, swollen with the human blood they had consumed. To his credit, Rossignol immediately obtained a large tin of creosote the contents of which were used to saturate the timbers of the entire bed. Escaping bugs were summarily dealt with and the problem was resolved. News spread around the camp rapidly and the demand for creosote soon exceeded the supply.

• • • • • •

Pincher, whose home was near Stockport, survived the war. Later, back in Civvy Street, he and I met and enjoyed several lunches together. He was employed as accountant with an electrical company that supplied the needs of the textile mill where I worked. A small world!

• • • • • •

Although the camp was indescribably filthy throughout, due to lack of hygiene facilities, there was no litter. There would be always a future use for every small scrap of paper, every empty Red Cross tin, every cigarette end, or fragment of torn clothing. Nothing was wasted.

Cigarettes, a high priority, were of very strong black tobacco and an issue strictly rationed. On the extremely rare occasion of a prisoner seen to discard a cigarette 'dimp,' it would be pounced upon by a fellow prisoner and added to his collection of 'dimps' for rolling into another cigarette. The outcome of this practice resulted in our smoking almost liquid nicotine with a total disregard for threatened lung cancer.

A few enlightened prisoners had reservations about continuous exposure to the strong sun and warned us of the attendant dangers from skin cancer. Their advice went unheeded; we believed the ultraviolet rays were beneficial.

Chapter Thirteen

WHAT DUPLICITY!

In 1940, General Huntziger on behalf of Marshal Pétain, had signed terms of the French surrender to the Germans and later in the same year endorsed the Italian Armistice. France, from being an ally, had become an enemy. Now, two years later he stood before us in Laghouat, addressing us on the pretext that he hoped for good relations with the British after the war!

When Huntziger departed it became the turn of the Foreign Legion Colonel and Garrison Commander, alias 'The Slug', to say a few words. Following Huntziger's hypocritical diatribe 'The Slug' had the temerity to add his personal barb. "I have told the North African Arabs that instead of the reward of one thousand francs for returning an escaped prisoner alive, they would receive two thousand francs for an escaped prisoner they brought back dead."

Later that afternoon the plane carrying General Huntziger back to France crashed in the desert killing all on board.

The weary days during the heat of summer wore on and with no tunnel work to occupy us, Bridge again became our salvation. We played all afternoons and evenings. To ward off the flies that swarmed in our room during daylight hours, we covered exposed parts of our bodies in towels or other suitable materials. At times, the flies nearly drove us to distraction and we would stop the game to have what we called a fly blitz. Three prisoners would position themselves, strategically, at the back of the room each holding a towel at arms length. At the word of command a fourth prisoner would open the door, the other three then advanced with flailing towels and drove the flies, literally in their thousands, through the open door. For a while we would have gained a little respite but it was quite normal practice to have three, or four blitzes every afternoon. Mercifully, after dark, the flies rested and we took advantage of this opportunity to slaughter them again, literally in their thousands.

I became mindful of the words of the Padre who had visited us a year ago, when he said,

"Every day is a new day, a day specially made for you and a day of opportunity."

Had we taken advantage of these three hundred and sixty-five opportunities?

I wonder!

This brings me to a quote from a letter I wrote to my relatives, also a year ago. It read,

"There is not a single man amongst us who would not sacrifice his dearest possession to be reinstated and back in the struggle to which we each and all belong. I will prove this to be true to you one day."

I wonder!

With the advent of autumn the heat became less trying and the flies began slowly to disappear. We were preparing to face, what would be for many of us, a second winter in Laghouat. How many more winters would we have to endure in captivity? Prospects were bleak. The possibility of starting another tunnel was discussed, if only to help pass the time, but where and how could we deposit the excavated sand? There was no spacious cellar at our disposal. Freshly excavated sand would be very noticeable even if carefully dispersed over the hard surface of the compound.

On 2nd November 1942, Sergeant Gibbins, our camp postman wrote a letter to my parents, which he thought I might like to read before posting. It was a lovely, thoughtful letter, extracts from which I quote,

'I pull Doug's leg quite a bit about his letters, I do believe he really thinks I read them at times, he at any rate never seems to get worried about it, I often wonder if he ever worries about anything, he always has a smile on his face, no matter how black things look, and, they look pretty black at times. I am sure you have no need to worry about him, he is a picture of health and his 'they won't get me down' attitude will bring him out OK.

Most men are quite well, I am looking forward to the day of our freedom, and feel sure it is not so very far off now.

PS

Have you found him a nice girl pen friend yet? Can you find me one?"

I read the letter, smiled and told him to send it off; it would buck up my folks no end.

Ironically, so shortly afterwards, remarkable news suddenly came from out of the blue. Early on Sunday morning 8th November 1942, we heard on our camp radio that the Americans had landed in North Africa and Algiers had surrendered. This turned out to be quite true but the Vichy French in Laghouat were disbelieving and at first could not be convinced. Their telephone lines from Algiers had been cut and they had no knowledge of the landings having taken place.

Meetings were arranged hastily between the Foreign Legion Colonel, alias 'The Slug', and our senior British officers, meetings that we were not privy to attend. I understand that the very frightened Foreign Legion Colonel made some absurd proposals that were turned down. He was not only fearful now of the Arab guards who really hated the French officers, but also of the British and Americans. He was in a no win situation, the biter was about to be bitten.

• • • • • •

I don't know how the situation became finally resolved between the British CO and the Vichy French, but I do know that a few days later, other old time prisoners and I were on the first lorry to head north for Djelfa. I experienced little feeling. My inside was numb. Could it be really true that those two and a quarter years of imprisonment were over and that I was on my way back to England to fly again in the war? Was I about to keep the promise I made in that letter to my relatives? I thought about Gibby's letter to my parents, posted on 2nd November, in which he said he was looking forward to the day of our freedom, and felt sure it was not so very far off. He must have been psychic! Would I arrive home before his letter reached my parents?

From Djelfa we were taken by train to a station outside Algiers. From there we were marched through narrow streets to the docks and taken on board HMS Keren, an old trading ship now painted battleship grey and flying the White Ensign. It had landed American troops and rather than return with an empty hold was loaded with oranges, a scarcity and delicacy in the UK.

• • • • •

193

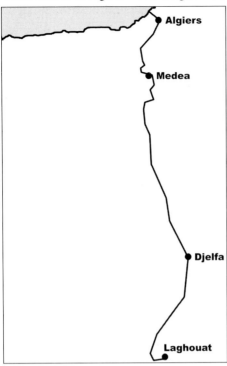

Homeward bound route, Laghouat-Djelfa-Algiers

A close Old Mancunian friend of mine since schoolboy days, John Clayton, then a lieutenant in the Army, had landed in Algeria with the invasion forces. On making hasty enquiries, he learned that several British prisoners from Laghouat were aboard the Keren, scheduled to sail to the UK and that the ship's departure was imminent. Unfortunately, an unexpected reunion, after a three years' separation, had been thwarted. Prior to the Keren sailing John was moved with his regiment eastwards towards Tunis.

It was ironical that his involvement with North Africa should start as mine finished. Fortunately, he survived the ensuing campaigns and we became reunited two and a half years later. Our friendship still endures, fifty-nine years on.

We took our last look at the lights of Algiers before becoming enveloped in a smoke screen prior to sailing. It was then I heard the splash in the water some fifty feet below. Was a British stalwart about to keep his vow and 'get' that CO Vichy bastard from Aumale? I believe he was and I understand he did. "Vive l'esprit Anglais!" ("Long live the English spirit!")

I shed no tears next month when I heard of the assassination of Admiral Darlan. Would it now be too late for the script writer to get busy amending "Oh! Vive de Gaulle"

On board I had a very comfortable hospital bed in which to relax throughout the journey home that took nearly a fortnight. The food was plentiful, more than my tired stomach could consume and of five star standard compared with the rubbish we had consumed in North Africa. Our ship docked at Gibraltar to refuel and we were allowed to go ashore for a few hours. It was on the Rock I bought a pair of fully-fashioned silk stockings, a present for mother and in the right size! After leaving Gibraltar the convoy sailed into stormy seas through the Bay of Biscay and continued in a westerly direction well out into the Atlantic to avoid the ever-present German U-boats.

We had been critical of the Royal Navy's attitude towards the RAF in Laghouat but it was at a time like this I learned to appreciate the value of their services. The crews were not exposed to extreme danger for a few hours, as say the time of a bombing mission, but for weeks, sometimes months on end. We witnessed at first hand the incredible performances of the destroyers whilst protecting the convoy and searching for enemy submarines. In the rough seas of the 'Bay' they would virtually disappear in the deep troughs then reappear and continue as if nothing had delayed them. The heroic sailors who manned them worked incessantly whilst enduring the most cramped living conditions. I shall remain indebted to them all for their continued protection during the long voyage home.

The serenity of the scene we viewed, of ships in convoy sailing so placidly, belied the reality of this stage, which could so easily have become a watery grave. It represented a stage fraught with dangers, sometimes from the air, but always from the continual threats of invisible lurking German U-boats. The crews in those destroyers could not relax for a brief moment, evidenced by the almost ever-present flotsam.

We first sighted land off southern Ireland and shortly afterwards, on a grey late November day, anchored safely in the Firth of Clyde off Greenock.

After disembarking we parted company with the Royal Navy and Army personnel, the former being taken to Portsmouth. I have no idea what happened to the army boys. The RAF personnel were taken to Glasgow St Enoch's railway station and marched, under guard, to an awaiting train that was to take us overnight to London. The guards remained with us throughout the journey and we were not allowed to make any contact with the public until we had been formally interrogated by senior RAF staff officers from the Air Ministry. Our imprisonment had ended but our freedom had not yet begun!

The following morning we were welcomed home by senior staff officers who enquired about our treatment and asked our opinion of the Vichy French. Questions we had no difficulty in answering in depth.

Then they asked did we think they would be supportive of the allies now? Our response was on these lines. In late August 1940, when we needed their support it was not forthcoming, a situation that never changed during the entire time of our imprisonment. Now, with the unexpected change of events in North Africa, we were convinced they would support whichever side they thought would win.

In the political arena the situation had become critical and it was explained to us how desperately Mr. Winston Churchill needed the backing of the entire French Nation. Retribution was understandable, but more important was the gaining of French co-operation. Restraint must be exercised, intimidation avoided and with a battle raging from Egypt westwards through Libya to the Tunisian frontier, we could not afford our relationship to become estranged.

So be it, or as we might have said in Laghouat, 'entendu.' Oh yes, we understood!

After the completion of interrogations, we were taken to stores and issued with new uniforms and other items of clothing. Later, we collected leave passes, travel warrants and a handsome sum in back pay. Now freedom had begun!

Then I returned to the Endsleigh Hotel where we had been billeted under guard during the last forty-eight hours, changed into my new uniform and prepared to return home. I was about to leave the hotel when I noticed my pilot, with his wife and colleagues, seated at a corner table near the bar. I went across to say farewell to a sick man. His charming wife knew she had welcomed home a husband, who was far from well, and most probably, whose service flying days were over. Sadness was written in her kind features when I held her tiny hand and said goodbye. It was the last time I was to see either of them.

Finally, I was really about to leave when I noticed an RAF serviceman sitting alone at a far table with a glass in his hand. On the table were several empty bottles. Something had to be wrong. I recognised him at once, one of the old time prisoners, a married man and a tough flight sergeant navigator, referred to by some senior officers in the camp as a leader of men. He looked at me with tears in his eyes. "What's the matter?" I asked. Distress was written all over his face when he replied, "She's bloody left me." He hadn't even reached home and his days of survival were numbered.

Feeling sad, I left the hotel on a miserable wet night and walked across to Euston Station to catch the night train for Manchester, where I would change trains and travel to my new home in Nelson. I had been unable to contact my parents, who were not aware I was even in the country, such had been the reticence of the authorities to broadcast news of our return.

Captured, Freed

By MARGOT BECK

AFTER tunnelling 187 feet to escape from an internment camp in Algeria 29 soldiers were recaptured.

The armistice signed after the fall of Algiers set them free again, and some have just reached Britain.

Their camp, they told me, was at Laghouat, an oasis on the edge of the Sahara, and its conditions were appalling.

But it was the terrible boredom that affected the prisoners most. All day they had nothing to do but sit in the blazing sun thinking.

They decided to plan their escape, and started to dig a tunnel from one of the prison cells.

Dug in relays

For seven long months they dug in relays for 24 hours a day. As they went further underground they had to deal with the problem of lighting their work. They solved this by stealing some wire and joining it to the electric power.

Soon they had burrowed under the inner wall — then underneath the courtyard — under the thick outer wall, and finally out into the desert and freedom!

But not for long. Arab guards soon tracked them down, and they were sent back to prison.

Yesterday Sergt. J. D. Shanahan, of Toronto, said to the "Sunday Chronicle": ' We heard the news of the Allied landings over the camp radio. At first it seemed too good to be true. The French, who were forbidden by the Germans to listen to Allied broadcasts, took a lot of convincing. We certainly were glad to leave that place."

1942 Article from the Sunday Chronicle It should be noted that the 'soldiers' were of the mixed services and the escape tunnel was started in the cellar

As the train moved slowly out of the station I realised that at last imprisonment was over. My thoughts turned to retribution. Yes, this had to come but not in the direction that caused Mr. Winston Churchill such concern.

We reached London Road Station at 04.00 hours and from here I had to walk across the city to Victoria Station to catch the milk train for Nelson. I had known the city streets like the back of my hand before the war, but now I was completely lost. Buildings that had been landmarks had disappeared and I witnessed in reality the destruction about which we had heard in the prison camps. Sitting alone in the dimly lit railway carriage, on the last leg of the journey home, my mind was made up. Retribution it had to be.

The effect of two years' anxiety, fear and worry were visibly and inextricably etched on Mother's face when she opened the door to welcome me home. It was a moment of emotion I shall not attempt to describe. Not until later in the day was I reunited with Father in whose face I read a similar story. Never had I become more determined to do all in my power to inflict on those guilty the suffering, which had been inflicted on my parents and on thousands of other completely defenceless civilians. If I had become weakened physically after more than two years of imprisonment, my resolution to seek revenge on the Germans was firm.

ᴸE LEADER.—FRIDAY, DECEMBER 4, 1942.

Two Years in Prison Camp

AIRMAN'S ORDEAL IN TUNISIA

Once more appreciatively sharing with his parents, Mr. and Mrs. Hudson, of 191, Halifax Road, Nelson, the comforts of his own fireside, Sgt. Observer J. Douglas Hudson, R.A.F., is now taking a well earned rest after suffering the ordeals of 2½ years spent in three North African prison camps and is, apparently, little the worse for his grim experience. It was through the timely arrival of the British and American armies in November that he was freed, following two unavailing attempts to escape. For a month his parents had no news of him, for he was believed missing.

About two years ago, the aircraft in which he and fellow members of the air-crew were flying, made a forced landing off Tunisia. A certain amount of damage was inflicted on the 'plane but apart from injuries sustained by the wireless operator all the crew were quite safe and sound. In Tunisia they were interned in a prison camp at Le Kef where they were held for eight months, being very closely confined and guarded. From six o'clock each evening until six o'clock next morning the young airmen (Sgt. Hudson is twenty-six years of age) were locked in their quarters, and there were no amenities. Asked by a "Leader" reporter how he and his colleagues passed the time away during these long months, Sgt. Hudson stated that apart from writing letters home which were restricted to one a fortnight, they read, and between them published a small newspaper of their own which they called "The Camp Echo." A friend of Hudson's edited the journal, he typed out the "copy" and with the co-operation of the others among whom were a number with an artistic flair, they turned out an interesting little publication periodically.

They also spent no little time in planning escapes, one of which such escapes he made from Tunisia but was later caught on his way to an Algerian port. The food in the prison camp was deplorable being the same as that supplied to the Arabs—macaroni and lentils (with a little additional Red Cross food)—but less in quantity. There were not many in this camp, beside Hudson, just a few members of air crews, about 16 R.A.F. and a few other services in all. They were then moved to Algeria to a camp at Aumale where they spent the summer. At this time the position of these men was raised in the House of Commons, for an attack of dysentery broke out there. They were later moved to Laghouat where they stayed until they were released by the arrival of our Forces on the 12th November. In common with 28 others, Hudson attempted to escape from this camp through a tunnel 187 feet in length and which took seven months to dig. This attempt too, proved unsuccessful. In the prison there was terrific overcrowding, latterly 100 prisoners being housed in a room originally designed to accommodate but 24 Arab soldiers. Sgt. Hudson and his colleagues were required to "sleep" in double-tiered wooden bunks which were bug-infested. Water was rationed during the summer months. The lack of food and of cleansing materials was due to the Germans and the Italians taking it over for their own use.

As was previously stated, the British and American armies invaded French North African territory on November 8th, and two days later liberated the prisoners of Laghouat. Sgt. Hudson reached home yesterday week and a few days later there arrived at his home a number of letters which he himself had written to his parents describing (as fully as censorship would allow) his ordeal many weeks ago. He little imagined when he wrote these letters that he would actually be home before they were delivered!

Article in the Nelson Leader

Chapter Fourteen
JOAN MORGAN

In November 1942, the time of my resolution to seek revenge on the Germans, Joan Morgan, from Lincoln, discovered the best way in which she could serve her country. Previously, she had been too young for call up, but was determined, that as soon as the opportunity arose, she would join the service of her choice. By volunteering as her registration number 25 drew nearer, she was accepted in the RAF to be trained for the trade, in which she was most interested.

After a few weeks of the inevitable square-bashing at Innsworth in Gloucestershire, she was posted to Cardington, Bedfordshire, home of the airships, to be trained as a driver, known as D.M.T. driver motor transport. The course was intensive and comprehensive.

With other Waafs, she was taught to drive on 3 ton lorries, to double declutch and use recognised hand signals in the absence of indicators. There was no heating in the cabs. Further instruction included how to carry out a daily inspection on any vehicle, to which they might be assigned, i.e. check the engine oil, lights, tyre pressures, radiator and battery levels and change a tyre, or wheel. They were responsible for the 10,000 miles' service, which included oil changes. This was carried out over a pit, with the Waaf lying underneath the vehicle to unscrew the nut and drain the oil. "I didn't always move my hand away quick enough. You've guessed it!"

Joan had discovered her metier as a highly qualified driver and was approached with a view to becoming a driving instructor. Although flattered, she declined, preferring, in her words "to be on the road myself and not teaching."

She was rewarded with a posting to a Lancaster operational station on 100 Squadron at Waltham, near Grimsby.

The girls slept in Nissen Huts on the Waaf site, situated close to the windmill, a famous landmark by the village. They used outside ablutions, but were issued with bicycles. No, no, not for travelling to the ablutions, but to enable them to travel more easily to and from the dispersed technical sites on the perimeter of the airfield!

Joan talks about the discipline, the domestic night, a time to polish shoes and buttons and wash hair, etc. A wonderful spirit of camaraderie prevailed between the girls. "I can honestly say that I enjoyed my time in the Waaf. The comradeship, the feeling we were doing something for our country. We just got on with it."

Chapter Fifteen

BACK IN THE UK

I had been granted six weeks rehabilitation leave, but after more than two years of malnutrition, I had to practise eating again! After experiencing three years of food rationing Mother had become adept at making a little go a long way. The meals she prepared from limited ingredients, were more than adequate for my weakened digestive system and I had difficulty in coping with the food she put before me. This concerned her but was no reflection on her standard of cooking.

For several weeks it was not easy adapting to the inclemency of the British winter climate. The North Country weather was cold, wet and dismal, a great contrast after the heat of the Sahara. I shivered and developed chilblains. The change had occurred too quickly and I had not become reacclimatized.

All my pre-war Mancunian friends were away, except one girlfriend and she had become engaged to a wealthy young businessman in a reserved occupation. I had no acquaintances near my new home and unbelievably, I felt lonely. I missed the comradeship of my old prisoner of war associates and the lighter social aspects of that communal life. Towards the end of my leave I developed a peculiar sickness and called our local doctor with whom my parents were on good terms. Through them he knew about my prisoner of war experiences and I looked forward to receiving some useful counselling. Unfortunately he had been called away and I was visited by a locum, a brusque man who gave me a rough yet thorough examination. After this manhandling, I asked when he thought I might be fit for flying duties. "Flying duties?" he retorted, "I wouldn't pass you C3 for the army until you get that off," and he grabbed a handful of flab on my still distended stomach. He then wrote out a medical certificate, adding, "Post this to your unit and report to them when it expires in two weeks' time." Without further ado he packed his little bag and departed.

I was suffering temporarily from nothing other than a post repatriation depression, exacerbated by inactivity and the aftermath condition arising from two years of malnutrition.

• • • • • •

A fortnight later I felt much better and reported to RAF Uxbridge, which acted as a holding station and a centre for the reassignment of temporarily redundant service personnel. Here I was reunited with Wilbur Wright and other ex Laghouat prisoners. On most evenings we travelled up to London and enjoyed pleasant evenings together at haunts off Piccadilly Circus and Oxford Street. Wilbur and I met two young females and became the envy of our Laghouat friends. During this short friendship we invited the young ladies to the Chevrons Club where Wilbur provided the pianoforte boogie-woogie entertainment. The girls loved him. The men enjoyed his piano playing and in consequence Wilbur never went short of a drink. Rarely had he to put his hand in his pocket. The top of the piano became lined with unconsumed pints!

We had to report back to Uxbridge before midnight and travelling by Underground witnessed the dreadful plights of many Londoners. The platforms down below were used as large communal dormitories where bombed out Londoners and others sought shelter. Crowded together in their hundreds were elderly folk, families with little children and women with young babies. There was no alternative than to climb over these sleeping citizens wrapped in their rolled up blankets. The platform was their pillow. They would sleep there night after night as the trains thundered by.

Whilst at Uxbridge we were not required to carry out any specific duties. Occasionally we would be detailed for a short route march. Nobody objected to this as it helped to pass the time. One morning, unexpectedly, we were summoned to the main gate where transport was waiting to take us to Elstree Studios. It was at the time they were shooting the film 'Millions Like Us', starring the up and coming young star Patricia Roc. We had been called in as extras, young servicemen, who for the purpose of the film, had to rush on to the set dance floor, supposed to be in a village hall, and act as partners for the local girls.

It was an interesting experience as none of us had been on a film set before. The 'shootings' were noisy. They appeared to be disjointed with many repetitive takes, stoppages and retakes accompanied by the loud shouts of, "Cut!" The scenes were short and did not conform to a particular sequence. Our extras' scene was shot twice, and later, when the film reached the cinemas, I was disappointed to discover that army boys had replaced the RAF personnel. I did not attain stardom but still retain pleasant recollections of young Patricia Roc, who was charmingly natural and had a smile for us all.

On leaving the set we were each paid the rewarding sum of seven shillings and sixpence, a sum that became liquidated without difficulty as the ensuing evening wore on. I had made a date with a young lady who worked off set. Freed from any further responsibilities towards Miss Roc, this young lady directed her attentions towards me and had become free to help me spend my money in the city. She took me to interesting and expensive haunts in the West End where we dined well and consumed many overpriced drinks. The latter might be more suitably described as concoctions and fortunately, my stomach had learned how to cope. Her talent for stopping a passing cab, when others failed, was commendable. She stood elegantly silhouetted at the kerbside; her left arm raised in a beckoning manner towards the approaching taxi driver, whom she hailed with a loud cry that sounded something like this, "Tayeksii." It never failed.

I had enjoyed a different experience and a rather expensive night out!

Chapter Sixteen

WYMESWOLD

From Uxbridge I was posted to Wymeswold OTU, a training station for heavy bomber crews. It was my first experience of a dispersed aerodrome with hard runways and Nissen hut accommodation. Gone were the mess waiters. We queued for food, which we carried to our tables. As a screened senior NCO, I was allowed to use the sergeants' mess, a privilege not permitted to trainee aircrews passing through.

I was billeted in a small Nissen hut designed to provide sleeping accommodation for ten personnel. Only five of the beds were occupied and after my arrival four beds remained permanently vacant. My companions were all screened senior NCOs, one of whom, 'Pop' Elton, was an elderly man, a veteran of the First World War who had joined up again to 'do his bit' in administration during World War Two. The others, all non-aircrew, were disciplined, well behaved men who exercised responsibility. I could not have wished to become associated with five more compatible comrades. I had to be careful of my own behaviour when I returned after a late night out with some of the screened aircrew boys!

Heated by a coke-burning stove in the centre of the room, it was a comfortable billet and we ensured it stayed that way. By employing a sensible, practical roster, we were able to keep the stove alight for twenty-four hours every day throughout the winter months.

One of the sergeants, an older man, married and with a young family, had domestic commitments. The responsibilities to his wife must have weighed heavily on his shoulders and whenever he returned from a few hours off duty in Loughborough, he would bring an assortment of household items, varying from a long handled sweeping brush, feather duster, zinc bucket and scrubbing brush to washing up bowl. Apparently, all prized possessions, virtually unobtainable in north London, such had become the wartime shortages. He had his leg pulled unmercifully when he set off on leave armed with this selection of domestic hardware.

On my first night at Wymeswold, standing alone at the bar in the sergeants' mess, I asked quite casually, if anyone played Bridge. The immediate response delighted me. At once, a new Bridge school was established. I had acquired three new enthusiastic comrades and we played together during the remainder of my posting. The Bridge therapy continued.

• • • • • •

My ground duties were with Flying Control as an Airfield Control Pilot (ACP) working in a caravan off the runway, controlling aircraft on take-offs and landings. I joined a team of four other senior NCOs, who, for some reason or other, were also on a ground tour. The senior NCO in charge of our team was Flight Sergeant Storey who had completed an operational flying tour on Wellingtons. We were left to our own devices and, provided the caravan was permanently manned, (a watertight cover-up was essential) we were able to arrange regular unofficial twenty-four hour passes. We all took advantage of this, in particular Sergeant Lomas, or Lomax who would shoot off to Macclesfield to visit his girlfriend.

This young sergeant was a very brave man, a stoic with indomitable courage who had suffered severe injuries from third degree burns when his aircraft returned in flames after an operational flight. He had spent months at Ely Burns Hospital where he underwent innumerable skin grafts by skilled surgeons who saved his life. The fortitude he displayed was exemplary. He had two wishes, firstly to get married to the young lady in Macclesfield and secondly to return to operational flying. Only his first wish became granted. I understand he did marry this lady and that they enjoyed many years of married life together until he died at the age of sixty-two.

I had completed a long stint on night duties by the morning of 19th February 1943 and was free to go on twenty-four hour pass. Tired from lack of sleep, I was undecided whether to travel home or relax on base. A colleague told me that a vehicle was scheduled to leave the guardroom for Loughborough station, so if I hurried, I could get a lift and catch the next train from London to Manchester. My mind was made up - I would travel home.

The train was crowded at Loughborough and I was fortunate to find a vacant aisle seat in a Pullman carriage. Although I was aware of the attractive young lady on my right, I settled quickly and being tired, promptly fell asleep. At Sheffield station I became wide awake and turned towards the young lady, who asked if the train was running late. I had no idea. It was not the question that attracted me but her lovely smile.

We began to talk and became completely engrossed in conversation until the train arrived, all too quickly it seemed, at Manchester. Here, we changed trains and crossed the city to Victoria station in an overcrowded taxi, which we shared with three complete strangers. A little later, standing on a draughty platform, it was time to act quickly, if we were to see each other again. Hurriedly we exchanged names and addresses. On the piece of paper handed to me I read: - Alice Ormerod, Prebendal School, Aylesbury, Buckinghamshire. This marked the beginning of a regular correspondence and it was not until later I learned that Alice's permanent home address was, Blackburn. I was to learn also that this talented young lady, when home on a recent weekend break, visited Preston, where a speech festival was being held. There was a national competition for speech and recitation, open to all comers, which Alice entered and won the first prize of a beautiful rosebowl.

Alice

Shortly afterwards, during a hastily arranged weekend leave to my home at Nelson, at my wish, Mother and I made a surprise visit to Blackburn. Fortunately, Alice and her two married sisters were at home, as was her Mother, a lady of grace with an endearing smile like her youngest daughter. The sisters' husbands were away on military service overseas.

My friendship with Alice deepened. I started on a refresher flying course during early May 1943 and we became engaged in the following month.

I flew in the Avro Anson aircraft on cross country training flights and it was on one of these exercises the route passed very near to Aylesbury. By arrangement with the pilot, I managed to arrange a slight diversion of course to take us directly over the town, and by using a hand held camera, took a very good photograph from about one thousand feet.

This shows the church quite clearly towards the centre of the town with the school close by, situated in about four acres of garden.

Miss Farmer, the school headmistress, employed a very useful handyman by the name of Titmarsh, who was an expert gardener. I got to know him very well from my visits to the school and thoroughly enjoyed his informative down to earth conversations. He was a fount of information on horticulture and certainly kept the school well provided with fruit and vegetables. Just one draw back, he had a penchant for growing parsnips. This  was outweighed by prolific yields of raspberries, strawberries, tomatoes and new potatoes, in season, and with hothouse grapes.

Some members of the teaching staff, including Alice, lived in school. I got to know them all and enjoyed their hospitality in the common room, where she and I would spend many an evening playing bridge. Little did I imagine, nine months ago in Laghouat, that I should be playing bridge in an English girls' boarding school! I was always assured of a welcome at Prebendal.

Alice was referred to by the staff as Dormouse, a nickname which stuck, because inadvertently, she once mentioned having played the part in Alice in Wonderland.

As my refresher training would lead to operational flying again we agreed to wait before rushing into marriage. In the meantime, whenever possible, we would meet on short leaves, either at Aylesbury, Blackburn or Nelson. It was on one of these occasions Alice and I climbed to the top of Pendle Hill, from the Barrowford/Nelson approach. I thought about her father's laboured attempt from the other side with the aid of a rope. What good fortune to be blessed with good health. The panoramic view from the long and flat summit was breathtakingly rewarding.

What fortune now lay ahead?

Shortly afterwards, travelling together on a night train, whilst peering through the carriage window, I noticed the bright star Regulus, clearly discernible beneath the belt of Orion. The position of the stars denoted the time. This started a conversation to lighten our journey in the early hours of the morning, when I mentioned the importance of being able to identify stars for the purpose of Astro navigation.

For a lay person, star identification may appear to be a daunting task. Light-heartedly I added that if approached in the right manner, it is not too difficult. Be prepared to stand out of doors on a frosty winter's evening, crane your neck and gaze skywards and make a few notes. Oh, and be prepared to get chilblains on fingers and toes! This will be a prerequisite if you are training to be an aircrew navigator. The RAF, to further the cause, will provide on loan a bubble sextant to be hand held for taking star shots and establishing position. I can assure readers that when the result is forthcoming, the position found will not be as expected. Errors of ten to fifteen miles are quite commonplace. Try it in an aeroplane, where it is much more difficult. Give me the assistance anytime of H2S radar, on which I comment later in the book.

Alice, however, became very adept at star recognition. She bought a book on stars and with the aid of this and the heavens, soon acquired a celestial library. It ranged from Aldebaran, Altair, Arcturus, Capella, Deneb, Vega and Pleiades to Ursa Major and Ursa Minor, plus a whole selection of others. I am surprised she did not suffer more from chilblains. The pronunciation of the name of one star was always controversial, namely, BETELGEUSE. Was it BETTELGEEZE, BEETLEJUICE, OR? I ask readers, because I don't know

● ● ● ● ● ●

Previously at Wymeswold, I met Jimmy Alexander quite unexpectedly for a few brief moments. His warrant officer promotion had come through. He would complete the OTU refresher course prior to being posted to Conversion Unit (CON Unit) way ahead of me. In a matter of weeks he would be back on an operational squadron. Lucky fellow I thought. I hadn't passed my damn medical yet. After seeing Jimmy, I decided again to make an official enquiry regarding my overdue promotion, but to no avail, I heard nothing.

I had enjoyed my three months' posting at Wymeswold but always regretted it had been only a ground duties' tour.

Chapter Seventeen

STAVERTON AND MORETON VALENCE

Fortunately, my distended stomach had now reverted to normal and in early May 1943, to my delight, I was passed medically fit to resume flying duties.

This resulted in my being posted to No.6 Advanced Flying Unit Staverton (No.6 A.F.U.) for a navigation refresher course on the dependable Avro Ansons. I was joined by Sergeant 'Joe' Pennington, a navigator who was to accompany me throughout the flying refresher courses and become a lasting staunch friend. During the period of astro/navigation training he acted as a valuable mentor and became an indispensable tutor when it came to star recognition. How easy it was to become confused when gazing at the stars in the sky at night, but Joe could pick them out. He was a brilliant navigator, plagued by airsickness. In spite of this he pressed on to reach a Lancaster Bomber squadron. Most deservedly he was later awarded the DFC after completing a full tour of operational flights from Elsham Wolds. As if that wasn't enough, he continued operational flying in the renowned twin-engined Mosquito Bomber until the cease of hostilities in Europe.

There was still no news of my overdue promotion so I took the matter into my own hands and went to RAF Records Office Gloucester. This followed a chance meeting with an RAF sergeant and his Waaf companion at a famous pub in Gloucester called the Monks' Retreat. On hearing my story they had no hesitation in advising me to make my own enquiries. They told me whom to approach and in which section I would find that person. My enquiries were received sympathetically and I was promised they would be investigated. Next day the Station Navigation Officer sent for me. He was a squadron leader who tore me off one hell of a strip for not making enquiries through the official channels. I told him politely I had been doing so without success for the last six months, whereupon I

No 6 A.F.U. RAF Staverton   May 1943

No 6 A.F.U. RAF Staverton   June 1943
(My second course for Astro Navigation)

was summarily dismissed. The following day he sent for me again. This time, with a broad smile on his face, he told me my promotion had been promulgated. I was a warrant officer first class and my promotion, with all pay increases would be backdated! There is a Yorkshire saying that goes something like this, "If tha wants owt doing, do it for thi'sen."

The rank of warrant officer first class was respected by officers and envied by many non-commissioned service personnel. To the majority of these it was never attainable. In peace time for most ground staff it would require many years of devoted service to attain this status. In wartime, even with more stations operating, the establishment on each was limited to a few warrant officer appointments, unless one served as aircrew. Dependent on survival, for them such promotion could be achieved probably in less than three years.

Proudly, I updated my uniform by sewing on the new rank badges. These badges by Royal Warrant displayed the Lion and the Unicorn and carried the motto 'Dieu et mon droit'. We referred to them rather irreverently as 'galloping horses' or 'Tate and Lyles', the latter after a similar 'emblem' which appeared on the tins of a well known treacle purveyor!

I was now classed as a pupil navigator whilst on this refresher training course and my training sergeant colleagues and I were not permitted to use the facilities of the sergeants' mess. In consequence, we queued for our meals at the canteen with the other airmen and airwomen and carried our own knife, fork, spoon and mug. I regarded this as a breakdown of protocol but at the same time great fun. These lads and lasses could give and take and had at their disposal an endless vocabulary of quips. I heard all, saw all, said very little but learned a lot. They certainly contributed to help win the war.

Soon I was to be deprived of their company.

On the day after my promotion I displayed my new symbol of rank whilst queuing for lunch as usual. The Station Warrant Officer who was passing, stopped and beckoned me to step out of the queue. He bore what I would describe as an almost unctuous expression on his face, as quietly, yet in a kindly manner, he informed me that as a warrant officer I was not required to use the airmen's canteen and should move to the sergeants' mess.

In reply I said something to the effect that today was no different from yesterday and that if I moved to the sergeants' mess the other pupil sergeant navigators should move with me. He explained the accommodation was insufficient to house all these men and that I alone should acquiesce to his request. He was instrumental in passing on an order that came from a higher authority.

My colleagues to a man urged me to comply. The opinion of one man was endorsed by them all. I should be put on a charge if I refused and I had been through enough already. They were a bunch of stalwarts and I do not know how many of them survived the operational flying towards which they were heading. Apart from Joe Pennington, I never saw or heard from any one of them after completion of the course.

I did use the sergeants' mess and never refused to take advantage of its facilities through the rest of my retraining.

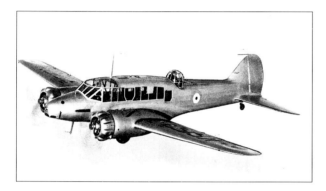

I refer to an entry in my new flying logbook dated 28th/29th June 1943. This referred to a night flight in Anson K4, in which take-off time from Moreton Valence turned out to be 23.45 hours. It was a training exercise, entered as Dead Reckoning (D.R.) navigation using radio aids and beacons. Joe Pennington and I were to fly together which was quite routine in training practices. Joe, as first navigator, was responsible for completing the flight plan and plotting the courses throughout the flight. My duties as second navigator were to obtain fixes from radio bearings, supplied by the wireless operator, and by map reading, a task that was more difficult at night. By take-off time the screened wireless operator had not arrived and the pilot was about to shut down the engines when the latecomer finally appeared. After receiving a strict reprimand from the pilot, the delinquent settled down by his radio and we were ready to take-off.

We flew immediately into an inversion layer, a meteorological condition in which the temperature of a layer of air increases with height, often causing poor visibility in the lower atmosphere. After

Joe and Nancie Pennington

climbing steadily, we levelled at 7,000 feet to find no break in the cloud. Visibility was nil, above and below. As this was an exercise that allowed for the use of radio aids, the pilot decided it was time to break radio silence. He tried to call up the wireless operator on the intercom, but there was no response. The man was asleep, in fact not only asleep but also in a drunken stupor. Eventually we succeeded in wakening him and although the predicament in which he was placed had a sobering effect, his efforts could not produce any signal from the radio. The set was unserviceable and beyond repair in the air. We continued without any radio aid.

Later, a decision was reached by us all to descend to 3,000 feet, below which we were reluctant to fly because of the proximity of the Welsh mountains. Unfortunately there was still no break in the obscurity; consequently we had no alternative than to continue flying by dead reckoning. Joe kept an immaculate flight chart and log and used dead reckoning fixes at turning points. He had applied, and continued to apply to his courses, the pre-flight forecast light airs winds (light air is a very light wind, force 1 on the Beaufort scale, 1-3 m.p.h.), so surely we should not be far off track when making the final descent towards base. Trusting we would be well clear of those dreaded Welsh mountains the pilot continued the descent until at 1,000 feet I caught a glimpse of water below. The shape suggested it could be the Bristol Channel. Had we been saved? Hopefully, if the pilot changed course he would fly up the Channel to Gloucester and base. Suddenly the water changed direction by almost ninety degrees to the right! It was not the Bristol Channel; it was the Solent. We were over the Isle of Wight!

Ford Aerodrome realised there was an aircraft in distress and very obligingly switched on the runway lights. Before making the final approach, we flew through a balloon barrage, which had been completely obscured in low cloud. Miraculously we cleared it without causing, or sustaining any damage. We landed safely at 03.30 hours, three and three-quarter hours after take-off. During this time we had drifted over one hundred miles south-south-east of track.

After landing, the wireless operator was interrogated by a senior officer and placed under arrest. The military police took him away and we never heard from him again. Overnight accommodation was provided for the rest of us, then the following morning we had to report to the navigation section for interrogation and debriefing.

Senior navigation officers scrutinized and analysed step by step Joe's entire flight's navigation chart and his flight plotting by dead reckoning. They could not find any faults. His calculations had been accurate throughout and he was commended for having kept an immaculate log.

At 12.00 hours we took off without a wireless operator on the return flight direct to base where we landed seventy minutes later. We never heard if there were any repercussions at a higher level.

The same night, 29th/30th June, we took off again on a D.R. navigation exercise using radio aids and beacons. This time I was 1st navigator, we flew with a competent wireless operator whose radio worked perfectly and we did not fly under inversion conditions. The flight was completed without any untoward incident and we landed back at base three and a half hours after take-off.

June had been a busy month in which I had carried out eleven similar cross-country flights.

One member of the permanent staff, a short-haired mongrel terrier, was everybody's friend. When the little fellow was not engaged in flying duties he could be found in the proximity of the sergeants' mess cookhouse, or outside the flights' office. It was alleged he had more day and night flying hours than any aircrew member. In fact one navigator tried to record his flights in a special flying dogbook! Twice he accompanied me on cross-country flights and after having a good sniff around the aircraft, which smelt horrible, he settled down comfortably and went to sleep. He was never airsick, thank goodness, which is more than could be said for some of the aircrew. I was fortunate and never suffered with this problem, so I had a strong admiration for those who did and in spite of it, pressed on in physical discomfort to carry out their duties.

Whilst on brief leave, quite unexpectedly, I met Bob Pine in Manchester. He was the navigator with whom I had shared billets during our earlier days of training at Prestwick in 1939/40. He had been discharged from the RAF suffering from diabetes, an illness from which he never recovered. In spite of this and suffering from chronic airsickness, he had pressed on heroically to complete forty-two operational sorties on Wellington Bombers. For this exceptional and commendable service he was never rewarded.

Chapter Eighteen

WYMESWOLD OTU REFRESHER COURSE

In July 1943 I returned to Wymeswold on the OTU refresher course. I went back to my old billet to find that three of the original occupants had been posted. It was not quite the same, one newcomer had arrived who did not stay long and the billet was very quiet. Members of the Bridge School had been posted and I no longer had the desire to seek new partners. I would be busy anyway with flying duties that would entail working unpredictable hours.

Here I met Pilot Officer Jack Hamilton, pilot and three senior NCOs, Sergeants Doug Chapman, bomb-aimer, 'Sparks' Dennis Lacey, wireless operator and Jack Duffett, air gunner, who were to become members of my new crew. We would train together until reaching my second operational squadron. Not knowing anything about these men, I enlightened them about my life in the POW camps and said I had no intention of undergoing such experiences again. They understood the message I was trying to convey and turned out to be the finest bunch of fellows with whom any navigator could wish to fly.

Our flying training was carried out in the twin-engined Wellington heavy bomber, a sturdy aircraft with a strong fuselage of geodetic construction obtained by an interlacing of short metal struts.

An incident occurred on 17th August 1943 that takes some telling but in which there is a touch of irony. We were flying on an interesting cross-country that included carrying out live bombing and air-to-air firing over Wainfleet. This exercise completed satisfactorily, we were continuing on a long cross-country flight westwards taking us over Anglesey, when our Wellington aircraft suddenly lost its starboard propeller. It just spiralled to earth leaving the aircraft unstable. Trouble was developing now in the port engine so the brave and talented, screened pilot Sergeant Coleman who, most fortunately had been detailed to fly with us, immediately assumed control and took over from our skipper. His handling of the aircraft, now completely out of normal control, was exemplary as he carried out a crash landing. The aircraft ploughed across two fields before breaking its back and finally coming to rest in two sections. Due to the pilot's first class talk down, not one of us was injured. We were braced in crash positions unable to see out, but always under his command. The nose of the aircraft was filled with earth up to the pilot's feet and poor old Jack Duffett ended up in isolated splendour in the rear gun turret. The back end of the plane had separated completely from the front portion and was pointing skywards at an angle of 45 degrees. Not until the rescue vehicle arrived was Doug Chapman able to climb up and help Jack out of his turret.

We were taken by truck, with all our flying gear, to Mona Airfield and reported to Flying Control. On arrival, I just could not believe what I saw parked outside. It was my BSA motorbike;

the registration plates RJ9739 positively identified it, the very machine that had taken Mother and me on holiday and to SELWORTHY in August 1939. My parents had sold it to a dealer in Manchester, at my suggestion, whilst I was in Le Kef. What a coincidence, but sadly I was not able to meet the flying

officer to whom it now belonged, as he was away on day pass.

After interrogation, our pilot Jack Hamilton retired to the officers' mess and we five senior NCOs departed to the sergeants' mess in search of a well deserved flying meal. Eight hours had elapsed since our early lunch at midday and we were looking forward to the accustomed bacon and eggs fry-up, generally available to aircrew following flying duties. Imagine our astonishment and annoyance when we found the kitchen had been closed. There was no food. The catering staff had been called elsewhere to prepare a buffet for a visiting ENSA Troupe. (Entertainments National Service Association was a body established in 1939 by Basil Dean that provided entertainment for British and Allied troops throughout the war. It was disbanded after the cease of hostilities in 1946.)

The buffet had been beautifully prepared and presented a well laid out appetising spread as we quickly discovered; almost as good as a flying meal we thought, as we tucked into succulent sandwiches.

"Hey! Put those down," roared an irate catering officer. "Those are not for you, they are for the ENSA Party."

"Is that so?" I retorted angrily, adding, "We haven't eaten since midday and a few hours ago we climbed out of a crashed aircraft that has been completely written off. The sergeants' mess kitchen is closed and there's no food available elsewhere." Grabbing another sandwich I went on, "What are you going to do about it,"

I was angry. I felt we had been 'pushed around' enough. I was not in a subservient mood, nor was I in a mood for servility. There wasn't much the officer could do, nor I, so we let the matter drop.

I shared a billet for the night with a squad of thirty army private soldiers who extended every courtesy and kindness imaginable with a complete disregard for protocol. They offered me the best bed in the overcrowded billet, a bed given up to me by the lance corporal in charge of the hut. In a corner of the room it offered a little more space but no more privacy.

I was immediately promoted from the rank of WO1 to 'mate'. Everybody was 'mate'; it was a common rank of bondage. We were all in the same boat, pulling together. They offered me 'fags', fruit, part of their rations. Their generosity was boundless. They represented the true backbone of everything that was British. There was no alcohol in the hut. On an army private's pay they could not afford more than one night out each week. (My pay for one day probably exceeded theirs for the week).

I left them next morning to a veritable hero's send off, to the accompanying shouts of, "All the best mate, good luck, happy landings mate and drop a bomb on Hitler with our names on it!" What a wonderful bunch of fellows!

Surely a return flight to Wymeswold would be arranged from either Mona, or Valley. No, the journey had to be undertaken by complicated overland cross-country; combining road and rail transport, starting from Bangor. This involved changing trains at Chester, Crewe, Birmingham and Leicester in the height of the holiday season. For most of the journey, which took all day, we had to stand in crowded corridors encumbered with parachutes, parachute harnesses, flying clothing, including my navigator's and other equipment.

It was approaching 21.00 hours when we reported back to flights at Wymeswold and discovered we had been detailed to fly on a five hours cross-country scheduled to take-off at 22.00 hours. Our skipper was not lost for words when he approached whoever was responsible for this planning and made his feelings clear. The flight was cancelled immediately and I returned to a cottage in the village where my fiancée was anxiously waiting. She and Joe Pennington's wife had come to stay for a few days during their holiday, and Joe and I had been granted a short, unexpected, temporary dispensation to live out when not on duty. Who could say the RAF was not caring?

• • • • • •

We completed the course without further incident and I was delighted with the report in my flying logbook by Chief Navigation Instructor Squadron Leader L.C. Pipkin DFC and Bar. I was proud and encouraged by his comments that I was a likely navigation instructor, but in particular by his personal remarks which read, "An above average navigator, has given every satisfaction, very keen and hard working." He was instructor and friend, we shared a common bond; we were both ex prisoners of war. This brave little man had the rare experience of making a break from a German POW camp, getting clean away and back safely to the UK. A success that only a man of great courage and initiative could have accomplished.

• • • • • •

At the beginning of October 1943 I received the tragic news concerning Tony Randall's death. After resuming operational flying, he had been killed when his Halifax bomber crashed near base returning from a raid over Germany. The tragedy was compounded by the fact that he had remarried shortly after repatriation.

ENFIELD AIRMAN'S DEATH AND FUNERAL

SERGT.-AIR-GUNNER D. W. RANDALL

A FELLOW-OFFICER'S TRIBUTE

The "Gazette" regrets to record the death on Active Service of Sgt. Air-Gunner Douglas William Randall, of 58 The Sunny Road, Enfield.

Aged 32, Sgt. Randall was for 2½ years an internee at Laghouat in Algeria, gaining his freedom in November, 1942, soon after which he was married.

In an interview with a "Gazette" reporter, a petty officer in the Royal Navy, who was in the same camp, spoke of the good work done by Sgt. Randall, who played a big part in the manning of the camps. He also produced a camp paper entitled the "Echo" and helped organise sports

in the camp. His final effort on behalf of the men who were held captive behind barbed wire, guarded by French native soldiers, was the part he played in organising an escape party.

Sgt. Randall joined the R.A.F. at the beginning of the war and had taken part in a number of operational flights over Germany.

Chapter Nineteen
LINDHOLME

The last stage in our training approached when we arrived at 1656 Conversion Unit Lindholme in early November 1943. We flew in Halifax and Lancaster bombers and were introduced to the sophisticated radar aids to navigation and enemy detection, namely Gee, H2S and Fishpond. These indicated the complete transformation that had taken place from the operational stage in 1940, to which I had been accustomed, to the stage in 1943 of mass four engined bomber raids, primed to destroy the German infrastructure.

One flight from Lindholme that stands out in my mind was carried out on 20th December 1943 in a Lancaster piloted by experienced Wing Commander St John. It was a five hours' square search from 2,000 feet over the North Sea. We were attempting to sight a dinghy with seven aircrew survivors on board from a bomber aircraft, which had ditched some eight hours earlier returning from a raid over Germany. Even flying at this low altitude it was difficult to envisage just what a dinghy would look like tossed about on a mountainous sea in probably twenty feet troughs. Exposed to the devastating, penetrating chill factor of the wind, conditions would be horrendous beyond imagination. We combed the area in vain for four hours and only then, reluctantly, abandoned the search. With heavy hearts, we returned to base and the welcome comforts of the mess.

Adverse weather conditions had interfered with the flying training programme throughout and in consequence completion of the course had been delayed. It was not until New Year's Eve that we arrived at 100 Squadron Waltham.

Halifax

220

Chapter Twenty

100 SQUADRON, WALTHAM

Our arrival was not greeted with a fanfare of trumpets. It coincided with a stand down and most of the fellows were out celebrating. Nobody in the orderly room wanted to know and as a temporary measure we were sent to some dispersed billets. I remember it was damn cold and there was no heat in the billets, nor any lights, nor hot water in the wash-house and toilets. So this was it, I had arrived at my second squadron! Shades of West Raynham! The situation could only improve and it did when we settled in.

Joan was still stationed on 100 Squadron when my crew arrived on 1st January 1944.

Each flight had its own Waaf driver with vehicle, to carry ground staff to and from the Lancasters. She describes the hive of activity on the airfield by ground staff when 'ops' were on. How they carried out checks on the aircraft, prior to it being 'bombed up', i.e. when the bombs were loaded into the bomb bay. It was then, and only then, when everything was O.K. that the pilot of each Lancaster would sign the Form 700.

The driving duties of the Waafs from the Motor Transport Section (M.T.) were manifold. They varied, from collecting the cocoa or tea urns for the de-briefing room, to driving the station ambulance, driving crew buses to take aircrew to and from their aircraft, and driving vehicles to carry technical staff, and others, to their places of work. Drivers were on permanent immediate standby at the radar section, where skilled staff could render prompt assistance if an aircraft had radar problems, prior to an operational flight take-off. The expertise of these radar technicians proved invaluable to me on more than one occasion. They never failed, at extremely short notice, to re-establish serviceability of the H2S equipment, which was an indispensable radar aid to navigation.

A regular duty of the Waaf drivers was to take the flying control officer of the day to inspect the runways. Joan says they drove him in a Standard van painted yellow. This vehicle was parked permanently at flying control, purely for this purpose, and nicknamed the 'The Yellow Peril'

Another of her experiences, whilst on duty driving round the airfield, coincided with a Flying Fortress approaching rapidly and very low, presumably making an approach for coming in to land. It must have been in serious trouble as it was losing height rapidly. Its wheels were not down, neither was the aircraft in line with a runway as it continued to lose height. Finally, it made an excellent belly landing on the grass, and miraculously the crew emerged safely.

This is what Joan had to say about Berlin. "Only the aircrew knew where they were going. Secrecy was paramount, but the expressions and quietness of the crews on taking them to their aircraft, made us feel they were going to Berlin for the first time. Whenever any of us came off night duty, the first words of the Waafs were, "Any missing?" If there were, they wanted to know who.

As a girl of twenty, she had a harrowing experience in the early hours one morning, when called out for ambulance driving duty. It was to take the medical staff to an aircraft where communication had been lost with the rear gunner. On arrival at the aircraft, they found he was dead with a bullet between the eyes. Next day, she had to drive him to the mortuary at Binbrook

On 1st May 1944 Joan had a special, unofficial, and more pleasant assignment. She was one of the Waafs from the M.T. Section, who formed a Guard of Honour at the wedding of Gerry Stanley and Betty Blyth at Waltham Church.

Although Joan and I met, when we served together on 100 Squadron, throughout the period of my operational tour, we never really knew each other, or became personally acquainted. She must have driven me and my crew to the aircraft and back on several occasions. Nevertheless, there is a destiny that shapes our ends.

In the meantime there was no fuel for the Nissen hut billet, which I shared with three other senior NCO crew members. (Our pilot was in officers' quarters, the two gunners never flew with us after our second 'op' and the spare gunners were billeted elsewhere.) To keep warm, we had no alternative than to 'raid' the coal compound, which was a risky and dirty routine. In this operation we were successful, but still required wood to ignite the coal to burn the coke. In consequence, the shower ablutions became somewhat denuded of wooden furniture. I am not aware of anyone being reprimanded for these misdemeanours.

A tour of 'ops' consisted of thirty operational flights, so I reached an understanding with Mother and my fiancée that after completion of each operational flight I would write a brief letter to both of them, prefixing the letters with a number, starting with one. The numbers would become progressive and would enable them to keep abreast of the number of completed sorties.

From 1st January 1944, my fiancée started to keep an independent, small diary. In this compact, little book she recorded brief details of the targets and losses sustained during operational flights, carried out by Bomber Command, obtained from daily news bulletins on the radio, until invasion day on 6th June 1944. The following year she became my wife and retains this small diary until the present day. Although a little faded, it lies open on the table before me now, fifty-seven years later.

The second day after our arrival was to be memorable for Doug 'Chappy' Chapman our young bomb-aimer. We were having lunch in the sergeants' mess when an attractive Sergeant Waaf passed our table. "Cor, I'm going to take her out tonight," said Chappy, or words to that effect, words that were treated with banter and light derision by the crew. However Chappy kept his word and did take the young lady out. He and Edna, as she was called, were married at Cleethorpes about ten months later and I was privileged to attend the wedding as best man. They were married for over fifty-six years, during which period we continued to keep in touch.

Sadly, I learned recently from Edna that after suffering a long illness Chappy had died at the age of seventy-seven. He had been one of our younger crew members.

The squadron was kept busy in early January and carried out two consecutive raids on Berlin during the nights of 1st/2nd and 2nd/3rd of the month. We did not have an aircraft and were stood down in enforced idleness.

From my point of view the situation did not improve when on 5th/6th January, members of the crew, myself excepted, were detailed to fly with four other crews to Stettin as 'second dickeys' to gain operational experience. Although this was often routine procedure with new crews, on this occasion it did expose them to the hazards confronting four aircraft, not one. Left behind I was most unhappy and not enjoying my early squadron life one little bit. Fortunately, all aircraft returned safely but with a casualty. The electrical heating in one of Jack Duffett's flying boots had failed; resulting in him sustaining severe frostbite, which prevented him from flying with us again. He accepted this misfortune philosophically and with fortitude. In between periods of hospital treatment he returned to the squadron and acted as 'nursemaid' to his old crew. He behaved quite magnanimously and went on later to complete a full tour with another crew.

After Stettin the squadron was placed on stand down until the 14th of the month.

We first set eyes on her on 10th January 1944. I think it was a question of adoption at first sight. She was a beauty standing alone at dispersal in her not too shiny armour to be inappropriately called 'R Roger'; a Lancaster Mark 111 aeroplane powered by four Merlin engines. She was ours and brand new. Her inaugural operational experience to Brunswick was to take place four nights later. After that she would soon become a very experienced lady.

With the exception of Oboe, she carried on board the following aids:-

Gee, which was introduced operationally in early 1942, became a great aid to navigation for distances as far as the enemy coastline, once the navigator had familiarised himself with the operation of the complicated innovation. Shortly afterwards the signals became jammed by the enemy. The navigator could fix position by consulting the Gee Box after reading the pulse signals on the radar screen received from three ground stations. These were not presented in the form of a map and had to be referred to and interpreted from a latticed Gee chart. Then they were transferred to the Mercator's projection chart on which the navigator plotted all courses to and from the target. On this projection, lines of longitude are parallel and do not converge towards the poles. In consequence the lines representing the aircraft's courses and tracks cut all meridians at the same angle. The aircraft was flown on rhumb-line bearings and not on the arcs of a great circle. This method of navigational plotting was adopted on all our operational flights.

Oboe, also dependent on ground signals' transmissions, was used operationally from the end of 1942 by Pathfinders. It was never successfully jammed by the enemy. Unfortunately its range was governed by the earth's curvature, restricting its use for targets beyond the Ruhr. When approaching the target area the pilot was guided by dots or dashes to the aiming point and the bombs were released with great accuracy on receipt of a radar signal.

H2S had an advantage of being independent of ground control. It had a limitless range and was incapable of being jammed. (The disadvantage was that it could be used as a homing device by the enemy who could detect in advance an approaching bomber stream.) By transmitting radar signals from a rotating scanner placed in a blister underneath the aircraft, returns were received and displayed on a cathode ray tube situated in the navigator's compartment. On striking a flat surface such as the sea the signals would be diverted through 90 degrees and not returned to the aircraft, thereby showing no feature on the cathode ray tube. If the aircraft was flying over a large built up area, or approaching a coastline where there was contrast between land and water, the signals would be diverted again by 90 degrees and returned to the aircraft. These would present on the screen an image, or outline, identifiable to a navigator who had kept an accurate plot. In this way a map of radar images could be created on the circular screen, which in radius represented a distance of thirty miles. The aircraft was always in the centre and in order to plot position, readings by distance and bearing could be taken of the images.

Fishpond was operated by the wireless operator and can be best described as a radar scanner looking backwards. It also had a circular screen representing a radius of ten thousand yards on which blips would appear from aircraft within this area. If the blips remained in the same relative position it could be assumed with confidence they were from other bombers in the stream. Fast moving enemy aircraft could be detected quickly as their blips would move rapidly along the screen and be seen by the wireless operator in time to alert the gunners.

Distance Reading Gyro-Magnetic compass, referred to as the 'DR' compass. This was a timely invention of great value to pilot and navigator. It was not disturbed by the extraneous forces present in an aircraft that could seriously affect the ordinary magnetic compass. The master unit was positioned in the rear of the aircraft in a position as remote as possible from the engines and other electrical influences. Repeater dials were located near the navigator, the pilot and bomb-aimer. Its readings

January 1944

Date	Hour	Aircraft Type and No.	Pilot	Duty	Remarks (including results of bombing, gunnery, exercises, etc.)	Flying Times Day	Night
		100 SQDN. WALTHAM			Time carried forward :—	120.55	101.05
4-1-44	1500	LANCASTER 3 W.	F/O HAMILTON	1ST NAVIGATOR	X. COUNTRY.		6.00
7-1-44	1405	"	"	"	BULLSEYE		4.25
10-1-44	10.00	LANCASTER R III	"	"	FIGHTER AFFILIATION	0.40	
14-1-44	17.05	LANCASTER R III	F/O HAMILTON	1ST NAVIGATOR	OPS. BRAUNSCHWEIG		5.10
16-1-44	1.55	LANCASTER U. III	"	"	'Y' INITIAL DEM X. COUNTRY.	1.40	
17-1-44	1.35	T. "	"	"	'Y' X. COUNTRY.	1.35	
20-1-44	16.35	LANCASTER R III	F/O HAMILTON	"	OPS. BERLIN		7.00
23-1-44	21.30	LANCASTER W. III	F/O HAMILTON	"	'Y' X COUNTRY		3.05
		SUMMARY UNIT. DATE. SIGNATURE	FOR JAN. 1944. 100 SQUADRON. 31-1-44 N. D. Hudson.	TYPES LANCASTER III	TOTAL HRS. DAY. TOTAL HRS. NIGHT O/C B.FLT. 100 SQN	3.55	25.40
					Total Time ...	124.50	126.45

February 1944

Date	Hour	Aircraft Type and No.	Pilot	Duty	Remarks (including results of bombing, gunnery, exercises, etc.)	Flying Times Day	Night
					Time carried forward :—	124.50	126.45
1-2-44	11.00	LANCASTER Q III	F/O HAMILTON	1ST NAVIGATOR	'Y' X. COUNTRY.	8.00	
1-2-44	18.00	LANCASTER N III	"	"	'Y' X. COUNTRY		1.40
2-2-44	14.30	LANCASTER R III	"	"	'Y' X. COUNTRY.	2.15	
2-2-44	20.20	LANCASTER S III	"	"	'Y' X. COUNTRY.		2.45
3-2-44	14.05	LANCASTER S III	"	"	'Y' X. COUNTRY + Y. BOMBING	4.10	
4-2-44	11.40	LANCASTER R III	"	"	'Y' BOMBING	2.05	
4-2-44	20.40	LANCASTER R III	"	"	'Y' X. COUNTRY		2.45
5-2-44	15.00	LANCASTER L III	"	"	'Y' BOMBING	2.45	
7-2-44	18.25	LANCASTER R III	"	"	'Y' BOMBING 'PASS OUT' O.K.	1.05	
9-2-44	10.45	LANCASTER S III	"	"	INSTRUCTING 'Y' INITIAL DEM.	0.25	
"	13.40					0.15	
					Total Time ...	140.50	133.55

226

were accurate as the instruments combined the properties of a gyro and compass and were not affected by sudden aircraft changes in direction, or accelerations. Occasionally it would go off heading, a symptom called precession, which could be rectified.

From the rear spar of the Lancaster along the port side, stretching beyond the wireless operator's compartment and along to that of the navigator, were located innumerable components relating to radar. Technology in this field had advanced beyond recognition and expectations since my days in the Blenheim, yet these represented only the forerunners of developments around the corner.

14th January 1944. I was now about to resume operational flying on that inaugural sortie to Brunswick. We did not experience any problems on the outward flight until H2S failed shortly before reaching the target. Fortunately we were able to identify it quite easily as the raid had already started. On the return flight we drifted thirty miles south of track before re-entering Gee range. Only then was I presented with an opportunity to establish a reliable fix but decided to carry on using the existing course until reaching the French coast. Then I made the necessary course alteration, which enabled us to maintain an accurate track to base. At the debrief, the navigation leader was not favourably impressed. He implied I had acted too late and suggested I should 'watch it' in future. I accepted the reprimand philosophically although a little grudgingly. He had no cause to admonish me again.

Perhaps I should explain that H2S, as relatively new equipment, was initially often operationally unpredictable. Somewhat complicated to master, it required involved and delicate tuning and had a habit of becoming unserviceable. Fortunately, the squadron had a team of expert technicians who rapidly overcame the maintenance and servicing problems. Thanks to their expertise the reliability of H2S was wonderfully improved. Not all aircraft were equipped with this device; we were one of the lucky ones.

H2S was not adversely affected by any conditions of poor visibility. Already I felt confident that when returning from future operational flights, I should be able to identify the tip of Spurn Head from a distance of twenty-five to thirty miles pointing towards Waltham aerodrome. My confidence later became justified. What a comfort this turned out to be. To relay our position to my crew, as I watched the outline of the Humber Estuary unfold, revealing Grimsby and Immingham docks, was a boost to six other tired, yet uncomplaining young men. The radar screen told us we were nearly home. Experience dictated - never be complacent until you are safely at home!

Our second mission on 20th January 1944 to Berlin was quite uneventful until we came to the bombing run. All bombs were released except the 'cookie' (four thousand pound bomb) that remained hung up. The pilot asked 'Chappy', the bomb-aimer, if he wished to go round again, a procedure not to be recommended, particularly over a target like the 'Big City', when a plaintive voice from one of the gunners came over the intercom, "If you go round again, you go round without me." The retort from the bomb-aimer, struggling with the reluctant 'electrics,' was unprintable. Alas, the second bombing run was unsuccessful, so we set course for base with a four thousand pound bomb in the bomb compartment.

Well over the North Sea and nearing the English coast a very serious situation had developed, when suddenly, for no logical reason, but to the great relief of us all, the 'electrics' inexplicably came back to life. The Lancaster, delighted to be relieved of its four thousand pounds' pregnancy, leaped upwards before settling down on course in the direction of the crew's eagerly anticipated bacon and eggs breakfast.

Neither gunner flew with us again and for the next few trips we relied on any replacements who were available. I should like to pay tribute to those men and thank them for their co-operation and help in times of danger.

On the 24th January we went home to enjoy a six days' leave. During this short period the squadron carried out three further raids on Berlin. Bomber Command lost one hundred and twelve heavy aircraft. It had been a busy month, for the squadron had been involved in nine operational sorties. On 30th/31st January tragedy struck when the Squadron lost three crews. We had participated in only two raids. For us it had been a slow and disappointing start.

For others it had been different. This is the story of Warrant Officer J.K. Ives and his crew of whom only the New Zealand bomb-aimer, Flight Sergeant Robert Fenton survived and was taken prisoner of war.

	TARGET	DURATION
1943		
29/30 Dec	Berlin	7.05 hrs
1944		
1/2 Jan	Berlin	8.05 hrs

2/3 Jan	Berlin	7.55 hrs
	landed at Croft	
4 Jan	Croft to base	1.30 hrs
5/6 Jan	Stettin	9.15 hrs
8 Jan	H2S X-Country	2.00 hrs
10 Jan	H2S X-Country	3.00 hrs
10 Jan	H2S night X-Country	2.40 hrs
20/21 Jan	Berlin	7.10 hrs
21/22 Jan	Magdeburg	6.10 hrs
22 Jan	H2S X-Country	2.00 hrs
26 Jan	H2S night X-Country	2.30 hrs
27/28 Jan	Berlin	8.05 hrs
28/29 Jan	Berlin	7.25 hrs
30/31 Jan	Berlin	No entry after take-off

• • • • • •

As a general aid to night bombing, route and target markings were carried out by experienced crews known as Pathfinders. They adopted three methods code named Oboe, Parramatta and Wanganui.

Oboe was the most accurate aid to navigation but being dependent upon signals transmitted from ground stations in England, its range was limited and also restricted by the earth's curvature. Other limitations confined its use initially to only one aircraft at a time. When the first aircraft had flown out of Oboe range another aircraft would take over and so on. The most successful markings were carried out by Mosquitoes to targets as far as the Ruhr. Using Oboe fixes they dropped their flares with a high degree of accuracy, probably within 150 yards of the aiming point.

Parramatta was not a navigational aid but the name given to flares used for ground illumination of target areas. Wanganui was the name given to the sky marker flares. The problems that would arise in attempts to obtain accurate markings were insurmountable and were created, as were most flying related problems, by the weather. Ground flares could easily become obscured by cloud, whereas sky markers, subjected to the movement of air, could be blown rapidly well away from the original aiming point. In addition, the Germans took advantage of these procedures by dropping their own dummy flares as decoys to add to the complications.

Over the target, an aircraft would be appointed specifically to fly above the main stream to which it gave continuous instructions regarding bombing procedure and aiming points relating to marker flares. It was referred to as the Master Bomber or Master of Ceremonies and its mission was highly dangerous and occupied the entire time taken to complete the raid, often twenty minutes or more.

On the occasion of one of our raids, this responsibility fell upon the shoulders of Squadron Leader H.F. Breakspear DFC and his crew attached to 1 Group's Special Duties Flight (SDF). After announcing the target the Briefing Officer continued with his address, "Gentlemen, your route markings for tonight will be by Musical Parramatta and your Master of Ceremonies will be Breakspear. I trust his commentary will be 'As you like it'!"

February 1944. With only two 'ops' carried out, we arrived at a moon stand down period. Flight Lieutenant George Pirie DFC was in charge of the H2S navigation section and took advantage of this stand down to fly the pants off me. I completed eight H2S training flights and three flights instructing and passing out squadron navigators who had operated the aid satisfactorily. These flights took place between 1st and 10th February and I thought George was a bit of a 'B' at the time. Later we became the best of friends and often got up to quite a few high jinks.

"George, you may have caused the seat of my pants to become somewhat threadbare, but H2S assuredly was not only our navigational salvation, but also I am sure our absolute salvation."

It was the duty of the navigator to carry a sextant for the purpose of taking star shots and hopefully to establish position lines in the event of radar aids' failure. Although I had no problem now with suitable stars recognition I never came to terms with astro navigation. The process was slow and the pilot was required to concentrate on flying straight and level for relatively long periods, which could be dangerous during operational flying. Furthermore I would not guarantee the accuracy of my astro fixes within say twenty miles. Neither would I dispute the fact that many crews owed their lives to astro navigation, nor would I dispute the fact that my attitude was wrong.

To obtain a fix, or fixes of questionable accuracy could be of some helpful guide to the navigator with no other aids at his disposal and enable him to get his crew back to the UK. I was one of the fortunate navigators, who with the exception of only one short occasion, did not require the option of astro insurance.

One evening, after final 'ops' briefing, I had collected together all my navigational and flying 'clobber' and was staggering out to the crew bus when someone called out, "Hey Doug you've forgotten your sextant." The chap was right, there it was still on the desk. "Thanks Joe," I replied and turned to collect the abandoned sextant. "I'd better take it to check the accuracy of H2S!"

It so happened that 'Traff, the squadron navigation officer overheard my remark and replied, "Quick, Hudson, enter that in the Line Book, if that's the last thing you do."

• • • • • •

My application for a commission had gone forward earlier and on 3rd February I was interviewed by Air Commodore Wray DSO DFC and Bar. He was an elderly officer with many distinguished awards plus First and Second World War experiences - the Commander Jessel type. In spite of being handicapped by a crippled leg, he still flew operationally from time to time accompanying new crews to help instil confidence and give them the benefit of his experience.

I was ushered into his thickly carpeted office where he was seated behind the inevitable large desk, ostensibly engrossed in the perusal of important papers. My footsteps were quite inaudible as I approached the desk and stood smartly to attention and saluted, according to my briefing. Was he aware of my presence? It seemed an eternity before he looked up and I became extremely nervous.

He fired the opening questions asking how long had I been on 100 Squadron, any abortive flights and so on? The answer to the second question, fortunately was no. Abortive flights were no recommendation. He asked about the time lapse since my days at West Raynham and what I had been doing? When he heard I had been a POW in North Africa, in Laghouat, his manner changed. He asked if I knew Lieutenant Commander Watkins? I told him I did and that for a time he was the British CO in Laghouat. That pleased him, he knew Watkins' father, a great man. From now on the interview developed into almost a chatty conversation and from my point of view was relieved of tension. Perhaps the Air Commodore had forgotten it was an interview and closed the conversation rather abruptly.

"All right Hudson, we'll let you know." I thought from his expression that it would be all right.

Within a few days I was a Pilot Officer.

The good news was broken to me in a pub near Grimsby by Flying Officer Beck, a 100 Squadron navigator, who earlier that evening, had read the announcement on the officers' mess notice board. He was almost as delighted as I. Only a few days earlier I had flown as his instructor on an H2S demonstration exercise. The exercise became interrupted when we encountered a heavy snowstorm and experienced severe icing, completely altering the aerodynamics of the aircraft. We lost the two inboard engines. Flight Lieutenant G.R. Ross piloted the aircraft on the serviceable outboard engines with commendable skill to make a brilliant diversionary landing, under blizzard conditions, at the nearest airfield. "Well done Flight Lieutenant Ross, you deserved an official mention that was never forthcoming."

● ● ● ● ● ●

I received a wonderful welcome to the officers' mess, particularly from the navigators with whom I was acquainted. It was a small, intimate mess, where often a hectic party took place following an unexpected operational 'scrub'. On these occasions I discovered George Pirie was industrious not only at work, but also at play! The 100 Squadron Male Voice Choir would find its voice and should the ladies show signs of lingering, a little prompting would be required. The opening phrase of 'Good Night Ladies' was generally sufficient, otherwise 'Bless 'em All' did the trick. Proceedings usually ended with the lusty chanting of the 100 Squadron Anthem, of which there were several verses, sung to the tune of McNamara's Band.

These are the opening lines.

> We are 100 Squadron -
> We're the boys who know the score,
> If anyone denies it,
> We'll spread him on the floor,
> At bombing and beer and billiards
> And all the Cleethorpe hops,
> We've got the gen; we're the leading men,
> We certainly are the tops.

Then the opening chorus followed by two of the many verses.

> While the bombs go bang and the flak bursts clang
> And the searchlights blaze away
> We weave all over the starlit sky
> And wish we'd gone by day.
> Pattison, Pattison, save us now
> We can't abide the noise,
> A credit to Butch Harris,
> The 100 Squadron boys.

> My name is Traff and I joined the RAF,
> Well pretty near the start,
> My trade is navigation,
> But I'm a bit of a wolf at heart.
> I've a popsy here and a popsy there
> And I don't care if they're wed,
> So long as their husbands don't come home
> And find me still in bed.

The huge battle scarred perspex nose of an American Flying Fortress had been cleverly inserted to form an extension to the bar counter and the gaping holes in the perspex, caused by enemy canon fire, told their own story. Many a glass was raised to our fallen American colleagues.

This little wayward episode is one George loved to relate. On one occasion when a mess party had been in full swing, he and other colleagues, with commendable navigation accuracy under the cover of darkness, broke into a nearby Womens' Royal Navy Service (WRNS) camp. Stealthily, they entered one of the sleeping quarters, where silently they caused considerable disarray by re-arranging the lingerie of the slumbering ladies. With total disregard for chivalrous support, George departed carrying a Wren's bra. The party was still in full swing when he and the others returned to the mess and the CO had just arrived.

"What's that you're brandishing, Pirie?" Asked the CO, looking rather amused. "It's a Wren's bra, Sir." George proudly handed over the spoil for the CO's closer inspection.

A young officer then approached and politely interrupted what promised to be an interesting conversation. "Excuse me, Sir, you're wanted on the phone, it's your wife."

Absent mindedly the CO thrust the bra into his pocket on his way to answer the phone. He was last seen dashing out of the room with the ribbons of the bra floating inelegantly in his wake! End of George's story.

••••••

Operational flying recommenced in mid-February and after the arrival of air gunners Flight Sergeant Johnny Hesp DFM and later, Sergeant B.R. Phillips, we became a balanced crew and flew together as an undivided team until the completion of our operational tour.

Johnny Hesp, now contemplating his second tour, approached me whilst enquiring anxiously about his new crew and mistakenly thought I was the bomb aimer. I still wore the original observer's 'O' brevet, not the 'N' brevet favoured by most navigators. Trying to reassure this experienced flight sergeant I began by extolling the virtues of Jack Hamilton, our pilot, explaining how reliable he was.

He interrupted and said, "I'm not bothered about t'pilot, what's navigator like?"

"You're talking to him!" I replied. "Now come with me and meet the others."

In February we added five more missions to our total. All these were as Pathfinder supporters and Chappy topped the squadron photographic ladder for his good bombing results. Bomber Command lost one hundred and eighty-four heavy bombers on these five raids alone. This included the loss of one hundred and twenty-one aircraft on just two raids, namely Berlin on 15th February and Leipzig on the 19th, a raid to which I now refer.

As Pathfinder supporters we flew in the first wave to render back up for their flares by ground marking with actual bombs. Due to a following wind, stronger than forecast, we ran well ahead of schedule requiring the pilot to reduce airspeed within sympathetic limits for aircraft safety. In addition we were obliged to carry out a 'dog-leg', an extremely dangerous practice for ourselves and one that could endanger other aircraft following closely in the stream.

The approach to the target was over ten tenths cloud resulting in zero downward visibility, therefore the bombing had to be carried out by H2S. It was an uncanny experience. All around and below was so quiet with no anti-aircraft fire, nor any sign of enemy combat aircraft.

Decision time had arrived and I had misgivings when I gave Chappy instructions to release the bombs. Could there have been some mistake? Were we really over Leipzig? According to H2S we were and a minute or so later this was confirmed by shouts from the gunners telling me that all hell had been let loose behind.

The main stream was arriving to the welcome of predicted and barrage anti-aircraft fire. Flak bursts were seen everywhere and stricken aircraft exploded on fire in mid-air creating a terrible pyrotechnic display of sparks and flames. Other bomber aircraft spiralled to earth in incandescent cocoons; balls of flame leaving trails of white-hot debris in their wake. The German defences were now fully alerted. Enemy fighters had arrived and over seven hundred heavy bombers were harassed relentlessly, attacked from the ground and in the air throughout their journey towards home. Seventy-eight aircraft failed to return. What a dreadful night's work!

After a few hours in bed we began preparations for a raid to Stuttgart on what turned out to be a long relatively uneventful flight. Losses for the night amounted to nine aircraft, the lowest for any long distance

raid in which we took part.

On the nights of 24th and 25th February we attacked Schweinfurt and Augsburg, ostensibly to cause industrial damage and interrupt ball-bearing production. Now we know that the Germans had anticipated such attacks and transferred some of their plant to shadow factories away from the area. Nevertheless, damage was inflicted upon other productive capacities and on the two towns. Bomber Command's loss was fifty-four aircraft over the two nights. 100 Squadron lost three aircraft on the Schweinfurt raid, including that of the squadron's commanding officer Wing Commander J.F. Dilworth DFC and his crew.

Two raids were carried out over Augsburg on the night of 25th February. We took part in the second after an interval of about two hours. The intensity of the fires caused by the first attack was so great we sighted the burning target from a distance of more than one hundred and fifty miles. Had it not been for flight planning we could have abandoned usual navigational practice and flown visually.

Flak

I have no photographic evidence to illustrate the picture we experienced from twenty thousand feet of burning cities such as this. When we approached the target, to carry out the second raid of the night, the glow from the flames below was changing from bright white to a more subdued red. Shortly after the second attack, as though fanned by a holocaust, we looked down on the return of an indescribable incandescence.

The enemy was stoic and never gave in. The picture above illustrates concentrated bursts of killer anti-aircraft fire (flak), as it appeared to crews looking down from their aircraft. A regular sight, experienced continuously on almost every operational flight.

Chapter Twenty One

OPERATIONAL FLYING CONTINUES

The new squadron commander, Wing Commander R.V.L. Pattison DSO DFC, soon became responsible for running the squadron affairs following the tragic death of his predecessor. I enjoyed an occasional quiet beer in the squadron mess bar with him and learned from our philosophical discussions about some of the demands these responsibilities entailed. Although at this time he was not as operationally experienced as some of the more senior aircrew, he had the well-being of all crews at heart. From him I learned that a senior officer could be very lonely.

I cannot over emphasize the importance we attached, during an operational tour, of flying with a crew which had become an undivided team, a situation in which we now found ourselves. When Doug Chapman suddenly fell ill to a most unpleasant stomach disorder (the Medical Officer called it diarrhoea, we had difficulty in spelling the word and said rather unkindly, that he'd got a dose of the ****s!) it appeared our team would be broken up, if only temporarily. The skipper pleaded with Doug to report sick and in his absence we would seek a replacement bomb-aimer. Doug would have none of it and in no fit condition to fly, insisted on accompanying us that night on a particularly long sortie.

Prepared with a toilet roll he boarded the aircraft and managed to check the settings of his bombsight whilst the pilot revved up his engines prior to take-off. Carrying a portable oxygen bottle he clambered over various spars and reached the safety of the Elsan (chemical lavatory) situated well down the fuselage, just in time to avoid personal disaster. Suitably disrobed he sat enthroned uncomfortably at a very chilly altitude of 20,000 feet. Three hours later he dressed and clambered back to his original bomb-aimer's compartment at the front of the aircraft to release the bombs. He returned to his 'throne', just in time to avoid another personal disaster, and stayed there for another three hours until landing. Charitably, or should I say magnanimously, he refused to be provoked by our proffered ribald suggestions. One suggestion was "Release the contents of the Elsan over the target and allow another crew member to release the bombs." Not in the best of taste, we tried to make levity out of an unpleasant experience. An unpleasant experience endured by a very young crew member, who had displayed an unsolicited, wonderful example of devotion to duty and the 'press-on' spirit.

• • • • • •

Spare a thought for the gunners, dependent on their electrically heated clothing to keep warm and stay alive. We up front enjoyed the luxury of the Lancaster's 'central heating' from the engines, whilst they, constantly on the alert sitting in their gun turrets, were exposed to outside air temperatures often of minus 40 degrees Centigrade, or lower.

Spare a thought also for the pilot and flight engineer on whom we relied absolutely at the dangerous times of take-off. A fully laden Mark 111 Lancaster could be required to leave terra firma hauling an overall weight of 68,000 pounds (over 30 tons) of which at least 32,000 pounds could be in 100% octane fuel and bombs, a highly combustible and explosive mélange. This does not take into account the thousands of rounds of .303 ammunition wrapped around the fuselage in which we were cocooned!

Spare a thought for our ground crew who had worked like Trojans, exposed to the rigours of all weathers, to ensure that R Roger would not let us down at this critical stage.

In trepidation and with the palms of my hands clammy, I would stand up front by the pilot and flight engineer to watch the take-off and marvel at the ability with which they handled this monstrous aeroplane and got it off the deck. The moment the air brakes were released R Roger would begin to thunder down the runway, striving and heaving to become airborne. At around 100/110 m.p.h. she would succeed and start the ascent, but not until we had reached 500 feet would I relax, wipe my sweaty hands and start work.

The Lancaster could be our salvation, our cradle or perhaps our coffin. She possessed weaponry of matchless peer. Loved or hated, her potential powers of destruction from the air were unequalled. She bolstered the morale of a British public, which had been tyrannized since 1940 by the Nazi aerial war machine, the enemy war machine, which had killed thousands of civilians and left countless thousands homeless. She bolstered the morale of an even greater European public, living under German occupation and subjected to the Nazi yoke. The roar of her engines and of her sisters' engines as they thundered overhead on their way to the German targets, gave those beleaguered citizens new hope. Now she was helping us to fight back and destroy the German infrastructure, their factories, lines of communications and all that contributed to the continuation of their war effort. Rugged, robust and reliable she remonstrated only when ill-treated. As the devil incarnate she terrorised and was feared and hated by the enemy. She obeyed our bidding.

Rocked in her cradle and in the warmth of her cabin I was able to suppress the dreaded fears of adverse possibilities. Calmed by the comforting continuous roar of her engines, which drowned all other extraneous noises, time would pass quickly for me as I worked incessantly until we reached the target. Then I would go up front, look around and take in the awesome proceedings. If we were flying in a later wave, the target would be already well alight and on nights of clear downward visibility burning buildings in the streets 20,000 feet below would be clearly discernible.

On bombing occasions, the aerial scene above most targets at around 20,000 feet was comparable with that I described over Leipzig. It was a scene we had learned to expect and to accept. As the observer, one's turn had not arrived, one felt almost detached from the horrors, yet every blazing bomber aircraft would become a 'crematorium'. Seven men entombed had to die.

What was our attitude after the bombs had been released? 'Sparks' Lacey and I would give the thumbs up sign. We had carried out further justifiable retaliation. Now it would be back to the navigational drawing board, to debriefing and what couldn't come too soon, rum, cocoa and bacon and eggs breakfast.

● ● ● ● ● ●

I always used the reliable Gee for fixing position on the early stages of flights, but as it was dependent on transmissions from ground based stations the range was restricted. The enemy had no difficulty in

FLIGHT ENGINEER'S PANEL, LANCASTER X

FIG 4

240

KEY TO *Fig. 1*

INSTRUMENT PANEL

1. Instrument flying panel.
2. D.F. Indicator.
3. Landing light switches.
4. Undercarriage indicator switch.
5. D.R. compass repeater.
6. D.R. compass deviation card holder.
7. Ignition switches.
8. Boost gauges.
9. R.p.m. indicators.
10. Booster coil switch.
11. Slow-running cut-out switches.
12. I.F.F. detonator buttons.
13. I.F.F. switch.
14. Engine starter switches.
15. Bomb containers jettison button.
16. Bomb jettison control.
17. Vacuum change-over cock.
18. Oxygen regulator.
19. Feathering buttons.
20. Triple pressure gauge.
21. Signalling switchbox (identification lamps).
22. Fire-extinguisher pushbuttons.
23. Suction gauge.
24. Starboard master engine cocks.
25. Supercharger gear change control panel.
26. Flaps position indicator.
27. Flaps position indicator switch.
28. Throttle levers.
29. Propeller speed control levers.
30. Port master engine cocks.
31. Rudder pedal.
32. Boost control cut-out.
33. Signalling switchbox (recognition lights).
34. Identification lights colour selector switches.
35. D.R. compass switches.
36. Auto controls steering lever.
37. P.4 compass deviation card-holder.
38. P.4 compass.
39. Undercarriage position indicator.
40. A.S.I. correction card hold.
41. Beam approach indicator.
42. Watch holder.

FIG 1

AP 2062 C PILOT'S NOTES PART V

INSTRUMENT PANEL

FIG 1

241

242

Date	Hour	Aircraft Type and No.	Pilot	Duty	REMARKS (including results of bombing, gunnery, exercises, etc.)	Flying Times Day	Flying Times Night
					Time carried forward :—	140.50	133.55
10.2.44	16.00	LANCASTER	F/L NOLL	1ST NAVIGATOR	INSTRUCTING 'Y' INITIAL J.C.M.	1.40	
15.2.44	17.20	LANCASTER R III	F/O HAMILTON	1ST NAVIGATOR	OPS. BERLIN P.F.F. SUPPORTERS		6.20
19.2.44	23.00	LANCASTER R III	F/O HAMILTON	1ST NAVIGATOR	OPS. LEIPSIG. P.F.F. SUPPORTERS		6.55
20.2.44	23.50	LANCASTER R III	"	"	OPS. STUTTGART. P.F.F. SUPPORTERS.		7.00
23.2.44	14.30	LANCASTER I	F/O SHERRIFF	1ST NAVIGATOR	INSTRUCTING 'Y' INITIAL J.C.M.	2.30	
24.2.44	10.00	LANCASTER R III	F/O HAMILTON	"	AIR FIRING	1.00	
24.2.44	18.20	LANCASTER R III	F/O HAMILTON	1ST NAVIGATOR	OPS. SCHWEINFURT P.F.F. SUPPORTERS		8.05
25.2.44	21.30	LANCASTER III			OPS. AUGSBURG P.F.F. SUPPORTERS.		7.15
		SUMMARY FOR FEBRUARY 1944 UNIT 100 SQDN. DATE 29.2.44 SIGNATURE [signature]	TYPES LANCASTER III		TOTAL HRS. DAY. [signature]	21.10	
					TOTAL TIME	166.00	

Mid to end of February 1944

jamming reception rendering the device useless beyond the Dutch and French coasts after which H2S came into use. This was when Chappy would help for a while, keeping a watch on the H2S screen. It enabled me to use six minute fixes, establish more reliable wind speeds and directions and a more accurate track and ground speed.

Although the Germans could not interfere with H2S transmissions, they could use it as a homing device and direct their fighters towards the bomber stream. Consequently we had to use it sparingly. It was, however, possible to confuse the enemy radar by dropping metallised strips, referred to as 'Window', a task normally the responsibility of the bomb-aimer. In the earlier stages of flights he would alternate duties to keep an eye on the H2S screen and share the 'Window' dropping task with Billy Bloomfield, our accomplished and co-operative flight engineer. On one of these occasions Chappy noticed a German searchlight beam hovering close, in fact too close for comfort. A complete package of the metallised strips had become jammed in the dropping aperture but were promptly released after receiving a hefty kick from the bomb-aimer's flying boot. This caused an instant wide dispersal of the strips and coincided with the searchlight moving rapidly across the sky and away from our aircraft. "Gosh, the ruddy stuff works!" an astonished bomb-aimer was heard to say over the intercom. We had unexpectedly acquired a reformed advocate of 'Window' dropping, a procedure always regarded as messy, even if effectual.

There was now, however, a device known as 'Airborne Cigar', more generally referred to as 'A.B.C.', fitted into the aircraft of only one Lancaster squadron. Ironically this was my old 101 Squadron now operating from Ludford Magna. It would fly mixed in with the main stream and carry a normal bomb load. The device operated with three transmitters and was manned by an eighth crew member who had to speak fluent German. Its object was to jam the German fighter-controllers' instructions. Although the German controllers soon became aware of its introduction, it created confusion, which required the undertaking of time-consuming counter measures.

● ● ● ● ● ●

March 1944.

During the month we carried out seven raids on large German cities commencing with a raid on Stuttgart on March 1st/2nd. The losses were fewer than on the previous Stuttgart raid, only four aircraft failed to return.

A briefing to follow caused much alarm. It would be about the beginning of the month, the day before our next scheduled leave. As I have no written record I cannot be precise, although I do recall that we stood by for an extremely long operational flight. After early morning met briefing we carried out all the usual aircraft checks including instruments and navigational aids with engine run-ups. Not until the petrol bowser arrived did we discover that we should be operating with maximum fuel load. The target would not be divulged until the crews assembled for briefings later in the afternoon. We had the rest of the day in which to ponder!

At the navigators' briefing we learned that the distant target was Königsberg. To economise on fuel consumption we would be required to fly at predetermined low heights according to terrain and anticipated meteorological conditions. Strict adherence to the most practical direct routes was essential. The scheduled flying time for the sortie exceeded nine hours, which afforded little latitude within the bounds of the Lancaster's maximum flying range.

Date	Hour	Aircraft Type and No.	Pilot	Duty	Remarks (including results of bombing, gunnery, exercises, etc.)	Flying Times Day	Flying Times Night
				Time carried forward :—		146.00	169.35
1·3·44	23.34	LANCASTER R. III	F/O HAMILTON	1ST NAVIGATOR	OPS. STUTTGART.		8.09
1·3·44		LANCASTER III	W/O COOK	NAVIGATOR	INSTRUCTOR ON 'Y' CNECK.	2.45	
15·3·44	19.05	LANCASTER R III	F/O HAMILTON	1ST NAVIGATOR	OPS. STUTTGART		7.50
18·3·44	19.05	LANCASTER R' III	F/O HAMILTON	1ST NAVIGATOR	OPS. FRANKFURT P.F.F. SUPPORTERS.		5.30
22·3·44	19.10	LANCASTER R' III	F/O HAMILTON	1ST NAVIGATOR	OPS. FRANKFURT.		5.20
25·3·44	18.55	LANCASTER R' III	F/O HAMILTON	1ST NAVIGATOR	OPS. BERLIN		6.50
26·3·44	20.00	LANCASTER R' III	F/O. HAMILTON	1ST NAVIGATOR	OPS. ESSEN.	-	4.45
30·3·44	22.05	LANCASTER R' III	F/O HAMILTON	1ST NAVIGATOR	OPS. NURNBERG.		7.55
		SUMMARY UNIT DATE SIGNATURE	FOR MARCH. 1944 100 SQDN. 3·4·44 M.C. Hadson.	TYPES LANCASTER III	TOTAL HRS. DAY TOTAL HRS. NIGHT O/C. B.FLT. 100 SQDN.	2.45	45.19.
					Total Time ...	148.45	215.54

March, 1944

I was ominously reminded of that fateful flight from Thorney Island in August 1940, which resulted in the crew spending two and a quarter years in prison camps. I felt most apprehensive. Was this going to happen again? The unpredictability of accurate weather forecasting, covering such a lengthy journey, offered no guarantee of success. I thought about Sergeant Parkinson back at West Raynham in July 1940 and the fateful experience prior to his scheduled honeymoon leave. Were we about to be confronted with a similar experience, or was this stupid superstition? The information received at main briefing and the unfolding of the navigators' flight plan did nothing to alleviate my concern. If ever there were to be a tight schedule on which to operate this would be it.

An hour later we were about to taxi out from dispersal, hoping to keep our appointment with Königsberg, when suddenly flares lighted the sky above the airfield. The 'op' had been cancelled at the last minute! I could not control myself and let out a loud 'whoop' of relief; the first and only time that I showed an emotional outburst in the presence of my crew. Two hours later we were on leave and I boarded a slow train from Grimsby heading towards Manchester. History had not repeated itself!

• • • • • •

After returning from leave we were kept extremely busy and in quick succession attacked Stuttgart twice and followed these assaults with two raids on Frankfurt.

The 24th March saw the last major assault on Berlin, which immediately preceded an attack on Essen, one of the most heavily defended areas in the Ruhr. By this time the colossal Krupps armament factories had become virtually obliterated.

On 30th March the infamous and catastrophic raid on Nuremberg took place. Bomber Command's toll on these seven raids totalled a loss of two hundred and seventy-four heavy bombers.

On the night of 24th March, the night of the Berlin raid, we had reached operational flying height when Chappy gave me a fix that I repudiated. I told him it was way out and to try again. In fact we both tried again and were satisfied that his fix had not been way out as subsequent events were to prove.

We were one of the wind finder aircraft required to broadcast to England every 30 minutes the latest wind speed and direction. Group radio stations in turn would send this information to Bomber Command Headquarters. There the Meteorological Staff would determine an average and send their findings back to the Groups, whose responsibility it was to transmit these findings, known as broadcast winds, to all the bombers.

This Berlin raid developed into a travesty. The Met Staff at Bomber Command HQ either were not prepared to recognise, or found difficulty in accepting the exceptionally high winds broadcast at thirty minute intervals sent back to England by many experienced navigators. These winds were almost twice the velocity of the forecast winds used in the navigators' flight plans; the discrepancy was about 70 m.p.h. I know, because I found and used winds of 140 m.p.h. from about 360 degrees in direction, at an operating height of 20,000 feet. We had encountered the jet stream, which remained constant in speed and direction, at altitudes of and immediately above 20,000 feet. Other navigators concurred when we discussed the matter back at base.

We had no difficulty reaching Berlin and approached the target area with a ground speed in excess of 360 m.p.h. on a heading of 180 degrees. At a height now of nearly 22,000 feet, we encountered few enemy fighters. The flight home passed with little untoward incident and we reached base unharmed at 01.45 hours. 100 Squadron lost one aircraft.

Crews who did not have the benefit of H2S, or whose navigators were inexperienced, or doubted their findings, continued to use the incorrect winds broadcast to the main stream and drifted hopelessly off track. Some failed to reach the target. On the return flight bombers far south of track encountered almost continuous heavy anti-aircraft fire from Magdeburg, Leipzig, Kassel, Munster to the Ruhr and beyond. Casualties grew and Bomber Command lost seventy-two aircraft on the night.

Why, oh why were our winds not accepted and retransmitted? How many lives could have been spared, were it not for this calamitous ineptitude?

At the Nuremberg briefing, six nights later, we were told many of the city's buildings were of wooden construction and that our bomb load would be mainly incendiaries. "Don't have to go there again, the city should be destroyed by a force of 795 heavy bombers!"

For many of us it had been a long eight hours' relatively uneventful trip. We were in the first wave and experienced few problems before reaching, or after leaving the target. There was some enemy action on the return flight and the Squadron sustained no losses although three aircraft had been damaged. From our crew's experience the sortie had been a 'piece of cake' and on hearing the news later, we could not understand why ninety-seven aircraft failed to return. Why did 101 Squadron lose seven A.B.C. Lancasters on the night? Was it because several of their aircraft had mixed with late arrivals in the main stream?

We had been completely oblivious of the nightmare this raid had become to the majority of crews. Nuremberg, the city, which it was thought should not require the bombers' further attentions, suffered only slight damage. Bomber Command suffered its heaviest losses of the war.

The reasons responsible are too manifold to chronicle in a few paragraphs. The main contributory factor was an unexpected, and allegedly impossible to forecast change in weather conditions resulting in an unexpected increase in wind velocity. Unsuspecting Schweinfurt received more attention from the bombers than Nuremberg!

The majority of the main force, using broadcast winds, became well north of target and when turning on the Nuremberg approach were not only late, but well off track. Much of the target marking became inaccurate and there was confusion amongst many of the pathfinders. The largest section of the bomber force presented sitting ducks for the

German defences in the target approaches area and all the way back, as they battled heroically on the return flight home.

Ahead of the main stream, the experienced crews of the 'Openers' were not seriously troubled by anti-aircraft fire, nor enemy fighters. I carried out navigation using H2S fixes and ignored the broadcast winds. We reached the target on time, bombed Nuremberg and set course for home well ahead of other unfortunate crews. Now we understood why, for us, it had been 'a piece of cake'.

What a night of travesty! What a planned? disgrace!

• • • • • •

About this time I read that Pilot Officer J.M. Alexander was reported missing and although I made enquiries afterwards never received any reassuring news. Why, oh why did it keep on happening to these fellows? But it did and continued to do so.

• • • • • •

On two separate occasions, each prior to operational take-off, an extremely depressed navigator stated in my presence that he would not return, so heavy were the odds against.

The first incident arose during afternoon tea in the mess when 'ops' had already been laid on for that evening. The navigator concerned had recently returned from leave. He appeared to be ill; his face carried a jaundiced, haunted look when he made the statement quite openly.

HIS CREW DID NOT RETURN.

The other incident arose after I had accepted George Pirie's challenge 'have at ye with the arrows'. (That was George's expression when asking if I would like a game of darts, a little last few minutes diversionary practice we often carried out before I joined my crew for 'ops' take off.) It was a beautiful late spring evening. In a nearby tree outside the mess a solitary blackbird sang, breaking an unrealistic silence as though the world were at peace.

I was joined by a fellow navigator, normally a rational thinker, well educated. He had served in a professional occupation in Civvy Street and was respected for being well qualified in his wartime navigational role.

Still listening to the blackbird, I commented simply, "Beautiful evening." His response was instantaneous. "Beautiful evening? It's a bloody awful evening. I know we shan't come back," to which I made some trite rejoinder about seeing him later over the bacon and eggs.

The silence was shattered. The ground reverberated as the Lancasters thundered down the runway on their mission of retaliation.

Date	Hour	Aircraft Type and No.	Pilot	Duty	Remarks (including results of bombing, gunnery, exercises, etc.)	Flying Times	
						Day	Night
				Time carried forward :—		148.45	215.54
1-4-44	14.00	LANCASTER B III	F/LT. INNES .	NAVIGATOR.	INSTRUCTOR ON 'Y' CHECK.	3.30	
9-4-44	23.25	LANCASTER R III	F/O. HAMILTON	NAVIGATOR.	OPS. DANZIG (MINE LAYING)		8.10
10-4-44	23.30	"	"	"	OPS. AULNOYE.		14.50
13-4-44	11.00	LANCASTER R III	"	"	AIR FIRING + FIGHTER AFFILIATION	1.55	
15-4-44	14.15	"	"	"	PRACTICE BOMBING.	1.35	
18-4-44	21.05	LANCASTER R III	"	"	OPS. POMMERAN BAY. (MINE LAYING)		6.55
20-4-44	23.35	R "	"	"	OPS. COLOGNE .		4.15
22-4-44	22.40	R "	"	"	OPS. DUSSELDORF		4.20
8-5		SUMMARY FOR APRIL 1944. TYPS. LANCASTER UNIT 100 SQDN. DATE 11-5-44. SIGNATURE A.D. Hudson.			TOTAL HRS. DAY. TOTAL HRS. NIGHT F/O. Hamilton F/LT B. FLT. 100 SQDN	7.00	28.30
					Total Time ...	155.45	244.24

April 1944

HIS CREW DID NOT RETURN.

Next evening a solitary blackbird sang in a tree outside the mess.

Another tragedy concerned a new crew about to embark on its first operational flight. During briefing the inexperienced navigator became so distracted he was unable to complete a single course on his flight plan. With only minutes to spare before the crew buses were due to depart and take us to our waiting aircraft at dispersal, I loaned him my flight plan from which to copy the courses. Abject despair was written on this young man's face when he thanked me. "You will be alright when you get up there," I tried to assure him. "You will have only one course to calculate at a time." This conversation took place in the presence of a senior officer with whom I exchanged a questioning glance. I was very disturbed. This navigator and his crew were allowed to go, but did not come back.

• • • • • •

Date	Hour	Aircraft Type and No.	Pilot	Duty	Remarks (including results of bombing, gunnery, exercises, etc.)	Flying Times Day	Flying Times Night
					Time carried forward :—	155.45	244.24
8-5-44	11.00	LANCASTER 'G'	F/LT EAMES	NAVIGATOR	'Y' PASS OUT CHECK.	4.00.	
10-5-44	22.25	LANCASTER 'R'	F/LT HAMILTON	NAVIGATOR	OPS. DIEPPE.		3.10
12-5-44	15.45	"	"	"	BASE – BINBROOK	00.10	
12-5-44	22.15	"	"	"	OPS. WILHELSMHAVEN MINELAYING.		4.10
14-5-44	14.45	LANCASTER Q.	S/LDR. HAMILTON	"	'Y' PASS OUT CHECK	2.15	
21-5-44	22.40	LANCASTER R	F/LT HAMILTON	"	OPS. DUISBURG.		4.05
22-5-44	22.40	LANCASTER R	"	"	OPS DORTMUND		4.35
24-5-44	22.40	LANCASTER R	"	"	OPS DUNKIRK		2.30
26-5-44	14.55	LANCASTER U.	P/O SMITH	"	'Y' PASS OUT CHECK	3.25	
27-5-44	23.50	LANCASTER R	F/LT. HAMILTON	"	OPS. MERVILLE		3.30
					TOTAL TIME ...	165.35	266.24

May 1944

Twice we were greatly indebted to 'Sparks' Lacey, who with his usual keen eye on fishpond, observed blips moving across the screen in our direction. He alerted the gunners on both occasions and they sighted the approaching enemy fighters in time to warn the pilot who took evasive action. To be in a heavy bomb laden, corkscrewing Lancaster is an experience not to be recommended and the smell of cordite in the fuselage compounds the unpleasantness. Happily, the enemy fighters missed their target on each occasion. Unhappily they got away.

My most frightening experience occurred on the night we were coned in the beam of a master searchlight, an almost ultraviolet light, just waiting for it to happen. Petrified, I had never been so frightened and could neither think, nor calculate and broke out into a cold sweat. The pilot struggled valiantly with the controls attempting evasive action. His efforts were in vain until suddenly and inexplicably the light went out and we regained our flying and mental equilibrium. Had we been flying higher than predicted by the enemy ack-ack, and had the flak burst beneath us? We shall never know.

•••••••

During April we completed another five sorties, two of which were minelaying trips, the most interesting being the assignment to Danzig Bay in the Baltic on the 9th/10th of the month. About one hundred heavy bombers took part on a clear night involving a crossing over the North sea in excess of three hundred miles. Navigation had to be carried out by dead reckoning until we approached the Danish coast and regained the benefit of H2S. From here to the target area excellent return echoes were displayed on the cathode ray tube and our minelaying was carried out by H2S run up to the aiming point. Chappy released the mines upon receipt of my instructions. We climbed to 26,000 feet for the return flight and landed safely at base after completing a trip lasting eight hours and ten minutes. Pilot Officer J.D. Mortimer and his crew had a miraculous escape after their aircraft had been badly damaged by cannon fire. The expertise of the pilot and flight engineer in their heroic struggle to fly the aircraft back to base saved the lives of this gallant crew, all of whom, with an injured rear gunner to look after, played a valiant part. Out of the near one hundred aircraft despatched by Bomber Command nine failed to return, a percentage loss bordering on that of Nuremberg!

About three weeks later the Squadron received a congratulatory telegram from The Admiralty informing us that all ships of the German Navy sheltering in Danzig Bay had been unable to sail during this period, pending clearance of the mines.

The next minelaying trip involved a fairly routine flight of seven hours to Pommeranian Bay on the 18th/19th April.

This was followed by two, what we referred to as Ruhr Bashes to 'Happy Valley'. On 20th/21st and 22nd/23rd April we carried out raids on Cologne and Dusseldorf. The 'Happy Valley' anti-aircraft batteries could be relied upon to give us a warm reception and these two occasions proved to be no exceptions. We were accorded the usual hostile welcomes resulting in damage to R Roger's starboard aileron.

•••••••

The crew of 'R' Roger of 100 Sqn Waltham 1944
L to R
Fg Off J.K. Hamilton, Sgt 'Billy' Bloomfield, Plt Off J.D. Hudson,   Sgt D.H. Chapman,   Sgt D. Lacey, Flt Sgt 'Bernie' Phillips, Flt Sgt J.M. Hesp DFM

Later to become:

Flt Lt J.K. Hamilton DFC,   Flt Sgt 'Billy' Bloomfield, Fg Off J.D. Hudson DFC,   Fg Off D.H. Chapman DFC, Flt Sgt D. Lacey,   Flt Sgt 'Bernie' Phillips DFM, Fg Off J.M. Hesp DFC DFM

May turned out to be another busy month during which we carried out seven more missions. A minelaying trip to Wilhelmshaven required our flying to Binbrook to be 'mined up'. Here, we met the Station CO, Group Captain Hugh I. Edwards VC DSO DFC, who, recognising us as a guest crew, very courteously chatted to the skipper and me during the pre-flight meal and later drove our crew out to dispersal in his staff car. We regarded this as a very friendly gesture from a great man, which gave us quite a morale boost before take-off.

The flight to Duisburg on 21st May, my birthday, was not entirely uneventful and deserves mentioning. We were still a long way from the target when one of the engines failed and with a full bomb load and still heavy fuel load on board, the aircraft began to lose altitude. Down to 12,000 feet and still descending, we made a quick alteration of course and from an H2S bombing run released the four thousand pound bomb on Munster. The previously unsuspecting German ground defences put up some light flak resistance, which we negotiated safely.

With the lighter aircraft load the pilot was able to maintain altitude and we continued at 12,000 feet towards our primary target to release the remainder of our bombs over Duisburg. The town presented a well-defined blazing target after having received the attentions of the main force a little earlier.

The pilot, with the valuable help of the flight engineer who never took his eyes off the instrument panel, nursed the aircraft back to base on three engines at a reduced air speed. We approached Waltham about twenty-five minutes overdue, just in time to witness the aerodrome lights go out. Fortunately, after call up from the skipper, the lights were restored and we returned to the welcome from a small 'reception' committee. Only a few minutes earlier they had given us up for lost and our names were about to be rubbed off the operations board!

At dispersal, a senior member of our devoted ground crew heard me make a rather silly observation. "There's one thing for sure, we shan't be on again tonight."

Came the reply. "I shouldn't be too sure of that sir."

22nd May 1944. We set course for the raid on Dortmund at 22.40 hours. What a devoted ground crew! In future keep your mouth shut Hudson!

Date	Hour	Aircraft Type and No.	Pilot	Duty	Remarks (including results of bombing, gunnery, exercises, etc.)	Flying Times Day	Night
					Time carried forward —	165.35	266.24
24-5-44	1435	LANCASTER 'U.' III	P/O MILLS	NAVIGATOR	'Y' PASS OUT CHECK.	3.05	
31-5-44	2350	LANCASTER 'R' III	F/LT HAMILTON	NAVIGATOR	OPS / ZEROWER		4.20
		SUMMARY	FOR MAY 1944	TYPES LANCASTER III			
		UNIT	100 SQD.		TOTAL HRS. DAY.	12.55	
		DATE	1-6-44		TOTAL HRS. NIGHT.		24.20
		Signature	J. Hudson.		O/C B.FLT. 100 SQDN.		
					O.J. Slemiff F/Lt.		
					TOTAL TIME —	168.40	290.44

May, 1944

Date	Hour	Aircraft Type and No.	Pilot	Duty	Remarks (including results of bombing, gunnery, exercises, etc.)	Flying Times Day	Night
					Time carried forward :—	168.40	290.44
2-6-44	11.50	LANCASTER R III	F/LT HAMILTON	NAVIGATOR	AIR TEST	1.00	
2-6-44	23.35	LANCASTER R III	F/LT HAMILTON	NAVIGATOR	OPS. DIEPPE BENEVAL.		3.45
5-6-44	21.20	"	"	"	OPS. CRISBECQ		4.20
6-6-44	22.15	"	"	"	OPS. VIRE		4.55
			SUMMARY FOR FLYING AT 100 SQDN. DATE 8-6-44 SIGNATURE W. Hudson.		TOTAL HRS. DAY. TOTAL HRS NIGHT SIGNED [signature] O/c B. FLT 100 SQDN	48.45	182.39
					COMPLETION OF TOUR OF OPERATIONS SIGNED [signature] W/CDR. O/c 100 SQDN.		
					Total Time ...	169.40	283.44

June, 1944

However, just over four and a half hours later we had another operational flight under our belt, but only just. The Luftwaffe had started a campaign of intruder raids in a last attempt to destroy more heavy bombers, by surprising the unsuspecting homeward bound crews as they approached base. On the return flight we were nearly caught out in the home circuit, only the timely sighting of a German fighter by our gunners saved R Roger. Our alerted pilot took prompt evasive action at a very low altitude and had the emergency under control. Chappy, still in the nose of the aircraft, obviously was not too sure and screamed - "Skipper for ******* sake look out, or you'll hit the bloody hangar." Thankfully, the hangar remained intact, as did R Roger. I was blissfully packing up my navigational gear when this took place. Never be complacent!

By the end of the month we had completed three assaults over Northern France attacking target areas on which the Germans relied to reinforce their ground forces in anticipation of the pending Allied invasion.

In between operational sorties I flew on four H2S instructional flights and passed for proficiency the navigators of four crews, namely those piloted by Flight Lieutenant E.L. Eames, Pilot Officer Smith, Pilot Officer D.G. Mills and Squadron Leader A.F. Hamilton DSO DFC, later to become Squadron Commander.

••••••

I was with Eric Norman, navigator of E Easy one of 100 Squadron's centenarian aircraft, when we met some friendly Petty Officers in The Navigation, a Grimsby dockside pub. At closing time they insisted we should accompany them back to their ship for a nightcap of Royal Navy rum. On arrival at the dock gates, Eric and I were refused entry on security grounds. Not to be deterred and fortified with ale from The Navigation, we succeeded with some dexterity in scaling the high fencing at a point well away from the guardroom gates. We joined our Royal Navy friends a little later on board their vessel, only to find the rum locker in the petty officers' mess had been placed 'out of bounds'. Our hosts were most upset and to make amends for enforced inhospitality beyond their control, insisted we should not depart empty handed. We were each given a large pure white loaf of bread, a luxury completely unobtainable then by the housewives in Civvy Street but alas of no practical use to us and a handicap when climbing back over the fence. What would we have given for such bounty in Laghouat?

Next morning, when wakening me with a welcome cup of tea, 'Taffy' my batman was surprised to see a large white loaf of bread on the bedside locker.

"Oh! Mr. Hudson, Sir, where did you get that and what are you going to do with it?"

After a few questionable explanations I enlightened him.

"Nothing at all 'Taffy', it's all yours if you want it."

'Taffy' was going on leave that morning and his wife would be delighted with such a prize. It turned out she was surprised and delighted and asked when next would Mr. Hudson be re-visiting his friends at the docks? I never returned to collect a second prize. The vessels had sailed before the 6th June. I often wonder what happened to those friendly petty officers.

••••••

2nd June 1944 and the tour was nearly finished. Only three more softening up tactical missions remained, all of which would be over Northern France again in preparation for the D. Day landings.

6th June 1944. The D. Day invasion had begun. At 22.15 hours we took-off for Vire on a flight that was to be our last softening up blow against the enemy. From the relative safety of our faithful Lancaster we saw the Allied invasion forces' armada below; thousands of brave men, who within the next few hours, would be facing gravest perils, for many, certain death, as they bravely confronted a formidable enemy. For them it was the beginning. For us it was the end. At 03.10 hours on the morning of 7th June 1944 our operational tour was over, we had come through physically unharmed. BOMBER COMMAND HAD LOST OVER ONE THOUSAND FIVE HUNDRED HEAVY BOMBERS DURING THIS PERIOD: LOSSES WHICH ACCOUNTED FOR OVER TEN THOUSAND FIVE HUNDRED AIRMEN EITHER KILLED, WOUNDED OR TAKEN PRISONERS OF WAR.

Later on 7th June 1944: We had been taken off the Squadron flying strength and had no wish to celebrate as we watched the crews take-off without us on a raid to assist the Allied forces in the battle for Europe. Unanimously we reached a decision and asked if we could resume operational flying. The Squadron Commander's agreement was overruled and quashed irrevocably by Squadron Leader 'Doc' Marshall, Station Medical Officer. Our tour had really ended.

Although perhaps understandable under these 'Flak Happy' circumstances, our request had been thoughtless and selfish. We had failed to consider the pain and anguish it would rekindle in the loved ones close to us, who had just been relieved of these anxieties.

Let us pause and reflect on the wisdom of Doc Marshall, who said "You don't realise how 'sick' you are."

BY THE END OF JUNE THE SQUADRON LOST A FURTHER SIX AIRCRAFT, BRINGING ITS LOSS TOTAL FOR THE HALF YEAR TO THIRTY-TWO LANCASTER BOMBERS.

Our aircraft was taken over by Flying Officer D.G. Mills and his crew whose navigator I had checked out on H2S proficiency only a few days previously. Sadly the aircraft crashed on 21st July at Aylesby in Lincolnshire, just outside Waltham base circuit, returning from an operational flight to Courtrai. Four of the crew were killed including the pilot. The other three, namely Flight sergeant A.J. Irwin and

Sergeants G.A. Wells and A.R. Fuller, although injured, survived. R Roger ND413 HW-R had completed fifty-five operational sorties.

I mentioned that when we joined 100 Squadron, my fiancée started to keep an independent small diary, in which little book she recorded brief details of the targets and losses during operational flights carried out by Bomber Command. I am now reading from its faded pages. These are extracts after we completed our operational tour.

1944

Jan 14	Brunswick	38 missing	1
Jan 20	Berlin	35 missing	2
Feb 15	Berlin	43 missing	3
Feb 19	Leipzig	79 missing	4
Feb 20	Stuttgart	10 missing	5
Feb 24	Schweinfurt	35 missing	6
Feb 25	Augsburg	24 missing	7
March 1	Stuttgart	4 missing	8
March 15	Stuttgart	37 missing	9
No record for number 10			
March 18	Frankfurt	22 missing	11
March 22	Frankfurt	33 missing	12
March 24	Berlin	73 missing	13
March 25	Essen	9 missing	14
March 30	Nuremberg	94 missing	15
April 9	Minelaying	11 missing	16
April 10	Railway Targets	22 missing	17
April 18	various targets	14 missing	18
April 20	Cologne	16 missing	19
April 22	Dusseldorf	42 missing	20
May 10	France	15 missing	21
May 12	Sea mining	14 missing	22
May 21	Duisburg	30 missing	23
May 22	Dortmund	35 missing	24
May 24	Dieppe	28 missing	25
May 27	Merville	27 missing	26
May 31	Tergnier	8 missing	27

June 2	Dieppe Beneval	17 missing	28
June 5	Crisbecq	losses not recorded	29
	Targets coast of France		
June 6	Battle area	13 missing	30

FINIS

The losses reported on some of the later French targets include those incurred on other targets in that area by Bomber Command aircraft.

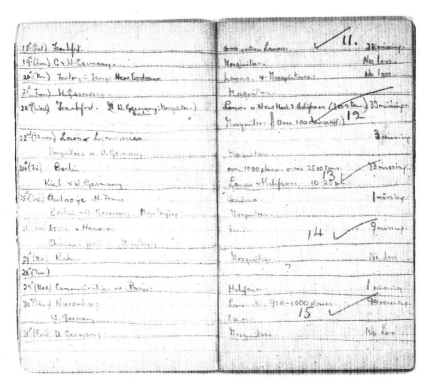

Extract from the diary which Alice kept and to which I refer in the text. Between 18/19th March to 30/31st March 1944

Chapter Twenty Two
SANDTOFT

Chappy, Eric Norman and I were subsequently posted to Sandtoft 1667 Conversion Unit, where flying in Halifaxes and Lancasters, we instructed pupil aircrews in H2S navigation.

Providentially Doc Marshall joined us at Sandtoft enabling my associates and I to enjoy and benefit from the wisdom of his conversations. They helped pass many an agreeable 'on duty' evening in the Mess until an unexpected early posting deprived us of his company.

19th September 1944. I was delighted to read in the National Press that I had been awarded the Distinguished Flying Cross. This was later confirmed in a letter of congratulation from Air Vice Marshal E.A.B. Rice CB CBE MC. Worthy compatriots Doug Chapman and Eric Norman received similar good news.

Before the Doc's posting, Flying Officer Danny Salt, a Canadian navigator who had completed a Lancaster tour of ops, joined us in the H2S navigation instructors' section. He was a 'Falstaff' of a man, gross in physical and mental stature. He hailed from Vancouver and was a university graduate. Engage him in repartee at your peril. Avoid at all cost becoming blameworthy of indiscretion, or stupidity. This would be an open invitation to be pilloried and accused of having descended from a dubious ancestral line. We became good friends and withstood each other's banter, which was never really serious. When I heard he was going on leave to Yorkshire, I asked jokingly, "To Saltaire?"

"As a matter of fact, I am," he replied. "I am going to see Salts Mill and to check on my ancestry!" He was not joking.

Sir Titus Salt had built this famous huge woollen textile manufacturing mill about one hundred years previously. Not only had Sir Titus Salt been responsible for building the mill but also for building the town around it to house his employees. This town, through which the river Aire flowed, was named Saltaire. It seemed ironical

From: A/V/M. E.A.B. Rice, C.B., C.B.E., M.C.

Royal Air Force,
Bawtry Hall,
Bawtry,
Yorks.

1G/EABR/DO.   20th September, 1944.

Dear *Hudson*

    I heartily congratulate you on the Award of the Distinguished Flying Cross.

    I am very glad your splendid achievements have received due recognition.

Yours sincerely,

P/O. J.D. Hudson, D.F.C.,
No.1667 H.C.U.,
R.A.F. Station,
Sandtoft.

that a young Canadian had come on a mission from Vancouver, to help the Allies destroy the enemy infrastructure, and arrived to see the industrial town created in the Salt family name in the West Riding of Yorkshire. Was he one of the family?

••••••

Most operational aircrew were proud of what they referred to as their operational hats. The more battered the headgear the more prestigious it became. Danny was proud of his veteran hat, which had been knocked about considerably and survived maltreatment to his satisfaction. However, disaster nearly struck one night when we were returning late from a night out at a country pub. As screened personnel we were all allowed the privilege of possessing a bicycle, a service issue, which became our responsibility and was strictly the property of the RAF. Great care had to be exercised to ensure these machines were well maintained and not stolen. Normal practice was to chain and padlock the bicycles together before entering a pub and remove all extras such as lights and pumps. It was not uncommon to remove tyre valves to prevent them being pilfered and then endure the tedium of reinflating the tyres before the return journey back to the Station.

On this night in question, five of us were cycling back to Sandtoft with Eric Norman leading the formation. He was the only man with a bicycle light and prudence dictated he should assume 'pole position'. All went well until Danny, who was following in the rear, acted impulsively and decided to take the lead. With head down and pedalling furiously he succeeded in taking over. Without lights, he cycled into the stone parapet of a bridge where the road narrowed and crossed a dyke. The huge frame of the rider was catapulted unceremoniously over the parapet, then described a perfect mid air parabola, before landing head first in the murky, weed strewn waters some ten feet below. After a resounding splash there were moments of absolute silence. We all feared for Danny's safety until the sound of splashes could be heard again. Then vituperations rent the Lincolnshire night air. Danny was safe and well but could not find his hat! He wallowed in slime above his waist for several minutes before most fortuitously under the circumstances, finding the errant headgear.

How we got him back to the Station I cannot recall. I know he spent the night in sick quarters, purely for precautionary observation, under the care of the long-suffering Doc Marshall. (It was not surprising that The Doc, when travelling back to Blackburn by train with my wife after her stay with me at Epworth, referred to us as his 'aircrew babies'!) We must have caused him many moments of anxiety, which he accepted with a rather wry and amused philosophy.

The episode cost Danny a new number one uniform. The old one had become a smelly, shrunken write-off. That did not distress Danny, his operational hat had survived and become more prestigious. The experience had been worth every moment of discomfort, if only for the hat!

• • • • • •

As a navigation and H2S instructor I completed thirty-six training flights with pupil aircrews. The pilots were relatively unaccustomed to handling four engined aircraft having only recently converted from twin engine flying. Each time I boarded an aircraft I was reminded of my first meeting with Johnny Hesp with whom I did not share the same apprehension. My concern was not about navigator, but what's pilot like?

It was not uncommon, when carrying out pre-flight tests, to find the aircraft developed a fault rendering it unserviceable. This would result in our being diverted to another aircraft. Occasionally the second aircraft developed problems requiring a third diversion before we could become airborne. It was no adverse reflection whatsoever on the ground crews or maintenance staff, simply the outcome of the high expectancy demanded from these machines in the rush to complete aircrews' training as quickly as possible and avoid backlogs.

Flying Control officers at Conversion Units were not subjected to the same periods of heavy concentration as were the controllers on operational squadrons where fifteen to twenty-five, or perhaps more aircraft could approach the circuit within a few minutes of each other and would require, or expect prompt instructions regarding landing procedure. At the Conversion Units normally only one or two aircraft would return and be in the circuit at the same time. Imagine the consternation therefore, when on one occasion at Sandtoft, some thirty American Liberators returning from operational flying, suddenly were diverted and required prompt landing instructions.

The cautious approach of the controller, who was taken by surprise, could have resulted in several heavy four engine bombers, rapidly running short of fuel, being stacked in the aerodrome circuit up to fifteen thousand feet. Eric Norman and I were present at the time and neither of us will forget the Liberator's Group Leader asking over the intercom, "What on earth goes on down there?" Not as politely as that I might add! In no uncertain terms he told our controller to get off the air and promptly began to talk down his squadron. At times there were three Liberators on the runway with a fourth entering the approach, something quite unheard of under normal Bomber Command circumstances. Incredibly, as far as I recall, there were no accidents and all aircraft were brought down safely in a few minutes. It was a remarkable display of efficiency albeit not without potential hazard.

I was finally taken off instructional flying on 21st March 1945 and went on leave to be married three days later. The day of our marriage, 24th March 1945, marked the first year's anniversary of the disastrous Berlin raid when Bomber Command lost seventy-two aircraft. The night of the hopelessly inaccurate forecast and broadcast winds from the meteorological office - an arranged calamity of the highest order. It will go down in the history archives as such and not be forgotten.

Neither will the marriage at St. Silas Church, Blackburn, of Alice Ormerod with Douglas Hudson on 24th March 1945 be forgotten, but for very different reasons. It was a blessing to be remembered

throughout our lives. The marriage took place during Lent, when music was not allowed at services This ruling was waived however, by a dispensation granted to meet Alice's special wish.

The picture of the altar shows the frontal tapestry, so beautifully embroidered by Alice's eldest sister Elizabeth, who gained a City and Guilds diploma for church embroidery. She was married at St. Silas Church in 1939 with Eric Stirrup, who was a very devoted worker for the Church and Sunday School Superintendent.

Sadly, Gilbert Ormerod, did not live to see the marriage of his daughters. Elizabeth, his widow, survived to witness

Frontal Tapestry embroidered by Elizabeth Stirrup, Alice's eldest sister

Douglas and Alice's Wedding

all three, a just reward for agreeing with Gilbert to encourage their daughters to attend the nearby Church of England church.

•••••

A few days after returning from leave I received orders to prepare for operational flying again. The pilot of my new crew was Flying Officer Don Palmer DFC with whom I was friendly. He had completed an earlier tour of 'ops' about the time I finished at Waltham and our scheduled posting, after completing a quick refresher course, was to the Far East, to the Japanese war zone!

It was not to be however. I contracted a severe throat infection, which led to gingivitis and mouth ulcers. At the same time a flying officer who occupied the next bed to me in station sick quarters contracted scarlet fever. Fortunately I escaped the infection but was placed in quarantine and isolated from all personnel other than the medical staff. During this period another navigator was chosen to take my place in Don's crew, but thankfully for all of us the operational orders for the Far East were subsequently cancelled.

Shortly before Doc Brown's appointment to Sandtoft, Alice returned by train to Blackburn from Epworth, where we had been living out after our marriage. Ironically, who should join her in the compartment but Doc Marshall, who was also travelling to Blackburn. They were not acquainted, nevertheless, soon entered into conversation and he was interested to learn that his travelling partner was Doug Hudson's wife. She was soon to hear that I was one of his aircrew 'babes', for all of whom he had a high regard. He said something to the effect that we were often a tediously irresponsible lot when off duty, but quite harmless. Then told her seriously, that as ex operational flyers, we didn't realise the stresses, to which we had been subjected on the squadrons. He did not need reminding of the Danny Salt episode and his submersion in the murky waters of the dyke. Danny was very lucky and could have been seriously hurt, or drowned, after his head first plunge over the parapet. All it cost him was a night in sick quarters and a new number one uniform, but not a new hat! It caused the Doc a lot of inconvenience, which he bore ungrudgingly.

Doc Brown had been appointed as the new Station Medical Officer, after Doc Marshall's posting. Whilst I was in sick quarters an aircraft on an H2S familiarization flight crashed and I shall never forget Doc Brown, with sleeves rolled up, bursting into the ward and shouting, "Doug, do you know Flying Officer 'S'?"

"Yes, he's a fellow instructor, I know him well."

"Describe him to me, his face, colour of hair."

After hearing my description the Doc uttered one word. "Was," and left the ward to complete his gruesome task.

The identification of another dead airman had been confirmed. This time the tragedy occurred on a training flight and was the last fatality concerning an aircrew member with whom I had been acquainted. The war in Europe ended a few days later.

•••••

On 19th June 1945 and 20th July 1945 I flew as navigator over Dutch and German territories in Mark 111 Lancasters piloted by Flight Lieutenant Atkinson and Flight Lieutenant Des Sergeant DFC. We carried an attractive payload of Waafs on sight seeing missions at 2,000 feet over fifteen devastated cities, two regrettably Dutch, namely Arnhem and Rotterdam. The other thirteen were cities of the German Reich. These flights were officially recognised by the authorities and were referred to as Cook's Tours. Their object was to enable certain ground staff personnel to see the damage that had been caused to the enemy as an indirect result of their efforts. Photographs on accompanying pages illustrate some of the areas of devastation.

1945

Emden

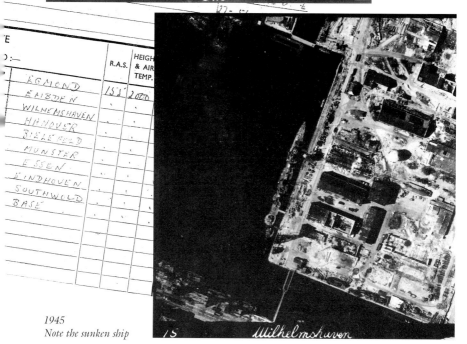

1945
Note the sunken ship

Wilhelmshaven

267

35

WATCH.................... fast / slow

ORDERS *T.O. 1*

s/c 1

rse)	Compass Corrn. for Devn.	Course (C)	ROUTE		
			FROM :—		TO :—
5	°		BASE	A — B	EG
0			EGMOND	B — C	EM
9			EMBDEN	C — D	WIL
5			WILHELMSHAVEN	D — E	HI
0			HANOVER	E — F	BI
9			BIELEFELD	F — G	M
3			MUNSTER	G — H	E
7			ESSEN	H — I	EI
8			EINDHOVEN	I — J	SO
9			SOUTHWOLD	J — A	BI
			—		

Bremen

1945

	R.A.S.	& AIR TEMP.	T.A.S.	D.R. G/S	TO RUN	TIME	E.T.A.
	26						
	155	2000	160	110	204	76	15.21
	"	"	"	110	103	39	1600-05
N	"	"	"	160	34	13	1618-23
	"	"	"	110	72	35	1658-170
	"	"	"	160	49	18	1721-26
	"	"	"	160	34	13	1739-44
	"	"	"	110	39	15	1759-180
L	"	"	"	160	57	21	1823-30
D	"	"	"	160	150	56	1926
	"	"	"	110	120	44	20.10

27   Bremen

20   Bremen

1945

On 6th and 9th August 1945 atom bombs were dropped on Hiroshima and Nagasaki. Five days afterwards the Japanese surrendered unconditionally. World War Two was effectively over by VJ day on 15th August 1945 and irrevocably on 2nd September 1945 when the Japanese finally surrendered. After these dates I did not fly in any service capacity again.

I had survived the war physically unimpaired and was demobbed at the end of October 1945. My wife and I returned to my home in Nelson and after a brief rest took Mother on a short celebration trip to London.

Mother died two weeks later.

It was then I learned from our family Doctor that throughout the war she fought bravely a battle against a painful and incurable cancer that slowly and relentlessly was destroying her body. He explained it was pure will power that had kept her alive. Her faith that one day I would return had bestowed upon her the will to live. If the war had continued another six months or even longer she would have continued to fight her battle. When at last she finally gave up the struggle, she knew the war was over and that I had found someone to take care of me.

Flying Officer J. D. Hudson DFC RAFVR

271

Chapter Twenty Three
CIVVY STREET

My wife and I spent most of the demob leave at Father's home in Nelson. On the employment front reality had dawned. Plum jobs and opportunities were not there for the picking and my old firm in Manchester could not offer a salary commensurate with married responsibilities. Fortunately, through Father's influence, I obtained my first job back in Civvy Street with the manufacturing firm where he was employed as an analytical chemist in charge of the dyehouse. The situation was useful for all of us. It provided a temporary home for my wife and me at a time of readjustment and escalating prices.

I thought I should enjoy my first duties, which were to call on Lancashire textile mills to buy materials suitable for resale. Combined with my new firm's own production, these should considerably increase the marketable selection. From my pre-war experience I had found buying to be relatively easy. Selling had been difficult.

Our mill manager was a brusque, hard-headed Yorkshireman, a real 'call a spade a spade' man! He knew his job, the trade and those with whom he had to deal. This is what he said before I set off on my first day's calls.

"Now remember this lad, just forget tha was ever in't officers' mess and use t'long 'a' sparingly. Let me know how you get on. It'll not be all that easy!"

How right he was. Did I detect a wry smile on his face?

I trudged the streets of those Lancashire towns, called on the mills with which I had been familiar before the war and sent in detailed weekly reports but never succeeded in buying a single yard of material. It was essentially a sellers' market. Those mills had not experienced short time working for over six years having been committed to executing Government contracts throughout the war. This had guaranteed full employment. They were damned if they would sell to a competitor now the war was over. I did not carry a passport to privilege.

At the end of those four weeks I was depressed and prepared for premature dismissal when I was called in to see the manager with my last detailed report.

"You've done all right lad. Your weekly reports have confirmed what I suspected and have told me quite a lot about the competition. The mills are not ready to sell to us yet. We must stand on our own feet for a while. Now, I'm going to give you a real chance. I am sending you to work in another of our mills south of Manchester to help the manager step up production. He's an elderly, pedantic sort of chap and doesn't find it easy to delegate responsibilities. You'll have your work cut out at first but you'll get there in the end, I'm sure. Remember it's still a sellers' market, but it won't last. We've got to make hay whilst the sun shines."

I was flabbergasted, overwhelmed and delighted. Five months later my wife and I bought our first home in Cheshire and paid nearly four times the price for which it was bought when new in 1939! At the time of our purchase I made a most inaccurate prophetic statement. "One thing is certain, house prices will never be so high again!" (As I now complete my memoirs, some fifty-six years later, house prices are probably forty times higher!)

Father came to live with us when he was also transferred to the south Manchester mill, where we worked together until his death in February 1949. Shortly afterwards I was appointed mill production manager.

The managing director previously lived in Germany. He was Jewish and spoke fluent German and English coming from a line of families who had avoided persecution and sought refuge in England before the outbreak of war. Dynamic, industrious and most impetuous, he was a hard taskmaster who taught me in a few months how to run the mill and stand up to the trades union. My response to his tuition combined with hard work brought quick financial rewards.

I learned how to overcome most difficulties but really thought these would become compounded when he appointed a German Doctor of Philosophy (Ph.D.) from Mönchen Gladbach who was a technical expert in textile machinery. Provided we could work in harmony our combined activities would be complementary and of great practical benefit to the mill.

My worst fears were realised shortly after his arrival when several operatives came to me to register their protests against his behaviour.

Some threatened to leave unless he approached them in a calmer manner. They remonstrated, "We are not here to be shouted at by any German so soon after the war."

A problem had arisen, which required immediate resolution. Quietly, I talked and reasoned with the Doctor to whom I explained their protests.

"You are not in Germany now. We behave differently towards our workpeople. We don't storm and shout at them. You will find they will respond to calm, sensible explanations and persuasion."

Although this may have sounded naive and trite, it was true. To his great credit he listened and subsequently modified his approaches to the operatives accordingly. His attitude changed so dramatically they began to like the man. They listened to him and carried out his suggestions. He began to joke with them and drink tea with them by the machines at their rest breaks.

It was a remarkable transformation and led to the forming of an incredible, anomalous triumvirate of authority as we ran that mill. The controller was a Jewish managing director supported by an ex Wehrmacht German officer, now textile spinning expert, who worked jointly with an ex RAF Bomber Command navigator. Our responsibilities were not only to the company but also to the workforce exceeding three hundred men and women who relied on the mill to earn their living.

The Doctor, who served most of the time during the war in the German Wehrmacht, was fully aware of my wartime activities and never showed any sign of animosity. In fact at times he would joke when explaining how all Germans had combined together, working with bare hands, to help repair the structural damage we had inflicted. He said, "The RAF knocked down the old buildings for us. All we had to do was rebuild them to modern standards!"

We worked together for some three years and it was with sadness I bade him farewell when he tendered his resignation to return to work in Germany. I believe this was due to the problems his boys had to face at their English boarding school.

Soon after his return to Germany I received a very sad letter asking if I could possibly help him find an appointment with a good sound English firm. Part of his letter read, "You used to say in England that I shouted too much. The problem here in Germany is that I do not shout enough!"

Photo of three daughters, Elizabeth, Evalyn and Alice with their mother Elizabeth Ormerod

The purchase of a motor car in 1947 was restricted to people who needed a vehicle for business purposes. Petrol for private motoring was not available and special application was required to obtain fuel for business travelling. Furthermore, cars were not readily obtainable.

Shortly after Alice and I moved into our first house at Cheadle Hulme, Cheshire, a friend suggested I should contact a Manchester car dealer and get on the waiting list to buy a new car. This was perhaps the surest way of acquiring one in the not too distant future. It was a measure he had taken and which I adopted. About a year later, a new car became available on the understanding that I was in receipt of petrol coupons. These I obtained without difficulty for business travelling and in March 1948 took delivery of my first new car, a Morris Eight Series E, which cost £355.00. I was required to sign an undertaking, or covenant, not to sell the vehicle at a profit, within a period of twelve months. This was a general rule. When these covenants began to expire, second-hand cars appeared in the showrooms at extremely inflated prices. Dealers temporarily enjoyed a bonanza.

My neighbour and banker colleague Bill Brimelow, who I introduce in a later paragraph, commented on this inverse economic situation. What is the logic in a second-hand article, whose functions have become impaired after use, realising a higher financial value when sold, than it cost when new? The answer of course was self evident, supply and demand. A situation, which was soon to change.

The rather unexpected end of petrol rationing in 1950 enabled

Morris Eight Series E JNC558 at Cheadle Hulme in 1948

my brother-in-law and me to take a touring holiday in the Scottish Highlands. We left our respective wives, Alice and her sister Evalyn, to look after our very young daughters, whilst we enjoyed a much deserved break! It was during June and the Scottish climate lived up to its reputation providing heavy rainfall every day. We commented upon this to a local Scot in Fort William who suggested we try July next year. We did and experienced the same climatic baptisms. You should have been here in June, we were told. The weather had been perfect!

Production of new cars gathered momentum and the inverse law of economics regarding car selling, was on the wane.

Aunty Maud Hudson and Alice Cheadle Hulme back garden 1949

Self and Alice in Cheadle Hulme back garden 1949

In 1949 Manchester City required urgently a new goalkeeper to replace the legendary Frank Swift, whose retirement from professional football left a hard act for any successor to follow. The club made a signing which was anomalous and highly controversial. They signed a German!

Their signing was ex prisoner of war Bernd Trautmann, who accepted the daunting challenge with exemplary fortitude and no mean professional expertise as a player. Bert, as he became known to the huge crowds, was soon accepted and a great favourite liked by all. He served Manchester City loyally for fifteen years and played in over 500 league matches and two Cup Finals at Wembley. I had the good fortune to attend these Finals in 1955 and 1956. City lost the 1955 match to Newcastle and won the next, beating Birmingham City by three goals to one. On the latter occasion Bert played in the closing stages with a broken neck. He was one of the all time greats, as a player and ambassador for sport, and in wider fields.

It was about the time Bert Trautmann signed for Manchester City that I developed a keen interest in home photography, which continued for the next twenty years. Our elder daughter was in her second year and I thought a photographic record would be rather nice, something of interest to keep in the family album! So, on a glorious late summer Saturday afternoon, my next door neighbour watched with amusement, as I, with a box camera, pursued my young offspring round the garden 'clicking' at every opportunity.

I thought it rather interfering, when he suggested I might do better by using a more 'versatile' camera, like the Kodak he possessed at the time, and which he would be delighted to bring round to demonstrate. He did come round and a half hour later, had exposed a roll of film. This was ready for the developing tank, which he used in a dark room under the stairs, at his home. He then invited me to his house, where I was to witness for the first time, the mysteries of roll film development. From that moment I had become completely 'hooked' on black and white photography, thanks to this neighbour, Bill Brimelow, who became my close friend.

I pursued this satisfying hobby using an Ensign Selfix camera, which enabled me to take either eight square, or six rectangular pictures per roll of film. With apertures ranging from F3.5 to F22, manual focussing and shutter speeds covering time exposure to a three-hundredth of a second, I found it sufficiently versatile for my

Ann feeding Yvonne at Cheadle Hulme in 1950

purposes. I carried out all my own developing and printing, and with the aid of an economically priced and very functional enlarger, completed the photographic record I had originally set out to establish. When our elder daughter reached the age of three, she referred to the developing tank as 'Daddy's little pressure cooker.' I practised for hours in the dark, threading a blank reel of film into the tank, until I became sufficiently accomplished to wind it smoothly. A faulty wind could ruin a film, which might be irreplaceable. There is another easier way, as you will see!

In late summer of 1951 our younger daughter was showing signs of taking her first walking steps. We were together in the garden and in anticipation of this possible achievement, I had the camera primed at the ready. Later that afternoon, I was rewarded by capturing on camera, the first steps she had ever made. This was followed by a succession

Alice and Ann at the front gate Cheadle Hulme

Grannie Ormerod and Ann at Cheadle Hulme

Yvonne standing

Alice and Yvonne on lawn Cheadle Hulme

of steps, followed by tumbles, all of which I succeeded in snapping.

Later that afternoon I developed and fixed the film, which now, only required washing in cold water for half an hour or so. However, I decided to have a quick look first, and held the film up to the window for examination. Each frame was perfect and in excellent focus. What a superb achievement for family posterity - UNTIL - in my excited haste, I rinsed the film under the hot water tap. The entire reel was stripped bare. It would not be politic to recall my comments.

Bill would be about twenty years older than me, a family man with two daughters and the friendship between our families developed into a deep sincerity. He was a photographic expert and member of the Cheadle Hulme photographic society. Tragically, he died in his early fifties of terrible abdominal cancer. It was my privilege to receive Bill's Rolliecord camera (excellent for portrait work) from his widow Elsie. I shall remember him for his great practical knowledge and profound honesty. He knew more than most men and would never bluff. He taught me how to take photographs of my family for posterity.

Ann at fence with Nicholas, the little boy from next door at Cheadle Hulme

Alice's priceless legacy
Children at Cheadle Hulme
(a, b, c) Yvonne and (d, e) Ann

*Enid Brimelow with
Ann at Cheadle Hulme*

His elder daughter Enid had passed the matric standard of education and would have been ready to take the higher school certificate exams (A levels today). I am delighted to have traced a lovely photograph of Enid and our daughter Ann, which I took about this time. I know Bill would have been delighted with it. Had it not been for his 'interference', this and many others to follow, never would have materialised.

On the 21st May 1953, my thirty-seventh birthday, an opportunity enabled me to move from the textile mill in south Manchester. I became producer sales manager and later wholesale director, with a public company in The Midlands, engaged in national wholesale distribution of household furnishing materials.

My wife and I bought a charming detached house with a large, magnificent garden, at Four Oaks, near Sutton Coldfield. We enjoyed sweeping views over the Staffordshire countryside to Lichfield Cathedral and beyond. The garden was paradise for our young daughters and their friends. There was room to play, to exercise their Border Collie dog and to get lost in their adventures of make believe. Round every corner, behind each bush, the winding steps of the intriguing rockery led to the unexpected in this enchanted garden.

Highclere and lily pond Four Oaks

Its beautifully designed lily pond was home for the most fascinating, curious and tame little newts. They never failed to entertain as they appeared, disappeared and reappeared in a glorious game of aquatic hide and seek. The garden was nature's habitat for the birds and nature's gift to the photographer.

At this stage, our daughters were too young to understand and appreciate the long term advantages to be derived from true motherhood. They were too young to understand the value of

Highclere Garden, 4 on the swing, the collie dog, Yvonne in the rockery and Ann on a bicycle on the back lawn (opposite).

enduring motherly counsel, love and affection. From her devoted care and attention, Alice established a solid platform for them. It nourished their future welfare, it created a confidence from which, in later years, they had become tutored to face responsibly the problems, which lay ahead.

Children are adept at making friends quickly, informally and without introduction. It was no surprise, when our daughters were joined in the garden by three young new arrivals, girls of similar ages to ours, whom they invited to come and play. They were the daughters of Margaret Tobitt, née Margaret Ide, who had married an Army officer during the war.

Fate had decreed that the paths of Margaret Ide and Alice Ormerod should become the paths of Margaret Tobitt and Alice Hudson, later to converge. Fate had also decreed that these paths should often travel, more or less in parallel, for many years to come.

The welfare of our two daughters now became of paramount importance. My wife and I wished them to have educational opportunities similar to our own. As Alice had a professional teaching background, we decided that she should supervise their schooling, a responsibility I was delighted to leave under her capable jurisdiction. After leaving private school, both girls profited from excellent tuition at the local John Willmott co-educational grammar school, where splendid facilities prevailed for academic and sporting pursuits. Under its Headmaster Bill Roberts, the school was organised by a highly qualified man of great wisdom. Bill was a shrewd, approachable, unbiased man, a keen disciplinarian, with a listening and sympathetic ear. He was popular with teaching staff, pupils and parents. Alice and I were privileged to know him well.

Activities at the nearby Saint James' Church helped to increase our daughters' circle of friends. They learnt the meaning of good fellowship, the importance of community spirit and how to develop social understanding. Our younger daughter Yvonne gained invaluable experience from five years in the Girl Guides, where she finished as a Ranger. Nevertheless, when problems arose, Mother's counsel was always readily forthcoming for them both. She was a lady of great wisdom, a priceless gift ascribed to and inherited from her mother. She lavished love and kindness on her daughters, but not to the exclusion of correction and discipline, when required.

There were local facilities where disabled children could receive day care and attention, affording a little temporary relief for their mothers. Alice and Margaret, who were now close friends, worked together regularly, taking two children back to their homes after day care. Margaret would drive, whilst Alice kept these high spirited, cheerful little

Alice

souls entertained on the journey. It was a tragically rewarding experience, serving as a stark reminder of the blessing, so easily taken for granted by parents with perfectly healthy and physically able children.

It is often attributed to the other person, that his or her grass is always greener. Is it? The city of Birmingham had undergone considerable building transformation, which had benefited some, but not all. Rebuilding and relocating could be prohibitively expensive for many businesses. The old established public company, for which I worked, became victim of both, resulting in heavy and unavoidable financial strain. In the late nineteen sixties, the company secretary and I would seek a little lunchtime relaxation in the Gun Room Bar of the Albany Hotel. Here, with the benison of some good draught ale and tasty well filled baps, we would endeavour to resolve the business problems of the day.

What I mention now will remain for ever in my mind. One day, on our way to the Albany, we witnessed a lady with a lame little child, trying to cross the road at a busy part of Smallbrook Ringway. The child's legs were withered to the ankles   Each leg was supported in an iron framework and the child struggled to walk with the aid of crutches. The lady's face bore evidence of an enduring sadness. I turned to my colleague and said, "We think we have problems!"

Chapter Twenty Four
SCOTTISH HIGHLANDS

In July 1965, my wife and I set off on a touring holiday of the Scottish Highlands. It was the first time we had left the girls at home to look after themselves and Alice's first visit to Scotland. From my own past experiences of Scottish Highland weather, I warned her to expect the worst. I could not have been more mistaken in my expectations. We enjoyed two weeks of glorious warm weather and the surface of the road to Mallaig was more sympathetic to vehicles' suspensions, than in 1938!

One evening, on the return from Tongue to our hotel at Lairg, we broke the journey for a drink at Altnaharra, where we listened to the weather forecast. This augured well, the weather was to continue fine and dry. Whilst enjoying our drink, we were rather surprised to hear other visitors grumbling about the weather forecast they had heard for the days ahead. I could not refrain from telling these strangers that this was not the forecast we had just heard. Rather peremptorily came the rejoinder, "You're obviously not up here for the fishing!"

Later that evening we were entertained by the Lairg Pipers, who played for the guests at the Sutherland Arms Hotel, where we enjoyed comfortable en suite accommodation and a high standard of cuisine. Bathing earlier that day, in the bay at Sheigra, suggested that the Gulf Stream had lost its way to the waters from the Arctic. The pictures suggest it is Mediterranean.

Our photographic record of this wonderful touring holiday, taken with the late Bill Brimelow's Rolliecord camera, is a delight, on which to look back.

During the sixteen years we lived at Four Oaks, Alice continued ceaselessly, to carry out welfare and charitable church and community work. In spite of these time consuming activities, nothing was neglected at home. They were never at the expense of her own domestic responsibilities to me and our daughters. She worked with a tireless energy and received few accolades.

By the end of the sixties, our daughters had left home in pursuit of their careers. I abandoned the office hot seat to be independent and enjoy freedom on the 'open' road! In this capacity I was to gain valuable new experience as a furnishing textiles' sales representative in London and the South East.

My early experience of the 'open' road occurred in a frustrating traffic jam somewhere off the Strand in London. Slowly, I edged the car towards Charing Cross Station forecourt with the intention of stopping to sort out my route. Unfortunately, being off sighted by a large vehicle, I failed to notice I was edging the car into the station forecourt exit. A London taxi driver, who was trying to get out, quickly drew my attention to the mistake. He put his head out of the cab window and bellowed: - "You must be a bleeding lunatic!"

We sold our lovely house at Four Oaks and moved to a pleasant detached property with a large garden at Caterham in Surrey. It had not the character and charm of the Four Oaks garden, but it offered scope for relaxing recreation. Alice derived much pleasure, one could refer to it as therapy, from the garden, but now the girls were away, she found time also to accompany me on my prospecting journeys in the Metropolis. With the aid of a London A to Z street guide, she became invaluable in map reading our way through the labyrinth of streets. Without her navigational skills in those early days, my journeys undoubtedly, would have been more frustrating and protracted. Together we discovered many an 'Aladdin's Cave' behind the closed doors of Brick Lane and in a large area around Curtain Road and Great Eastern Street. Upholsterers thrived in this East End of the City and turned out beautiful furniture.

Restoration of genuine old furniture was a profitable and rewarding craft. In many an upholsterer's yard, open to all weathers, I have seen dilapidated old chairs and sofas, which I believed were destined for the scrap heap. Many of these would appear later in West End showrooms, having been judiciously repaired, beautifully renovated and polished, or tastefully reupholstered. They attracted wealthy American tourists in a market that was insatiable.

●●●●●●

My younger daughter joined the RAF and was commissioned for seven years in the General Duties (Ground) Branch as an air traffic controller. An early posting took her to RAF Prestwick, my first training station thirty years previously, where ironically, she shared the facilities of HMS Gannet's Wardroom with officers of two Royal Navy helicopter squadrons.

Glen Orchy

Glencoe

Source of two rivers near Tarbert

Mallaig

Ring of Bright Water

Loch Assynt

290

River near Loch More

West end of Loch More

Lairg Pipers Sutherland Arms Hotel

Arkle across Loch Stack

Bay near Sheigra

Bay near Sheigra

In March 1974 she was posted to West Raynham, coincidentally, where I had served on 101 Squadron for two months in 1940 and from where, in 1974 by further irony, 100 Squadron was flying Canberras. It was a proud moment for my daughter when she discovered her father's name on the 100 Squadron Honours Board. A proud moment for both of us, when, after the kind invitation to the Squadron by Wing Commander Brian Harcourt-Smith, she was able to point out my name to me in the presence of my wife and elder daughter, who were both privileged to receive invitations.

Afterwards, as guests of the Squadron for the day, we were shown around by a young flying officer navigator and later, enjoying the hospitality of the mess, learned more from him about modern air force life.

He married our younger daughter in the following year and now, as a squadron leader at the age of fifty four, continues to fly the 'traditional flag'.

100 Squadron RAF West Raynham 1974, inspecting a BAC Canberra B2 engine.
Left to Right: Fg Off A.W. Puncher, Fg Off J.D. Hudson DFC (Retired), Fg Off Y.F. Hudson

100 SQN HONOURS BOARD RAF WEST RAYNHAM 1974 Fg Off Y.F. HUDSON (WRAF) Fg Off J.D. HUDSON DFC (Rtd)

Flying Officer Yvonne Hudson WRAF RAF West Raynham Local Controller Air Traffic Control. RAF Raynham was the base for 100 & 85 Squadrons in 1974 and the base for 101 & 18 Squadrons in 1940 where one of the hangars was bombed in July 1940

293

Yvonne and Alan's Wedding

Chapter Twenty Five
SOMERSET

By April 1975, I had established sales in the London and South East territory. A younger man was appointed to serve the area and I moved on to exploit business prospects in the South West.

Alice and I became country dwellers on the southern outskirts of Bridgwater in Somerset. We bought an attractive bungalow near Durleigh, with uninterrupted, magnificent views over open countryside to the Quantock Hills. The grandeur of the elms enhanced the scenic beauty. They epitomised the splendour of landscaping, ours to behold each day, by drawing back the curtains. In their changing mantles, they were foretellers of the seasons.

This was before disaster struck. They were to be ruthlessly and insidiously ravaged, by a killer called Dutch elm disease, caused by a bark beetle.

Dutch elm disease struck aggressively, relentlessly and was almost one hundred per cent destructive. The brown skeletal remains of its elm tree victims bore testimony. Professional tree surgeons, farmers and others equipped with chain saws soon became busy felling these lifeless giants. I understand that main trunks were cut for making load storing pallets. With a small electric chain saw I cut several hundred logs, probably a few thousand, from large branches lying around in our neighbour's adjacent fields. The logs were compactly stacked, as can been seen from the photograph, and provided several years fuel for our open lounge fire and that of the farmer neighbour. She was delighted to receive the fuel. It was acceptable, but no reward for the trees she would never see again.

From the huge well stocked garden, we were completely self-supporting in fruit and vegetables throughout each year. The benefits of our home produce were not reaped however, without many hours spent harvesting and processing. Alice undertook the majority of these rewarding, but sometimes tedious tasks to maintain a well stocked freezer. She was always on the lookout for an occasional rotten fruit, which could easily develop in the cartons of keeping apples and other hard fruits, wrapped and stored in an outside building.

The success of our crops depended on a regular supply of nutrients from combined sources. We worked on an annual rotation basis from three general compost heaps, to allow sufficient time for thorough decomposition. All deciduous leaves were bagged for two years before use, to ensure they had become well rotted. Wood ash, a source of potash from the occasional bonfire, was stored and kept dry. Farmyard manure was an additional bonus, which helped to improve yield, but was used only for deep trenching, well in advance of planting. Surface dressing brought on too many weeds. Grass mowings were used sparingly as heavy mulching encouraged mildew. Diseased plants and leaves were burnt, as were the haulms of peas and potatoes. We adhered strongly to the rotation of most crops.

Matter being indestructible, nature's recycling is irrevocable. It creates, destroys and then recreates, ad infinitum. An eternal provider, it is an open free book without words, affording the opportunity for everyone to learn by observing. Go out into the garden, or the fields, read the portents, make use of what it has to tell and be rewarded. Ignore what it has to tell and reap the barren consequences.

We had mains supply drinking and household water but relied on treatment by septic tank for waste disposal. For this purpose, a huge concrete tank, with a heavy removable inspection lid, had been sunk discretely in the orchard area of the garden. The process was fascinating. I inspected the contents regularly to check that they did not rise, nor fall, below acceptable levels. During our eleven years tenure at the bungalow, an odourless and efficient, biological, natural break down of waste materials had ensured that the tank never required any attention. It did not attract flies, even in the heat of late summers.

Easy access to the M5 motorway, which in those days was relatively quiet on weekdays, facilitated long distance travel. It was ideal for my business journeys, on many of which, initially, Alice accompanied me. She was able to make valuable reports, record essential details of interviews and prepare what we would call today, a customers' data base.

During my navigational training I had learned the importance of thoroughness, application and accuracy to detail, in order to be successful. In those early days, Flight Lieutenant Dawson had forcibly reminded me that there was no short cut to success. In 1975, at the age of fifty-nine, with the invaluable help of my patient wife, I was back at the 'drawing board' planning the next steps in sales research and psychology. When travelling away from home, we worked together most evenings in our modest hotels, preparing the next day's calls. It paid off for eleven years.

On 8th July 1978, our elder daughter Ann married David Smith, at Oadby near Leicester. David, a keen sportsman, played union rugby, cricket

Littlecroft Bungalow

and tennis for local teams. To illustrate the benefits derived from regular, controlled and often strenuous exercises, he still participates in sport twenty-six years on.

For readers unaccustomed to the rigours of strenuous exercise, but who wish to ensure bodily fitness during advancing years, I suggest you seek professional advice, or tread warily, before taking a leaf out of David's physical fitness book. Few men, at the age of sixty-three, will turn out regularly for a game of rugby.

Earlier I mentioned Gilbert Ormerod's devotion and support to the St. John Ambulance Brigade in Blackburn. David's father, Eric Heywood Smith, leant considerable support to the Order of St. John in Leicestershire. He became County Cadet Commissioner and was appointed Honorary Serving Brother of the Order of St. John, for which he received the long service medal.

Ann, who is fifty-seven, almost six years younger than her husband, teaches physical education, activities which require great control and expert supervision. Correctly carried out they are extremely beneficial to the pupils' physical upbringing. In the hands of a novice they could be damaging. Following in Alice's footsteps, she teaches English as her second subject.

I find it gratifying that she, and her sister Yvonne, have their Mother's gift for elocution and her natural articulate ability of expression in the English language.

Our first grandson Andrew was born in 1979 to our younger daughter Yvonne, whilst her husband Alan was serving with the RAF in Norfolk. At the age of thirteen months, the child was diagnosed as a chronic asthmatic to the great concern of his parents. Fortunately, they received excellent support and advice from the local hospital and The Asthma Society in Norfolk. With suitable medications, professional guidance and a lot of care, they were able to rear the boy through this early critical stage. Later, the family moved north of the border when Alan was posted to RAF Lossiemouth, where there was no Asthma Society Branch.

By now both parents, completely dedicated to their cause, had gained invaluable experience in the nursing required to combat Andrew's persisting chronic asthma. They acquired and exercised an expertise beyond the lay. To her great credit, Yvonne, supported by Alan, founded and became chairman (until 1991), of the Moray Branch of what was known then, as the Asthma Society. Later, it became The National Asthma Campaign and is now ASTHMA UK.

My days of business travelling were drawing to a conclusion in September 1986. At the age of seventy, when most men had been long retired, we moved to East Devon. I still enjoyed my job, but this was to be the last throw of the business dice. With retirement now in mind, we bought a small bungalow, situated in an outstandingly beautiful garden, at Colyford. It was in an area described as 'of outstanding natural beauty', about a mile from the Seaton sea front in Lyme Bay.

For some years I had been travelling on a part time basis and by 1986 could conduct most business from home, having established, what I would describe, as a creamed off clientele of trustworthy, reliable and friendly customers. Why should I have retired earlier? I enjoyed relative freedom with little interference, until one year later, it was decreed by head office, that I should finish. I shall always remember the words of the lady secretary of one of my manufacturing upholstery customers, when I finally said good bye. She told me very simply that members of the board, who had been talking together, concluded and commented that it was the end of an era. Sales representation was changing rapidly. Personal contact between supplier and customer was disappearing. Impersonal, computerised selling had started to take over. Clients had to adapt accordingly.

For me it was the end of an era - Per ardua ad - retirement in 1987.

Following Alan's posting to RAF Waddington in 1991, the family moved to Heighington in Lincolnshire. Andrew still required well monitored care and medications. Despite this, he was determined to lead as normal a life as possible, becoming extremely accomplished in various sporting activities. By choosing his sports carefully, he was able to maintain a high level of fitness. Golf and cricket proved better than football or other sports requiring sustained running, which tended to make him breathless, particularly in the cold weather. He was also a very keen scout and achieved his Chief Scout's Award, as did his younger brother David. This award required the development of a variety of skills and character building challenges and was the highest award a scout could achieve, before moving up into Venture Scouts, where other challenges like the Duke of Edinburgh's Award or Queen's Scout Award could be undertaken. As I write this manuscript in 2004 Andrew's asthma is usually under control, but he always carries an inhaler. I hope this story may be of encouragement to readers who are asthma sufferers, or have friends or relations who are.

In the seaboard and rural areas of East Devon the climate was relaxing, remarkably clean, but relatively mild and humid. Could it have been the latter that took its toll on Alice, who sadly developed asthmatic symptoms? Perhaps it was hereditary? In this context, remember her father Gilbert Ormerod.

Ann and David's Wedding (and opposite page)

Pianist protégé Emma, tutor Grannie Alice

David with baby daughter Emma

302

Davington Colyford

303

Andrew and ...

...David receiving their awards

Urgently she sought medical advice, as her outdoor activities in the garden, from which she had always derived so much pleasure, became increasingly restricted. It was now that her daughter Yvonne's many years of practical experience with Andrew, was extremely helpful She was able to offer useful guidance. Medications were more beneficial and the medical profession had gained a wider experience of the illness since the days of Gilbert Ormerod. Perhaps asthma could not be cured, but its distressing effects could be alleviated and enable most sufferers to lead normal lives.

Our large partly walled garden, which included an excellent productive vegetable area, presented me with a relaxing and rewarding retirement therapy until September 1993, when I became the victim of prostate cancer. Two months later, I underwent keyhole surgery, referred to as trans-urethral prostatectomy. My recovery was slow and for several months Alice became a devoted and competent nurse. The garden workload became too much and beyond our joint capabilities, so sadly, we prepared to move again, a move which was to mark the end of our in depth gardening era.

We sold our property in Devon quickly and bought another, with a much smaller featureless garden in Lincolnshire, near our younger married daughter and family. By mutual agreements with the purchasers and vendors, we were able to delay exchange of contracts by six months, to end March 1994. This gave me time in which to recuperate prior to the move.

I shall never forget my disillusionment on the first morning after our arrival. There was no panoramic view, when I drew back the curtains this time. I took one look out of the kitchen window and said, "Hudson, what the hell have you done?" My wife overheard and commented simply and without hesitation, "Put up a fence." As usual, how right she was.

Now in better health, I erected a castellated wooden fence shielding the full length of the back garden. The fence varied in height from about six to eight feet with trellis, and was painted in golden chestnut. It immediately altered the climate in that area of the garden enabling us to create a microcosmic replica of a small part of the Devon garden. We planted a variety of trees and shrubs, mostly evergreen, some deciduous, two of which included a Ginkgo Biloba, noted for its fan shaped green leaves. Biloba is the sole survivor of a Chinese and Japanese tree family going back, it is alleged, some two-hundred million years! The second, a Cornus alba Elegantissima (Dog Wood), which has beautiful red stems in winter.

Here is a cross section of our colourful evergreen choices: - Abelia Gold Spot: Stranvaesia davidii Palettte: Photinia fraseri Red Robin: Leucothoe Heishei Royal Ruby: Choisya ternata Sundance: Escallonia Donard Seedling and Apple Blossom: Viburnum tinus Laurustinus: and Berberis darwinii:

Other evergreen prolific growers, not as colourful, but offering a wonderful variation in shades of green, include:- Arbutus unedo (Strawberry Tree): Aucuba japonica Variegata: Buxus Sempirvirens (Box): Euonymus several varieties): Rhamnus alaterna Argenteo variegata Italian Buckthorn (the birds love this one): Prunus laurocerasus (Cherry or Common Laurel): Prunus lusitanica (Portugal Laurel): Laurus nobilis Bay Laurel: Elaeagnus ebbingei: Elaeagnus maculata: A controlled Eucalyptus gunnii, whose delicate, decorative small leaves, are the result of drastic spring pruning, followed by lighter pruning in summer: The not to be maligned Ligustrum ovalifolium Auream Golden Privet: Pittosporum crassifolium variegatum: Two Buxus (Box) hedges, an Escallonia hedge, a controlled Leylandii hedge plus a variety of other conifers.

The stark, featureless, small garden was transformed into an attractive small garden of great feature, with all the year round interest and colour. It has become a paradise and nesting habitat for the birds, who find food and protection, afforded by the shrubs, in this aviary of nature's creation.

During early 1994 Alice experienced eyesight problems. An early examination diagnosed that she required operations for cataracts on both eyes. These operations carried out expeditiously, painlessly and with expertise by her consultant surgeon, resulted in immediate restoration to clarity of vision, from which she benefited for the remaining ten years of her life. The improvement in vision was a revelation, reinstating a quality of life that had begun to slip away. She could enjoy reading again without eye strain. Another example of the benefits derived from continued medical research and advancement, from which those who do grow old can take advantage.

Her distressing asthma became relieved with regular careful monitoring and knowledgeable use of improved medications. From anticipation and awareness gained by earlier experiences, she learned how to overcome serious breathing problems. This enabled her to take care of me.

I relied on Alice's cooperation and sympathetic help and understanding over a period of seven years from November 1993, when I became plagued with recurring cancers of the prostate gland and bladder. These problems required nine diathermy operations and several cystoscopic investigations, in spite of which, I have managed to retain a high standard of general fitness. For this, I attribute sustained, sensible and practical exercise, derived from walking and gardening activities, which continue to give me pleasure. These are activities I strongly recommend to those whose youth is beginning to be a memory. Don't delay, lest the memory fades!

I stated a little earlier that the move from East Devon was to mark the end of our in depth gardening era. Imagine our delight, when a few years after the move, we received a rather special Christmas letter. It came from the retired farming couple, who bought our Devon bungalow, to let us know that the previous summer, they opened the garden to the public for two days. What a joy to learn they were taking good care of that beautiful garden. What a sadness to learn a little later, that they had to move. The workload had become too much and beyond their joint capabilities.

It was an unexpected and great pleasure, for my wife and me, to welcome Joan Highfield to our home at Heighington near Lincoln, in February 2002. Although Joan and I had become reunited previously, when we were interviewed for a broadcast on Radio Lincolnshire, this second visit presented us with a wonderful opportunity to reminisce. As ex World War Two contemporaries, who had served together with 100 Squadron during 1944, we had much in common to talk about. We jogged each other's memories on experiences we had both forgotten. With the passing of nearly sixty years, it was flattering to be reminded by Joan of the aircrews' nickname the 'Brylcreem Boys' and to hear her say, that to them, her Waaf contemporaries, we were the 'cream of the crop'. She did not need remindng of the heavy losses. She and her colleagues were there on the ground, waiting and waiting, after each operational flight, hoping for all the boys to come back, which so often, was not the case.

The transformed garden at Sheppard's Close

Joan Highfield   *by courtesy of the Lincolnshire Echo*

STOICISM AND DETERMINATION REAP SUCCESS

In April 2002 our families experienced a domestic tragedy when my granddaughter, Emma, whom I mentioned in earlier editions of my book, was critically injured in a horrific car accident, shortly before she was due to complete her B.Sc. degree. The injuries sustained resulted in brain damage, paralysis to her right side and a fractured pelvis. She was not expected to recover.

Her survival has been miraculous. She was operated on, when in coma, for the fractured pelvis. Helped by the advancement in medical science, unsurpassed expertise in surgery was accomplished. Medical care was always available, administered by dedicated and devoted staff in three NHS Hospitals. Cooperation by the patient, combined with her dogged determination, helped her enormously on the road to recovery.

In September 2004 she resumed university studies on a part-time basis. Such was the confidence she inspired in her devoted tutors, she achieved her goal.

Emma's graduation

309

It is my good fortune and privilege, as her grandfather and author of this book, to include a photo of Emma in her graduate's gown, taken on her proud day of graduation in November 2006. A proud day for her parents, who with stoicism overcame the uncertainties at a time when graduation was a pipedream.

Dr. Denis Culver of Pain Management Service, Kitchener, Ontario wrote of an earlier edition of my book - which I quote below, and also under the heading THESE DID GROW OLD :

"This whole book has been an unfolding story of encouragement, no matter what will challenge us from Day to Day, with truth and ultimate faith in our creator, we will come through whatever trials beset us.

"Life is not fair to us," I hear from my patients. However with encouragement that people like you imparted, survival is possible always."

Shortly after the publication of the First Edition of my book it was brought to the attention of Allan Newman, a gentleman closely associated with the 428 Bradford V.C. Mess. I was delighted to learn that Captain Annand V.C., who has recently celebrated his ninetieth birthday, was able to present the book as their annual raffle prize in March 2004.

Fellowship of the Services

Bradford V.C. Mess

June 2003

Brigadier General
Roland Boys Bradford VC MC

428 MESS NEWSLETTER

AN OFFICER AND A GENTLEMAN　　(from ...Allan Newman)

Our Raffle Prize Table for the March 2004 Bowls Event already has its star attraction. Flying Officer James Douglas Hudson D.F.C. R.A.F.V.R. has written a truly wonderful book "There and back again a navigator's story". It was published in 2001 and received rave notices so much so that it went into three editions, which is remarkable for a self published effort. The author, a sprightly 87 year old takes the reader through a most exciting six years starting as war breaks out in September 1939. From trainee navigator to eventually top class instructor. Promotion from Sergeant, W.O., Pilot officer, Flying Officer and the award of the val-

ued 'Distinguished Flying Cross'. His two years as a P.O.W. reveal an aspect of wartime confinement seldom mentioned as the camp in North Africa was Vichy-French controlled. As Pathfinder support his operations over Germany are thrilling but all told with that aspect of good comradeship that we in Fellowship understand. We wish the author all the very best and hope that he and his wife of 58 years, Alice, have many more together. Incidentally F.O. Hudson appears to have flown several types of aircraft but never a 'Hudson'

Epilogue

I owe a debt of gratitude to: -

Miss Joan B. Morton who offered Bob Pine and me a second home, her home, at Prestwick.

The International Red Cross and others who, in the cause of humanity, helped to alleviate our sufferings during the period of imprisonment.

My crew who supported me throughout the tour and without whose co-operation my job would not have been possible. They always said they put their faith in me; I assuredly put my faith in them.

Our devoted ground crew who, often working exposed under dreadful weather conditions, kept R Roger flying.

Those expert radar technicians whose service to, and maintenance of Gee, H2S and Fishpond was quite exemplary.

All other Squadron personnel who contributed so much to our well-being.

The German anti-aircraft gunners and the Luftwaffe fighter pilots who did their damnedest to shoot us down and FAILED.

IN LIGHTER VEIN

1945. We thank the mums and dads of Grimsby and Lincolnshire outlying villages, who in their profound wisdom, allowed their daughters out on the town, knowing quite rightly, they would be safe under our protective care and attention!

IN SERIOUS VEIN.

Reflect seriously and spare thoughts for: -

Those at home whose sufferings endured the war years, to those killed, or injured, or who lost their homes and possessions at the hand's of the Luftwaffe.

For all others who lost their lives, or were injured in the defence of their country, at home and abroad.

The innocent German and other civilians killed and injured in Allied raids of mass destruction.

21st October 2000
It is more than Fifty-Six Years since that
Infamous Nuremberg Raid I recall so vividly.

It was now, when Bomber Command had stepped up its major offensive against the major German cities and industrial targets, Fred Panton and his brother, Lincolnshire boys, would stand outside their home, look towards the sky and listen to the thundering roar from the four engined bombers as they headed towards their targets.

They showed a passionate interest in these aeroplanes for many reasons, but one reason in particular, their elder brother was a flight engineer and member of an operational Halifax bomber crew. On the fateful night of March 30th/31st during the raid on Nuremberg, Pilot Officer C.W. Panton, only nineteen years old, was killed when his aircraft was shot down over the target area.

Ironically, as I am just about to finish writing my war time memoirs, how rewarding it was to be invited to visit the LINCOLNSHIRE AVIATION HERITAGE CENTRE at EAST KIRKBY and meet one of the boys who watched the aeroplanes thunder overhead in 1944. Now a man, FRED PANTON who, with his brother HAROLD, is responsible for creating this HERITAGE MUSEUM. I am indebted to FRED for such a courteous reception to this wonderful MEMORIAL for their brother CHRIS and the other airmen who lost their lives for the same cause.

What a privilege it was to hear those wonderfully tuned four Merlin engines of Lancaster NX611 and watch this veteran aeroplane taxi away and return under the control of Mike Chatterton and his team of experts, reminding us how rhythmically she could 'PURR'. A great credit to all those involved in several years' hard work.

Words from me are quite inadequate to express the emotional joy and satisfaction of being allowed to clamber on board, accompanied by my daughter, and negotiate all those spars to arrive, where for me, it all began, at the navigator's table..

Lancaster NX611 at Lincolnshire Aviation Heritage Centre East Kirkby

EXTRACT FROM
DIARY OF 100 SQUADRON WALTHAM'S
LANCASTER 'R Roger' FOR MARCH 1944.

1/2	March	Stuttgart
15/16	March	Stuttgart
18/19	March	Frankfurt
22/23	March	Frankfurt
24/25	March	Berlin
25/26	March	Essen
30/31	March	Nuremberg

30th March 2004 marked the sixtieth anniversary of the disastrous Nuremberg raid by the RAF, when Bomber Command lost ninety-seven heavy bombers. The attached picture, taken at the East Kirkby Lincolnshire Aviation Heritage Centre, speaks for itself. It appears by 'Courtesy of the Lincolnshire Echo' and also by kind permission of Mr Fred and Mr Harold Panton.

Self in centre with Fred and Harold Panton at their East Kirkby Lincolnshire Aviation Centre

WALTHAM REVISITED

Travelling on the A16 in the direction of Grimsby, my younger daughter and I passed the 'Jug & Bottle', a post-war pub at Holton le Clay. Built on a former aircraft dispersal site, this pub displays interesting photographs and memorabilia of the Second World War. A little further along this road we stopped at a small lay-by to pay our respects at the Memorial, erected in 1978, in memory of those airmen who gave their lives for their country whilst serving on 100 Squadron. On the day of the Memorial's unveiling ceremony by Wing Commander Le Marquand, two 100 Squadron Canberras from RAF Marham flew over in salute. My son-in-law was privileged to be a navigator on one of these aircraft.

We then continued through Waltham and arrived at the site of the old guard room entrance to the airfield where a commemorative plaque had been commissioned in 1987 by Mr F.W. Bury, who had served during the war in the Intelligence Section. The inscription carries an emotional reminder for all generations to read.

The plaque which Mr. F.W.Bury erected in1987

RAF· GRIMSBY (WALTHAM) 1941–1945
TO FIGHT FOR OUR FREEDOM AND TO
END THE NAZI TYRANNY. YOUNG PEOPLE
FROM ALL OVER THE WORLD CAME TO
THIS AIRFIELD TO SERVE AND TO FLY
THE WELLINGTONS AND LANCASTERS
OF 142 & 100 SQUADRONS.
OVER 1000 BRAVE YOUNG MEN CAME
THROUGH THIS ENTRANCE—
NEVER TO RETURN. MANY MORE WERE
✢ SHOT DOWN AND CAPTURED ✢
WE WILL REMEMBER THEM
AND SALUTE ALL WHO SERVED HERE.
F.W.B. 1987.

The 'Jug & Bottle' Pub built on the site of one of
RAF Waltham's dispersal Sites

315

THESE DID GROW OLD

I have been moved profoundly by the wonderful letters, received in appreciation, from readers of the earlier editions of my book. Although it has not been possible to reply to them personally, I treasure them all. Here are extracts from two.

Mr Bernard Barker of Orton Brimbles wrote:-

"I felt as though I were looking over your shoulder by the fireside as you pointed out the various illustrations and diagrams; and could hear the inflection of your voice and the manner of your talk."

"Sixty years is not such a long time in the sweep of historical events.... But you bring those moments of time close again - Europe in ruins; young men spiralling to their deaths in aerial crematoria; young French women writing letters to prisoners in the desert."

"So thank you once more for your book and the effort of writing it - and we shall remember you and the men who flew with you, our memories lent reality by your faithful words."

Dr. Denis Culver of Pain Management Service, Kitchener, Ontario, wrote:-

"This whole book has been an unfolding story of encouragement, no matter what will challenge us from Day to Day, with truth and ultimate faith in our creator, we will come through whatever trials beset us."

"Life is not fair to us", I hear from my patients. However with encouragement that people like you imparted, survival is possible always."

In the Introduction to my book I refer to my granddaughter's remarks of enlightenment two years ago, whilst at university, studying for her BSC degree.

Before the degree was completed, she was seriously injured in a car accident, resulting in brain damage, paralysis to her right side and a shattered pelvis. She was not expected to survive. However with expert medical care, great courage and enormous will power, she has learned to walk and talk again. She continues to fight a battle against adversity but is determined, when all appeared lost, to complete her degree. The same spirit and resolution epitomised the young people of World Wars One and Two, as they were prepared to make, or made the ultimate sacrifice to save their countries.

I have become reunited with readers who were my wartime contemporaries. Four of these shared some of my experiences in the Laghouat Sahara desert prison camp. This is what I have learned from Seaman Ray Davies living in retirement with his wife in Ledbury.

He was serving on the destroyer HMS Cossack when she was sunk by a German U-boat in the North Atlantic in 1941. One of 58 survivors, from a complement of 240, he was picked up by another destroyer HMS Legion under the command of Commander Jessel. During six hours in the water, Ray helped in the rescue of a young Lieutenant who carried on to become Rear Admiral Anthony Davies. (As President of the Swindon Branch, R.N.A and until his death in January 2003, he continued to maintain contact with his rescuer.) Ray Davies went on to serve on the Cruiser HMS Manchester, which was sunk whilst escorting a Malta convoy in August 1942.

After repatriation from Laghouat, Ray joined the light cruiser HMS Emerald. It sailed for the Far East in January 1943 patrolling the Indian Ocean for about 18 months before being recalled post haste to the UK. Then he sailed from Rosyth and when at sea, the ship's company was informed it was D Day - Operation Neptune to the Navy. Their beachhead was 'Sword' and 'Juno', where they were attacked by a German bomber. It dropped five bombs, two to port and two to starboard buckling the port and starboard plates. The fifth landed on a gun deck and remarkably did not explode. They spent ten days on the beachhead.

Afterwards he joined a Hunter Class Destroyer HMS Talybont and saw out the war in Europe. He continued to see service elsewhere until 1951.

A man of great philosophy he wrote to me saying: - "After 12 years would I change it? - Never. Wonderful mates and there is no doubt that the good times outweigh the bad."

Let us all take a leaf out of this man's book.

One of the prisoners in my room at Laghouat, and a bridge playing enthusiast, was a Master-at-Arms whose name had escaped me. I read only the other day from a newspaper cutting sent to me by Ray, dating back to November 1942, that he was W. E. Terry, a Londoner. This is what he had told the reporter about Laghouat.

"There we suffered atrociously from under-feeding, bad sanitation, dirt and flies. Through it all Captain Drew R.N. stayed with the ship's company."

Like the rest of us Captain Drew had little alternative.

I am indebted to Air Commodore Graham Pitchfork who, after reading my book, which he saw on display at Waddington International Air Show - 29/30 June 2002, wrote a splendid review in 'INTERCOM' Autumn 2002 Magazine of the AIRCREW ASSOCIATION.

Singing 'Oh vive de Gaulle' with Donald Gray...

As a result I became reunited with 88 years old widower Donald Gray, an ex Hurricane pilot and prisoner of war in Laghouat during 1941/1942. (See page 114 fourth from left on front row, with dark beard.) His last flying mission was scheduled to take him to Malta from the aircraft carrier Ark Royal, then sailing in the Mediterranean. Take-off from the carrier's short flight deck presented a hazard, compounded by the fact that his aircraft had been loaded with spare parts destined

...and Sharing Memories

for Malta. Fuel limitations left no reserve for emergencies, the aircraft ran out of petrol and crashed near Tunis where Don was captured and taken to Laghouat. Other aircraft failed to make the journey and shortly afterwards the Ark Royal was sunk.

During a memorable meeting at my home, he highlighted experiences in Laghouat with an almost whimsical humour, not failing to disguise his disgust and contempt towards our captors the Vichy French. He shared my views of disdain towards the Royal Navy's arrogant attitude towards the RAF junior service personnel, who had the misfortune to be imprisoned in a camp subjected to Royal Navy discipline. No adverse reflection on their bravery!

He participated in the hazardous work of tunnel digging but was suffering from serious dysentery when the break out took place. We each had our diversionary pastimes in the prison camp from which we gained some solace. Mine was bridge, whilst Donald found relaxation from the game of chess. These activities provided us with the required mental stimulus and helped to mask the tedium of prison life.

Nineteen years old midshipman George Yorke, from HMS Manchester, had quite a different pastime. In the Laghouat camp library he discovered a Hall & Knight's book, in which he became absorbed and studied higher algebra! These were his words to me on the phone: "This helped preserve my sanity as a young, naive man in a hostile environment." After a short leave following repatriation, from the heat of the Sahara he was sent to Scapa Flow and subsequently joined a destroyer patrolling the Russian convoys. Now, at the age of eighty, he undertakes the full responsibility of caring for his invalid wife, to whom he is totally devoted.

What a wonderful surprise to make contact again, after sixty-one years, with ex POW Ted Clayton, now OBE, whom I knew in Médéa, Aumale and Laghouat. Ted, an eighty-five years old widower and great grandparent, remains active. Time has not dulled his memory of many prisoner of war experiences we shared together.

With other army personnel, Sergeant Bob Turner, Sergeant R. E. Knight, Lance Corporal Williams, Bill Ballard and Daffy Watson, he escaped across France after Dunkirk in May 1940 and reached Marseilles. They crossed to North Africa where Ted, Turner, Knight, and Ballard spent time in a civilian gaol at Oran. The journey across France, whilst fraught with considerable danger, required resource and resilience. What was their reward for such an achievement? - Imprisonment in filthy North African prisoner of war camps until liberation and repatriation to the UK in November 1942.

Lance Corporal Williams and Daffy Watson, deservedly learned upon their return to England in November 1942 from the North African Prisoner of War Camps, that they had both been awarded the Military Medal for bravery in 1940 at the time of Dunkirk.

Ted was a great participator in Laghouat. He boxed regularly and was an enthusiastic member and adviser of the camp concert party. He spoke highly of Flight Lieutenant Bertie Brain DFC, whose organising ability was invaluable. Wilbur Wright, dear Wilbur, who inflicted damage to my nose in the ring, was another of Ted's great friends. His brilliant impromptu piano playing was a prime asset for rehearsals and shows alike.

The appalling conditions of prison life could not diminish POWs' outlook and attitude to keeping mentally fit. Men of foresight established 'Laghouat University', in which Ted also showed an active interest. It was run by young service personnel of high intellect, men who had knowledge and wisdom to impart to others. He reminded me, that in his 'university' capacity, he was styled 'registrar'.

Ted is to be seen on page 102 Blessing the Witches' Brew, pages 103, 108* and 115. (*Regrettably, in my earlier editions, I referred to No 1 Back Row as Bob Wilson. This should have read Bob Turner an escapee after Dunkirk).

My sincere thanks go to Nigel Parker, Editor of Bomber Command Newsletter, for printing a two pages article about my book in the April 2003 Newsletter. I was delighted in consequence, to make the acquaintance of Wing Commander Jim Wright DFC RAF (Ret). Jim, seven years younger than I, is an ex Lancaster navigator with two operational tours to his credit. It was an unexpected experience and a pleasure to welcome him to my home.

He told me about Verner N. Andersen a Danish gentleman, (with whom I have since corresponded) who is the leader of a Museum in Skarrild, DK 6933 Kibak, Denmark. On 27th August 1944 a Lancaster bomber of 630 Squadron, returning from a raid on Königsberg, crashed at Skarrild and the entire crew perished. They were buried by the villagers and lie in a grave in Skarrild Churchyard, permanently tended by the local people. I had the honour of sending my book, suitably inscribed, to Verner. He has displayed it in the Museum with a copy of my recent portrait painted in oils by Joan Highfield to whom I now refer.

Mrs Joan Highfield, née 'Dizzy' Morgan and Mrs Marjorie Grey, née Markham, were drivers in the MT section at Waltham 100 Squadron, when I was stationed there in 1944. Joan would be about twenty at the time. Amongst other driving duties, she had the demanding task of driving a station ambulance and also the crew trucks, carrying aircrew to and from their operational aircraft. Emotional experiences for such

a young person. The young MT Waaf personnel carried out their driving duties in all weathers unflinchingly and without complaint. There was no heating in the vehicles. As Joan said, "It was our job and we got on with it, just as you got on with your job up top."

Recently, I met these two ladies again when I discovered that Joan, in late retirement, had taken up portrait painting. Her excellent portrait of me hangs in the lounge and is my daily reminder of how others see me.

Both ladies had the honour of cutting the tape at the opening ceremony of the RAF Grimsby Exhibition at the Waltham Museum of Rural Life, where much 100 Squadron memorabilia is on display.

I have become reacquainted with three 100 Squadron Waltham aircrew contemporaries. The youngest is ex pilot Terry Cook DFC now living in Christchurch New Zealand. He runs the local Bomber Command Association from whose members he gets interesting and moving experiences.

This one is from New Zealander Bob Fenton, bomb-aimer and only survivor of Warrant Officer J. K. Ives' Lancaster crew mentioned on page 149. Miraculously, Bob succeeded in baling out of the blazing Lancaster over Berlin. Taken prisoner of war, he had a series of horrendous experiences after seven hundred men were evacuated from Lithuania Stalag Luft 6. They were chained, bayoneted, clubbed and injured by bites from dogs assisting the guards in the notorious 'run up the road' treatment. Terry sent me a detailed transcript of Bob's experiences of perfidy, depicting the most unbelievable evil and inhumane treatment by the Germans towards prisoners of war, helpless to retaliate.

"I know him very well," says Terry, "but he is ailing like the rest of us."

I was delighted to learn from Terry's navigator, Eric Norman DFC, now in his early eighties, that he is fit and well and living with his sister Betty in Warwickshire. Each year they travel for the Armistice Day

Memorial Service to Fiskerton, where Eric served towards the end of the war. He talks of the period we were together on 100 Squadron with E Easy and R Roger and later at Sandtoft when our paths crossed again. "Our time at Waltham was operationally identical. We both kicked off on 14th January 1944 with the Braunschweig operation and achieved our thirtieth with the trip to Vire on 6th June 1944, in support of the D Day landings and invasion of Germany. In between we had different targets, but I remember most vividly five trips to Berlin, (three in four nights) mining to Stettin and Danzig and a memorable run up to the target at

Sqn Ldr H. Hugh Grant Dalton DFC*

Friedrichshafen when we were bombed by a Lancaster!"

Terry who was twenty years old brought the stricken aircraft safely back to base. What pressures! Eric continues, "We all managed to cope adequately with the pressures and dangers of the times and survive."

I was very saddened to learn of the death of 'Terry' Terence Frank Cook DFC DipEd MRCVS on 13th September 2004 at the age of eighty-one, in Christchurch, New Zealand. Although we have never met it is comforting to be in touch by correspondence with his widow Colleen. She and I share a common sadness, each having recently lost our dearest one.

On page 214 of the Fourth Edition of my book 'There and Back Again - A NAVIGATOR'S STORY' - I refer to my colleague Wing Commander Jim Wright DFC RAFVR (Ret), stating that Jim, an ex Lancaster and Mosquito navigator, had two operational tours to his credit. This should have read that both tours were carried out on the Lancaster bomber.

Squadron Leader H. Hugh Grant-Dalton DFC and Bar was a pilot and one time my flight commander on 100 Squadron. Sixty years later, it was wonderful to talk together again and to learn that he, in his early

Wedding of my bomb-aimer October 1944. Left to right: Self, Margaret, Doug Chapman and Edna

eighties, is also fit and well and lives with his sister in Devon. He still enjoys classical music, to which it was difficult to listen in the squadron mess. There was a bigger preference by most aircrew for Joe Loss, Glenn Miller, the Andrews Sisters and Dinah Shore.

Having already completed a full operational tour on Hampdens, Hugh went on to complete a second tour (not without incidents) on Lancasters at 100 Squadron Waltham. When his aircraft was caught by a night fighter and badly shot up near Strasbourg, the crew returned on three engines. On the way to Leipzig in December 1943, his aircraft collided with another plane but continued to the target and bombed. Both aircraft returned safely! Later, after Arnhem, he did glider towing on 38 Group Stirlings, dropping paratroops and supplies. In peacetime he went into civil flying with BOAC until 1972, completing an outstanding pilot's aviation career.

What a joy for my wife and I to welcome Edna, my bomb-aimer's widow and her sister Margaret and husband. I had not seen Margaret since she was bridesmaid in October 1944 at her sister's wedding in Cleethorpes, when I was privileged to be best man.

I was delighted to be reacquainted unexpectedly with someone called Peter, whom I remember as a little boy in short trousers and a madcap on a bicycle. We first met in 1930 during our Manchester schooldays, when we had a mutual friend in John Clayton (mentioned on earlier pages). Peter's great chum was Louis Murray, one of our schoolboy quartet, sadly killed at the age of twenty-three, in a Blenheim forced landing, soon after he had graduated from Oxford University (page 98 refers).

Gaining his civilian pilot's licence at the age of 16 (before he was old enough to have a driving licence), this little boy was to become Air Commodore Peter M. Brothers CBE DSO DFC & Bar RAF, a well known figure since the Battle of Britain days, when he earned distinction as an ace fighter pilot. Retired now and in his eighties, he still attends public engagements, remembrance services and important ceremonial occasions.

****

This book will continue to be an unfolding story of encouragement, a challenge from day to day with truth and ultimate faith in our Creator. We shall come through whatever trials beset us.

October 2003

WE HAD BEEN MARRIED NEARLY SIXTY YEARS...

...when I lost my wife on 30th May 2004. She died peacefully after seventeen days in hospital, where she received loving care from the nursing staff, who ensured she was kept as comfortable as possible to the end. It was then I saw her asleep, completely composed at rest and blessed with the relief of no more pain.

My granddaughter says, "I look up to the sky. Grannie has gone to a happy place".

SO BE IT

'Joe' Sydney Pennington DFC, my closest wartime friend and fellow navigator, and his wife Nancie, met Alice in May 1943 when 'Joe' and I were stationed at Wymeswold. This was prior to our successful operational flying on Lancaster bombers and shortly after their marriage. Alice and Nancie spent many happy hours together at Wymeswold while 'Joe' and I were flying. The friendship with Nancie and her families continues, although sadly 'Joe' died twelve years ago. This is what his family said on their card of sympathy at the time I lost my wife.

"We were very sorry to hear about Alice, - she was a very friendly lady - her lovely smile is how we remember her best."

SO DO WE ALL

One of the earlier purchasers of my book was Douglas Shorrock of Huntroyde near Burnley, whom I mention earlier in this edition. He was born and educated in Blackburn and ironically, shortly after the war, moved to Cheadle Hulme. Unknown to Alice and me, he and his wife were our near neighbours in the early nineteen fifties. In consequence of the book, we established a friendly relationship, which enabled Douglas and Alice to share many memories of Blackburn and the surrounding area, they both knew so well. This is what he said in a recent letter to me.

"I am sure you will miss your dear wife but I trust your efforts to write a book of her life will help you to remain close to her and stimulate your fond memories. It should be a fitting tribute to a wonderful lady."

My daughters say,

"Our memories of her go back over fifty years. When we were children she was strict but fair and we thank her for that now.

She had a deep Christian faith, which sustained her throughout her life and gave us the foundation for ours. She was unselfish, loving, caring and compassionate. She encouraged us and always showed an interest in everything we did. In fact her entire married life was devoted to her family.

Her love of music and simple delight in her garden were a great influence in our lives. She gave us so much, that although she may not be here any more, she will remain with us always."

Alice

24TH MARCH 2005

This is the day on which I complete the final chapter of There and Back Again - A NAVIGATOR'S STORY. The day when Alice and I would have celebrated our diamond wedding anniversary together, had it not been for her sad passing on 30th May last year. Instead, I shall spend the day quietly and give thanks to God for his priceless gift, which was mine to hold on this earth for more than sixty years. I believe she is mine to hold for ever in a world, the dimension of which is beyond comprehension.

On 30th May 2004, I set course on the most difficult journey of my life, as 'pilot' and 'navigator' to an unknown destiny. I am reminded constantly of my comments made earlier in this book - "spare a thought for the other members of the crew," but in a much broader context, spare a thought for the countless men and women who have experienced and will continue to experience, the indescribable sadness of losing loved ones.

In July 1954, on a grey cloudy morning, I took my wife and two young daughters to Selworthy. Unexpectedly, the sun shone suddenly through a gap in the clouds creating a pool of great light. Beyond the gap it was as though a great circle celestial journey had begun, a great circle celestial journey that would encompass the firmament and eternity, a great circle celestial journey that would end where it began.

The stories related in this book represent merely a microcosmic arc of this celestial great circle journey, in which we all are involved. World without end.

"AT THE GOING DOWN OF THE SUN
AND IN THE MORNING
WE WILL REMEMBER THEM"

RE-UNITED

After my demob from Bomber Command at the end of World War Two, I made no attempt to attend any reunions, join any RAF associations or re-contact wartime contemporaries. I put my wartime experiences out of mind for the next fifty-four years. That was to change in December 2000 after publication of the First Edition of my book 'There and Back Again - A NAVIGATOR'S STORY.' Now, in November 2006, I am preparing additional script for an augmented Sixth Edition.

In consequence of the book I recently became re-united with some ex allied prisoners of war from camps in Vichy French North Africa, and also ex 100 Lancaster Squadron contemporaries, sadly only one of whom is alive today.

I learned that two senior Royal Navy officers, both ex prisoners of war in Laghouat, were court-martialled and relieved of their commands on repatriation to England. Lieutenant Commander Watkins, Captain of the destroyer HMS Havock, which ran aground in the Mediterranean in April 1942 and Captain Drew, Captain of the cruiser HMS Manchester, which after being torpedoed in the Mediterranean was scuttled later in August 1942. The action of Captain Drew saved the lives of about one thousand men, five hundred of whom were ferried to Gibraltar and five hundred became prisoners of war and taken to Laghouat.

After repatriation in November 1942, Commander R F Jessel, ex Captain of HMS Legion, pursued his wartime service career with distinction to become Commander RN OBE DSO DSC and Bar and three times Mentioned in Despatches.

Through the internet I became associated with the family, in St. John's Newfoundland, of the late Jim Templeton, a Canadian rear gunner of a Wellington bomber shot down in the Mediterranean by a Royal Navy Fleet Air Arm pilot!! Three of the crew were killed. Jim survived to be taken prisoner of war by the Vichy French and joined the allied prisoners of war in Aumale, before we were transferred to

Sgt Bob Turner, Petty Officer Crash Wines and Jim Templeton. Bob escaped from Dunkirk via Marseilles to Oran to be imprisoned later in Laghouat. Crash Wines Fleet Air Arm Pilot. Jim Templeton, see page 331 under 're-united' also Michael and Jessica's letter below.

Michael and Jessica Templeton

A letter just received from Gladys's grandson Michael reads:-

---

Dear Mr Hudson,

Deepest thanks for meeting with me and telling me your Laghouat story - in many ways, it was like the discussion with my grandfather that I never got to have. I really appreciated it. The courage and perseverance displayed by you and your generation is really remarkable. While Laghouat was a terrible experience for you and my grandfather, the fact that we could meet 60 years later for you to pass on your story is inspiring. I certainly won't forget it.

You've likely heard the saying that "Those who forget history are destined to repeat it." That is why it is so important for you to tell your story - your book is therefore extremely valuable. While there are still Laghouats in the world today, your story provides hope and the motivation to stand up for what is right. For that I am very grateful!

Best regards,
Michael Templeton
(and Jessica)

329

Laghouat in the desert. There we remained until the allied invasion of Algeria in November 1942.

I was delighted to welcome Jim's grandson Michael and his charming wife Jessica to my home here in Heighington near Lincoln on 18th November 2006. I communicate regularly with Jim's widow Gladys, whose son Ken, a QC, obtained a pension, index linked and back dated from 1942, for all Canadian prisoners of war in the Laghouat prisoner of war camp. I am an ex British prisoner from the same camp but do not receive a penny. My tentative enquiries for support in this direction fell on ground as stony as the desert.

Gladys phoned from St. John's yesterday, 20th November 2006. She told me Jim spent four months in hospital upon repatriation to the UK in November 1942 before returning home. For the rest of his life he suffered from the effects of claustrophobia as a result of participation in digging the Laghouat escape tunnel, which was 60 metres in length, 60 centimetres in width and 60 centimetres rising in places arched to avoid collapse, to 90 centimetres in height. The effects of ongoing dysentery took its toll and Jim died in 1988.

In my home village of Heighington, I have made the acquaintance of Pauline Harris, widow of Ron Harris, a 61 Squadron Lancaster bomb-aimer, who carried out thirty-one operational sorties. Pauline and I are now able to exchange interesting reminiscences. Mickey the Moocher of 61 Squadron completed 120 operational sorties, in which I understand three crews succeeded in completing their operational tour of thirty missions. After finishing operational flying Ron later flew to India with his squadron on Dakotas. Their flights in the Far East were on missions of manna, dropping grain to famine areas.

The picture of the only Lancaster in the UK flying today, 'The City of Lincoln', speaks for itself. Currently with the emblematic markings 'Mickey the Moocher', this Lancaster is based with a Dakota, Spitfires and Hurricanes and two Chipmunks at the Battle of Britain Memorial Flight, RAF Coningsby. I have been privileged to become an Honorary Member of the Battle of Britain Memorial Flight. In consequence, I met the 'Boss' Squadron Leader Al Pinner MBE Spitfire and Hurricane pilot. I also met the Lancaster crew of the day - Flight Lieutenants Miles Davey co-pilot, Ed Straw pilot, Wing Commander Colin Reeves flight engineer and Flight Lieutenant Bill Williams navigator. What a responsibility for these men, who have volunteered to be selected for this dedicated work after passing stringent flying tests. The 'Boss' is a permanent member of the flight at Coningsby; the others have responsible duties elsewhere.

Jeanette O'Connell was my charming escort when I was introduced to the members of the Flight and she took great care to ensure that I did not slip on the immaculately clean polished hangar floor. Her duties as Public Relations Officer are manifold in coordinating very complex programmes.

April 27th 2007 will mark the launch of the fiftieth season at BBMF, when after her return from major maintenance the Lancaster will be seen under her new name 'Phantom of the Ruhr'. She was initially of 100 Squadron and latterly of 550 Squadron. In consequence she will display the colours of both Squadrons. On the left hand side 100 Squadron of HW-R showing 31 missions and on the right hand side BQ-B of 550 Squadron where she flew a further 90 missions.

Away from the hangar is the Visitors' Centre, where memorabilia is displayed and updated and topical souvenirs are available for purchase. It is from here that experienced guides conduct the visitors to the hangar to see the aircraft, returning to the Merlin and History Rooms, where they explain the significance of display pictures and other items. The Visitors' Centre is controlled by the very experienced Manager Rod Sanders, ably supported by his deputy Mrs Margaret Trickett. Margaret, like Jeanette, always takes great care of me when I carry out frequent book signings, which can become very emotional. It is on these occasions I find the visiting public interested, appreciative and many express their thanks to the men and women of Bomber Command of whom 55,888, mostly aircrew, gave their lives during World War Two, in defence of our liberty.

I met many other dedicated people who are all part of a splendid team. They ensure that the Battle of Britain Memorial Flight is well maintained and a 'Mecca' for enquiring visitors seeking awareness of the RAF's participation in World War Two.

Douglas and Pauline, widow of Ron Harris ex 61 Sqn. Lancaster full tour

Douglas acknowledging BBMF visitors in front of City of Lincoln Lancaster

Douglas and Sqn Ldr Al Pinner

Douglas with Al Pinner and Lancaster crew

Lancaster displaying emblem of Mickey the Moocher

City of Lincoln at BBMF

Spitfire at BBMF

Douglas and Sqn Ldr Gerald Stapleton DFC & DFC (Dutch) Ex Ace fighter pilot

Douglas and Rod Sanders Manager BBMF Visitors Centre

Douglas and Margaret Trickett Deputy to Rod

BBMF book signing with Yvonne

Coningsby book signing BBMF

East Kirkby book signing with Yvonne

"Just Jane" East Kirkby

My elder daughter Ann in "Just Jane's" cockpit

Fred Panton towing "Just Jane" out of the hangar

Section of instrument panel

Ann with H2S radar aid at navigator's table

Ironically, only eight miles up the road at the Lincolnshire Aviation Heritage Centre, East Kirkby, is another Lancaster 'Just Jane' bought by Fred and Harold Panton in 1983. They established a museum at this Centre in 1988 in memory of their elder brother Chris, who at the age of nineteen, was killed when his Halifax was shot down over Nuremberg on 30/31st March 1944. This was the night Bomber Command lost ninety-seven heavy bombers, over seven-hundred aircrew.

East Kirkby was the wartime base of 57 and 630 Squadrons, from which 'Just Jane' now does regular taxi runs. This creates an opportunity for visitors to have the unique experience of boarding a moving Lancaster. Only then do they have some conception of the noise of the engines and experience the cramped, uncomfortable conditions under which wartime aircrew had to work and fly, sometimes for eight hours or longer.

There is an excellent and well maintained hangar containing extensive items of memorabilia and in which 'Just Jane' is housed and where considerable and expensive maintenance work is carried out during the winter months.

The flying control building must not be overlooked, nor the excellent catering facilities in the NAAFI, where a considerable collection of books and topical items of interest and emblematic toys for the collectors, young and old, are available.

Visitors cannot fail to be moved by the Chapel where names are listed of those from the two Squadrons at this base who made the ultimate sacrifice and gave their lives for their countries.

By courtesy of the Panton family, I am now acquainted with their three generations, I have carried out several book signings in the hangar and have always had the privilege and pleasure of meeting sincere and interested visitors.

'Just Jane', who is now quite an elderly lady, always likes to look her best to attract her admirers. Make-up, expensive and applied with precision is the very best. She is a real beauty and has not lost her 'voice'. You should hear her when she fires on all four engines before her taxi runs.

Apart from a short break over Christmas and New Year the museum is open all the year round with the exception of Sundays.

It was during a book signing at East Kirkby, I met Doreen Ainscough, previously a complete stranger, but a lady who I quickly discovered was deeply interested in all matters concerning the Royal Air Force. This is her tribute to the men and women who served in Bomber Command during World War Two.

"Whilst a war baby exercising my lungs during the later stages of World War Two, young men and women were volunteering for service with the Royal Air Force.

I later learned to read of the many sacrificial exploits of the personnel of Bomber Command and they became my heroes. With over 55,000 men and women killed, their part in the war effort was of the greatest magnitude.

Later, when teaching history from the immediate past, I used family veterans and artefacts to give children a complete hands-on history education. I determined that Bomber Command history would be faithfully retold.

According to the comments of Winston Churchill the fighters were our salvation, but the bombers alone provided the means of victory.

Sadly, no official Bomber Command medal in recognition has ever been forthcoming.

Those alive, with their continuing modesty, still deserve my total respect and gratitude, as does the remembrance of those who died with life stretching before them.

THEY ARE MY HEROES STILL."

DOREEN AINSCOUGH

101 SQUADRON LUDFORD MAGNA

The aircrew who flew from here paid a tragic price in loss of lives as they fought the enemy from the skies during World War Two. They epitomized the bravery of all gallant young men from other squadrons, who carried on regardless of danger, until the Nazi war machine had been destroyed.

As readers will have learned, I spent July and August 1940, with 101 Squadron as navigator on the twin engined Bristol Blenheim fighter bomber based at West Raynham. A great change took place in 1943 when this Squadron moved to Ludford Magna to fly Lancaster heavy bombers. From October 1943 these Lancasters flew using a system named 'Airborne Cigar'. With a German speaking operator on board they were able to disrupt the German controllers' transmissions causing chaos to their interceptor fighter aircraft.

I have become acquainted with Royston Clarke from Wragby, Lincolnshire, who served with 101 Squadron during a period from 1943 to 15th/16th February 1944, when his Lancaster was shot down over Berlin. It was a raid in which we took part and the Command lost forty-three heavy bombers. For Royston it was his thirteenth operational flight to Berlin and the thirtieth, and what would have been the last, of his tour.

He told me about his horrific experiences from the time their aircraft was initially struck, killing five crew members, including the pilot, to the time of the second strike when it burst into flames. With the help of the navigator, he managed to move the dead pilot from the cockpit and take over the controls, but now had to bale out of the stricken aircraft over the 'Big City', whilst the raid was in progress. Can you imagine his experience as the wireless operator air gunner, at the age of twenty, in that stricken aircraft? The memory of five dead crew members on board, the mid upper gunner's head blown to pieces and appearing as though a pot of red paint had been tipped over the remains, has haunted him for sixty-three years.

During his parachute descent, miraculously, he avoided the bombs raining down from our attacking aircraft, the barrages of flak directed at the bomber stream from the German ground defences and attacks from their fighter aircraft, regardless of the Geneva Convention. After landing in the burning city he was captured, taken to an air raid shelter where he was molested and threatened to be thrown into the burning buildings when the raid was over. He managed to escape only to be recaptured later and imprisoned. He escaped again on an enforced march and made his way to freedom in advance of the final invasion. A remarkable story of one very young man's wartime experiences, which should be documented for compulsory reading in schools.

This is what Mr. Stanley Baldwin, a Lincoln gentleman, wrote to me after he heard about the publication of the First Edition of 'There and Back Again - A NAVIGATOR'S STORY'.

"TO THOSE WHO GAVE THEIR ALL

Remembering Douglas Hudson DFC RAFVR and his many thousands of comrades of RAF Bomber Command 1939 - 1945.

These men flew into hell and back, time after time and played a major part in destroying the evil Nazi war machine.

Also remembering the thousands of dedicated RAF women and men who toiled day and night with great skill and determination to keep the aircraft flying.

As a young schoolboy, I was witness to much of the air activity in Lincolnshire and I watched in awe and great admiration.

I can never thank these heroes enough for giving me and millions of people like me, the right to live in peace and freedom.

We must never forget them."

Stanley Baldwin - Lincolnshire

There and Back Again
A Navigator's Story

"Dramatic account of author's experience in Bomber Command and over two years as a prisoner of war in Africa. Well written."
Lincolnshire Life. The County Magazine.

"Some war memoirs are interesting because of the experiences they record, others because they are well written.
The book by Douglas is both. We are delighted to have a copy. I have no doubt it will soon wear out through overuse."
The High Master, The Manchester Grammar School.

"If when someone tells you, regarding a book 'I couldn't put it down', it's common practice to take the comment as a direct invitation to read it yourself. I therefore have no hesitation in recommending that course of action with this wonderfully entertaining work by Douglas Hudson."
Kevin Webster. Editor 100 Squadron Association Website.

"Although we are familiar with Hollywood depictions of death, of losing comrades during wartime, the unsentimentality of this book adds a poignancy to the reality of having just got to know someone and noticing they are absent at breakfast the next morning. This was the reality for thousands of servicemen and women at that time.
There and Back Again is a well-written account of one man's war experiences. It is not just an enjoyable read, but also an invaluable history lesson."
From a review by Sally Frecklington of Ottaker's Bookshop.
Lincolnshire Gazette.

"Packed with previously unpublished photos that tell a tale themselves, this is a fitting tribute by Douglas Hudson to his comrades who did not live to see the peace that we have all since enjoyed."
Leicester Mercury

LOSSES

In July/August 1940, when I was stationed at West Raynham navigating Blenheims, the Station lost 20 Blenheims from 18 and 101 Squadrons.

From 27th August 1940 to 12th November 1942 I spent 2 ¼ years in three Vichy French North African prisoner of war camps controlled by the Deuxième Bureau, who were collaborators with the German/ Italian Commissions. These camps were in Le Kef Tunisia, Aumale Algeria and Laghouat in the Sahara Desert. I made two escapes only to be recaptured and as a result and for other 'misdemeanours' such as aiding other escapers, spent in total several weeks in cells and 3 days in a dungeon below ground with no amenities. During captivity I suffered ongoing dysentery.

Upon repatriation I had to practise eating. My stomach was distended and it took six months to get fit for flying again. I succeeded to complete a full tour of 30 operational flights on the Lancaster heavy bomber at 100 Squadron Waltham near Grimsby. In addition I flew 46 missions instructing or passing out navigators on the use of H2S a navigational radar aid. Most of these missions were with different pilots the majority of whom had just converted from flying twin engine (Wellingtons) to four engine bombers (Halifaxes or Lancasters).

At my guest talks and on BBC Radio interviews I have often been asked if we were frightened.

We were not a frightened crew generally nor when we were taken to and climbed on board our aircraft. There were times in the air when we were very frightened.

Some crews, young men 19 to 21 years old and others, you could read from the fear in their eyes, were frightened when they boarded the crew bus to be taken out to their aircraft. They did not talk about their fear. They were the bravest of all and never came back or only survived a few sorties.

Aircrews have been maligned by the pundits who were not there and by some professional biographers.

Dresden, Dresden, Dresden is often all the media can ask me about. So I say; the crews who went to Dresden were carrying out their duty as instructed by their superiors, who were responsible. Who gave the instructions? Answer – the government of the day, Churchill, under pressure from the American Government, which was under pressure from the Russians, who were advancing in Germany, and Dresden was in the way of the invasion forces.

During part of the period I was operating on Lancasters from 100 Squadron, i.e. during January 1944 to June 1944, D Day, our chance of completing a tour was about 6 to 1 against. Numerically, 100 Squadron was wiped out twice, losing thirty heavy bombers. My crew and I flew on three raids of the heaviest losses in Bomber Command, namely: 19th/20th February 1944 Leipsig losing 79 heavy bombers. 24th/25th March 1944 Berlin losing 73 heavy bombers. 30th/31st March 1944 Nuremberg losing 97 heavy bombers.

On my recent talks or interviews on BBC Radio or BBC and ITV Television, I enlightened listeners and viewers to this sort of ongoing experience. Typically at 21,000 feet on looking out of the aircraft, I would see an aircraft blow up on the starboard beam. This followed with another hit by flak and bursting into flames. With one voice the crew would shout "Jesus Christ another seven poor sods just bought it", as their aircraft in flames started spiralling to earth with seven men inside, entombed, incarcerated and being burned alive. On average, about this time Bomber Command would lose 35 heavy bombers on each operational sortie prior to D Day. (About 1500 aircraft from 1st January 1944 to 6th June 1944 - 10,500 aircrew).

The following introduction appeared on the first two pages of *LINCOLN CATHEDRAL booklet - CHORAL EVENSONG and dedication of the Bomber Command Ledger Stone - Sunday 27th August 2006.*

It was The Eleventh Sunday after Trinity and the occasion was the unveiling of a Memorial Ledger Stone by Veteran Bomber Command WAAF Mrs Sylvia Watts and me, in the North West Transept.

INTRODUCTION

On 3rd September 1939 the British Prime Minister Neville Chamberlain, stated that our country was at war with Germany. Our small island stood alone facing an implacable enemy, the ruthless strongly fortified Nazi Germany war-machine. Heroically brave young men and women, aged nineteen to twenty-three years, prepared to sacrifice their lives in defence of freedom. Supported by other dedicated men and women, they volunteered to fly and take the fight to the enemy. World War Two Bomber Command was created by necessity and nurtured by expediency.

Young men and women left their civilian occupations and entered extensive training in the Royal Air Force. They joined the regular trained aircrew officers, senior NCOs and other serving personnel. Early in 1940 many volunteer reservists had qualified to combine with regular serving personnel to fly operationally against the enemy. Volunteers from Australia, New Zealand, Canada, South Africa, India, Poland and Czechoslovakia, who had evaded the Nazis, together with Free Frenchmen and others from occupied Europe, swelled the increasing numbers in Bomber Command. A combined force, to be reckoned with by the enemy, was growing despite horrific losses sustained in training and operational missions.

During the early years of the war, the difficulties of long-distance hazardous day and night-time operational sorties were exacerbated by a lack of navigational aids, yet these continued with growing intensity. Nevertheless, the activities of crews, often dissatisfied with the inaccuracy of bombing and distressed by growing losses, proved to be of great public relations value. Bomber Command received accolades when Sir Arthur Harris launched the Thousand Bomber Raid on Cologne in May 1942. This was followed one year later by the Dambuster Raid from Scampton, when fifty-six brave airmen failed to return after dropping the bouncing bomb and breaching three dams. A similar number of men from 101 Squadron at Ludford Magna was lost on the infamous Nuremberg Raid on 30th/31st March 1944.

The raids on Nazi Germany and occupied territories became considerably intensified in 1943 and 1944. Bombing was difficult from 23,000 feet, but accuracy improved with the advent of more sophisticated radio and radar navigational aids, causing significant damage to the German infrastructure and paving the way for the D-Day invasion. Losses were tragically high and from 16th February to 31st March 1944 458 heavy bombers were lost, accounting for over 3000 aircrew. Between 1st January 1944 to the time of the D-Day landings on 6th June 1944 the Command lost over 1,500 heavy bombers, a toll of 10,500 men.

Undaunted, brave aircrew continued to fly, determined to fulfil their dangerous missions in support of the ground invasion forces in Europe. By 5th May 1945 the Nazi war machine had been destroyed and Germany surrendered to the Allies. The offensive task of Bomber Command in Europe was over, followed in the Far East on 15th August 1945 when the Japanese surrendered.

The task of Bomber Command in World War Two was completed at the cost of 55,888 lives.

J Douglas Hudson DFC, RAFVR

THE MEMORIAL LEDGER STONE

On the 25ᵗʰ October 2005 I read full front page and inside front page articles in the Lincolnshire Echo describing the project. The campaign, always under tight control, was chaired and organised by 'Scotty' as he preferred to be known, supported by two members forming the undermentioned small committee.

Chairman Mr R A 'Scotty' Scott, ex Flight Lieutenant RAF, Vulcan Air Electronics Officer.
Squadron Leader Alastair Scott RAF ('Scotty' Scott's son)
Treasurer Mr Roy Fleckney, ex Warrant Officer RAF and Adjutant of the Red Arrows.
Mr Eric Moss-Wright, Accountant and advisor to the committee.

'Scotty' had the sincerity, foresight and desire to seek a lasting Memorial for over 55,000 men and women who paid the ultimate sacrifice defending their countries against the tyrannical Nazi war machine. He attempted and succeeded in ten months, what no government, authority or influential power had brought about in more than sixty years.

I was deeply impressed on hearing about his activities and quickly became involved as his 'chief ally'. The publicity I had received from the earlier editions of my book was helpful and the Lincolnshire Echo Newspaper was an ongoing supporter as was BBC Radio Lincolnshire. 'Scotty' and his committee beavered away continuously. There was no let up.

A large monument of Lord Tennyson exists in the grounds of Lincoln Cathedral. He was a close friend of Queen Victoria, but The Church of England authorities in London will not permit any other monument, or edifice of remembrance, to be erected in these grounds. Unenlightened persons suggested there should be an ostentatious and elaborate memorial with fountains. Others suggested something similar in public places. I am a ninety years old aircrew veteran of Bomber Command and have no hesitation in stating that such a Memorial would not be in keeping and would be rife for vandalism.

Success came Scotty's way from the Chapter of Lincoln Cathedral, three members of whom I am privileged to mention below and to whom I extend my sincere thanks and appreciation for their support to the campaign:--

The Very Reverend Doctor Alec Knight - the former Dean
The Reverend Canon Gavin Kirk - Precentor of Lincoln
Mr Roy Bentham - Chapter Clerk and Chief Executive

Chapter agreed to a Memorial Ledger Stone being placed in the North West Transept by the Airmen's Chapel, where there exists a Bomber Command stained glass window. The words of dedication are sincere and simple and in what more hallowed and protected place could the Memorial Ledger Stone rest?

Nevertheless, one man wrote to the press stating that a cheap and quick option had been decided upon. Many other persons expressed adverse criticism leaning in the direction of pretentious display. Let us pause and reflect. To whom should these people offer thanks for freedom of speech, which today is readily taken for granted?

The Precentor thought differently. This is an extract from his words written to me, "The stone will lie within the ultimate symbol of sacrifice and resurrection to which we all aspire." To which I say, "Amen."

On 6th February 2006 it was victory at last for 'Scotty' Scott, his campaigners, the heroes of Bomber Command and their families when Lincoln Cathedral agreed in principle to the Memorial being engraved. This important duty became the responsibility of Lincoln Cathedral sculptor Mr Michael Morris, who achieved the engraving to perfection for the unveiling ceremony on Sunday August 27th 2006.

Shortly after hearing this positive decision, 'Scotty' was determined that the unveiling ceremony should be undertaken by two Bomber Command veterans, who had served in The Second World War. Veteran WAAF Mrs Sylvia Watts and I were the two privileged persons chosen by 'Scotty' to carry out this duty of the highest honour.

Sylvia and I were strangers. Our introduction arose from a telephone call I made to her shortly after hearing the above incredible news. Thereafter, I was taken to visit her by my elder daughter Ann and friend Doreen. We have since become close friends. In our reminiscences we share a lifetime of varied experiences, many similar and others very different, covering more than eighty years.

Sylvia and I enjoy a similar accomplishment. She has published two successful autobiographical books under her maiden name of Sylvia Pickering entitled:

'Tales of a BOMBER COMMAND WAAF (& her horse)'
and
'More Tales of a BOMBER COMMAND WAAF (& her horse)'

During the intervening period leading to the unveiling date, 'Scotty' worked tirelessly in attempts to get the message of the pending event to Bomber Command veterans at home and overseas. The event was one which most veterans believed would not occur in their lifetime. I supported 'Scotty' closely and we were both successful in Lincolnshire, thanks to publicity throughout by the Lincolnshire Echo newspaper. Latterly, the event was also given publicity by BBC Radio Lincolnshire, Look North Television and ITV Central.

The Battle of Britain Memorial Flight at RAF Coningsby and the Lincolnshire Aviation Heritage Centre at East Kirkby provided me with opportunities to draw notice of the unveiling to a wide public who attended my book signings. Apart from an excellent article in the Times Newspaper I had little success on a national basis until virtually the eve of the unveiling day.

It was encouraging to read and hear of a greater awareness being directed to the younger generation and to the schools, of the tragic losses suffered by the young volunteer aircrews of Bomber Command 1939 - 1945. Nobody was conscripted for flying duties in the Royal Air Force.

At the age of ten, Felix Hammett, the younger of two brothers, wrote a project about the Second World War for Yardley Court School, Tonbridge.

In this project he describes the evacuation of children, of whom there was a total of one and a half million, mostly from vulnerable cities. On the subject of food rationing, he states that in 1941 one person could buy 2oz (60 grams) of butter and 4oz (120 grams) of meat, which is how much a child today would eat in one meal! Bananas, oranges and other exotic fruits were almost impossible to get hold of because the ships importing them were bombed or used for more important cargo. Whale meat was plentiful and not rationed! Referring to The Royal Air Force, he mentions in particular the Spitfire and Lancaster aircraft, the latter carrying out 156,000 missions.

How did I know about Felix? His mother is a free-lance journalist and also writes for The Times newspaper. Under her maiden name of Catherine O'Brien, and authorised by Erica Wagner literary editor, Catherine wrote a splendid review in Times 2 on 10th December 2002. This was shortly after the release of the Second Edition of my book. It is appropriate and certainly in keeping that reference should be made to Felix's project in this Sixth Edition.

My Alma Maters Ermysted's Grammar School Skipton and The Manchester Grammar School have taken books for their libraries and history reading. The William Farr Church of England Comprehensive School, built on the site of RAF Dunholme Lodge WW2 bomber station, has placed books in its libraries, museum and chapel and for history reading.

Books have been placed in thirty units of Trent Wing Air Training Corps (ATC) to many of whom I have given 'Guest Talks.' I have found the young cadets most interested and receptive. I explained there is no 'I' in team, that there was no most important member in an aircrew; we worked together as a team. We relied on the cooperation of all members on the station. Our aircraft would not have flown without the support of our groundcrew. They could not have done their jobs without the help of the WAAFS and other service personnel carrying out a host of different duties. The whole Bomber Command station worked as a team.

Cadets outside Cathedral

Douglas and Mollie

Douglas, Mollie and Jeanette

Yvonne, Ann and the two Davids

ATC in Cathedral before unveiling

David, Sandra, Emma and her cousin David

Mrs Dawn Bowskill, Ben Hudston, Sylvia and Douglas

347

Standards in readiness before unveiling

Altar and wreaths

Michael Morris the sculptor of the Bomber Command Memorial.

Scotty and Douglas in the Chapter House

Scotty, Douglas and Sylvia after unveiling

Autographing booklet with Jim Wright and Rebecca Brice BBC

Douglas and Wing Commander Jim Wright

BBC TV Interview

Ann, Douglas and Yvonne

Ann, Emma and Douglas by wreaths after departure of congregation

Barnes Wallis family wreath

Sylvia Watts, Air Marshall Sir Clive Loader and Sylvia's book

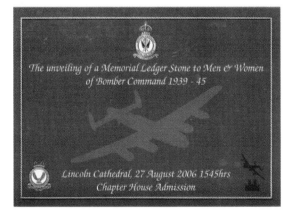

The unveiling of a Memorial Ledger Stone to Men & Women of Bomber Command 1939 - 45

Lincoln Cathedral, 27 August 2006 1545hrs
Chapter House Admission

For safety reasons admission to the Chapter House had to be restricted

Our Lancaster bomber crew typified the average aircrew. On the ground, when not on duty, most aircrew were wanton, irresponsible, irreverent but not irreligious. They were not insensitive to a tactile association with the opposite sex. In the air, when flying operationally, they were highly responsible, efficient and extremely brave.

I say today that wartime aircrew were not made, they were born. Of course they had to be tutored to perform their respective duties, but would not be expected to stand a chance of achieving success had they not been 'born to fly'. I know because I was one of them, I was there! They had to be prepared to face horrific dangers. The odds in favour of survival were almost insuperable.

I told the ATC that what I am about to mention happened ON AVERAGE to thirty heavy bombers on every operational sortie, in which my crew and I took part in the Lancaster bomber, from early January 1944 during the run up to the D DAY LANDINGS in early June 1944.

Somewhere over Nazi Germany at 20,000 feet, Johnny Hesp, our rear gunner, suggested I should take a look out. I did, to see a heavy bomber being blown to pieces. Immediately afterwards another heavy bomber was hit by flak and burst into flames. I and all the crew shouted, "Jesus Christ, another seven poor sods just bought it!" Inside their flaming aircraft seven men were entombed, incarcerated, incinerated being burnt alive before the plane would hit the ground and disintegrate.

The dawn broke on Sunday 27th August 2006 to herald a day that would be pleasantly warm, dry and sunny. In the morning I visited my wife's grave in Washingborough. She was already with the 55,888 men and women of Bomber Command on their great circle celestial journey that would encompass the firmament and eternity.

It was a day of great incredulity for me, as I am sure it must have been for Mrs. Sylvia Watts, who would accompany me later to unveil the Memorial Ledger Stone. For 'Scotty' Scott and his team it must also have been a day of wonderful disbelief.

In the early afternoon the congregation began to arrive at Lincoln Cathedral, where twelve-hundred seats had been allocated for the unveiling ceremony. The crowd assembled in the Cathedral grounds to witness the fly past of the Lancaster, which made three passes over the spires exactly on schedule at 15.05 hours.

Several Air Training Corps Cadets were in attendance performing manifold duties. One particular responsibility was escorting veterans, some of whom were disabled and in wheelchairs, or walking gingerly with the aid of sticks.

Sylvia arrived in a wheelchair, ably controlled by Ben, her close young friend and neighbour. He would be her carer today. Later she and I took our places seated in the front row nearest to the curtained Memorial Stone, temporarily supported on an easel in readiness for the unveiling.

Before Evensong, Canon Nugent stood up and welcomed the veterans to 'Bomber Command's Cathedral'. The Choral Evensong and dedication of the Bomber Command Ledger Stone commenced at 15.45 hours in the awe inspiring atmosphere of the massive Cathedral.

The dedication of the Memorial began with Mr Jack Jones reading the verses of 'Lie in the Dark and Listen' by the late Sir Noel Coward. Following this reading, Sylvia, escorted by two female cadets, rose from her wheelchair and using two sticks, walked slowly towards the Ledger Stone. I joined her, accompanied by two male cadet escorts. With the congregation standing, we then jointly unveiled the Memorial Ledger Stone to reveal the Bomber Command Crest and the following words:-

'Dedicated to the men and women of
BOMBER COMMAND
1939 - 1945
over 55,000 of whom gave their lives
in defence of our liberty'

It was a highly emotional experience for Sylvia and me as we turned to face the massive congregation, whilst the Subdean cited the prayer in praise of Almighty and eternal God, Lord of the universe and maker of all that is.

After the prayer we returned to our seats as a trumpeter played the Evening Hymn while wreaths were laid. Air Marshal Sir Clive Loader KCB OBE FRAeS RAF, Deputy Commander-in-Chief Strike Command laid the wreath on behalf of the Air Force Board and the Royal Air Force. By the time this book is published on 1st April 2007, he will be Air Chief Marshal, Commander-in-Chief Strike Command.

The climax was reached as bearers paraded ten Standards to a crescendo of sound from the drums, band and trumpeters of the Air Training Corps. Appropriately, the band played the tune of the Lincolnshire Poacher. The atmosphere in that massive awe-inspiring Cathedral had to be experienced to be comprehended.

A day in history had been created. The men and women of Bomber Command 1939 - 1945 had been recognised. Their bravery and dedication recorded in the hallowed archives for posterity. For this, a debt of gratitude is owed to Mr R A 'Scotty' Scott and his committee.

Dedicated to the men and women of

BOMBER COMMAND 1939-1945

over 55,000 of whom gave their lives in defence of our liberty

---

FLIGHT LIEUTENANT ERIC NORMAN DFC

In my earlier editions I referred to navigator Flight Lieutenant Eric Norman DFC. In 1944 he and his crew completed a full tour of operational flights on the Lancaster bomber from 100 Squadron Waltham during the identical period my crew and I had the same success. Sadly Eric died in the late summer 2006. He lived with his sister Betty, to whom I spoke just before he died. I learned that she was able to read to him the account, from the Choral Evensong and dedication of the Bomber Command Ledger Stone booklet, of the unveiling ceremony on 27th August 2006 in Lincoln Cathedral. He listened with eyes closed and passed away peacefully shortly afterwards.

Late post war fulfilment enjoyed in Somerset by my wife and I and our son-in-law David from the productive garden at Littlecroft. This was part of the legacy we inherited from the 55,888 men and women of Bomber Command 1939-1945 who gave their lives in the defence of our liberty. A privilege they never lived to enjoy, but inherited by veterans like myself, by other World War Two survivors and their descendants. We owe a debt of gratitude that can never be repaid.

Alice with two specimen vegetable marrows

Alice and David by the branch of the prolific early fruiting apple tree

353

Alice and self on Littlecroft front lawn

Self and David laying paving stones in rear courtyard

ACKNOWLEDGEMENTS

It was not until the year 2000 I decided to write my wartime memoirs. Fifty-five to sixty years later may seem a long time before recording this chapter in my life's history. Motivation arrived from an unexpected source, from two very dedicated people, who were previously unknown to me. I am indebted to my bomb-aimer Douglas Chapman who was responsible for our introduction.

Nick and Carol Carter had devoted a great deal of their time in detailed research to compile and publish a register of all recipients of The Distinguished Flying Cross 1918-1995. Two copies of this register they kindly donated to the Royal Air Force Benevolent Fund to be auctioned to raise funds for this cause.

I was delighted, a little later, to welcome them to our home and it was during this visit they suggested that if I were to chronicle my wartime experiences, they might be of interest to others.

Thank you Nick and Carol.

I also acknowledge the help of my immediate family and thank them for their patience, co-operation and advice; also my son-in-law Alan, whose expertise on computer and scanner was responsible initially for the upgrading and reproduction of photographs.

I mention Fred and Harold Panton, who bought and subsequently considerably restored Lancaster NX611, which now occupies pride of place at their Lincolnshire Aviation Heritage Centre.   I thank them for allowing me to include in my Memoirs references to their wonderful Memorial Museum.

Here I met John Proctor, a complete stranger who had a deep and sincere interest in 100 Squadron. He talked to me about his relative Warrant Officer Pilot J.K. Ives, who had an impeccable short record of operational flying on the Squadron from late December 1943 to the end of January 1944. Entries taken from his flying logbook and reproduced in my Memoirs illustrate the enormous pressure enforced on Bomber Command aircrew at this period.

I thank Mr T.R. Padfield, Copyright Officer of the Public Record Office, The National Archives, for permission to use the photographs of the bomb damage of German cities in 1945 and other photographs of air publications.

I thank my nieces Eileen Margaret Stirrup and Judith Lyn Park for information regarding the Ormerod family. Also Douglas Shorrock for information regarding Blackburn.

DURING MY NAVIGATIONAL JOURNEY I MET MANY
PEOPLE OF FASCINATING AND DIFFERENT
PERSUASIONS. WITHOUT THE HELPFUL INFLUENCE
OF THE UNDERMENTIONED, MY MEMOIRS COULD NOT
HAVE BEEN COMPLETED.

Joan B. Morton	Prestwick
'Old Man' Danks	Prestwick
Sergeant 'Bob' R.B. Pine	Manchester RAFVR
Flight Lieutenant Dawson	Manchester RAFVR
Sergeant Alec Buckley	Manchester RAFVR
Sergeant Harry Bowers	Manchester RAFVR
Sergeant J. Parkinson	Manchester RAFVR
	101 Squadron
	West Raynham
Sergeant Norman Giblin DFM	Manchester RAFVR
Flight Lieutenant Don Chadwick DFC	Manchester RAFVR
Sergeant Julius Holland	Belfast RAFVR
Air Marshal Sir Charles Portal KCB CB DSO & BAR MC	
	AOC-in-C Bomber Command
Later to become: Marshall of the Royal Air Force,	
Lord Portal of Hungerford KG GCB OM KCB CB DSO & BAR MC	
	Chief of the Air Staff
Sergeant W.B. Gingell to become	101 Squadron
Pilot Officer W.B. Gingell DFC, DFM	West Raynham
Sergeant Ted Hart	North Africa
Flight Sergeant Stevens DFM BEM	North Africa
Sergeant John Riddick	101 Squadron
	West Raynham and North Africa
Sergeant 'Tony' D.W.G. Randall	101 Squadron
	West Raynham and North Africa
French Lieutenant (Name unknown)	Le Kef (see page 68)
Flight Lieutenant 'Cap' Cooper	North Africa
Private 'Daffy' Watson MM	North Africa
Lance Corporal Fred Williams MM	North Africa
Corporal Ted Clayton OBE	North Africa
Flight Lieutenant 'Bertie' Brain DFC	North Africa
Lieutenant Commander Watkins	North Africa
Sergeant 'Wilbur' Wright	North Africa
Commander R.F. Jessel DSO	North Africa
Pilot Officer J.M. Alexander	North Africa

Captain Montgomery	North Africa
Squadron Leader Brickell	North Africa
Sergeant Claude Belcher NZ	North Africa
Commandant Jeunechamp	Laghouat
Eight Premier Spahis Cavalry Soldiers	Laghouat
Sergeant 'Digger' Aubrey Latter Australian	North Africa
Sergeant H.C. Gibbins	North Africa
Flight Sergeant Storey	Wymeswold
Sergeant Lomas, or Lomax	Wymeswold
Flying Officer 'Joe' S.S. Pennington DFC	Wymeswold
Sergeant Coleman	Wymeswold
Flight Lieutenant J.K. Hamilton DFC	Wymeswold
	100 Squadron Waltham
Sergeant W.F. Bloomfield	Wymeswold
	100 Squadron Waltham
Flying Officer D.H. Chapman DFC	Wymeswold
	100 Squadron Waltham
Flight Sergeant 'Sparks' Denis F.H. Lacey	Wymeswold
	100 Squadron Waltham
Pilot Officer 'Jack' I.J. Duffett	Wymeswold
	100 Squadron Waltham
Squadron Leader L.C. Pipkin DFC & Bar	Wymeswold
Pilot Officer J.M. Hesp DFC DFM	100 Squadron Waltham
Sergeant B.R. Phillips DFM	100 Squadron Waltham
Flight Lieutenant G.M. Pirie DFC	100 Squadron Waltham
Air Commodore A. Wray DSO MC DFC AFC	Binbrook
Flight Lieutenant G.R. Ross	100 Squadron Waltham
Flying Officer Beck	100 Squadron Waltham
Wing Commander R.V.L. Pattison DSO DFC	100 Squadron Waltham
Group Captain Hugh I. Edwards VC DSO DFC	460 RAAF

Squadron Binbrook, Later to become Air Commodore H.I. Edwards
VC KCMG CB OBE DSO DFC

Squadron Leader H.H. Grant Dalton DFC & Bar	100 Squadron Waltham
Pilot Officer T.F. Cook DFC	100 Squadron Waltham
Flight Lieutenant Eric W. Norman DFC	100 Squadron Waltham
Flying Officer J.M. Galloway DFC	100 Squadron Waltham
Pilot Officer J.D. Mortimer DFC	100 Squadron Waltham
Pilot Officer John B.Raper DFC	100 Squadron Waltham
Flight Lieutenant K.A. Drury DFC	100 Squadron Waltham
Squadron Leader 'Doc' Marshall	100 Squadron Waltham
	and Sandtoft Station Medical Officer

The ranks of the services' personnel are, as I knew them.

Air Chief Marshal Sir Clive Loader KCB OBE ADC FRAeS RAF
                          Commander-in-Chief Strike Command
The Very Reverend Dr Alec Knight   former Dean of Lincoln Cathedral
Canon Gavin Kirk   Precentor of Lincoln
Canon Alan Nugent   Subdean of Lincoln Cathedral
Mr Roy Bentham   Chapter Clerk and Chief Executive, Lincoln Cathedral
Mr Michael Morris   Sculptor, Lincoln Cathedral
Mr R A 'Scotty' Scott Flight Lieutenant RAF Retired
                          Chairman Bomber Command Memorial Committee
Squadron Leader Alastair Scott   Bomber Command Memorial Committee
Mr Roy Fleckney Warrant Officer RAF Retired
                          Bomber Command Memorial Committee
Mr Eric Moss-Wright   Accountant & Advisor to
                          Bomber Command Memorial Committee
Mrs J Sylvia Watts   Veteran Bomber Command WAAF
Mrs Dawn Bowskill   Welton Lincoln
Mr Ben Hudston   Welton Lincoln
Squadron Leader David Hortop RAFVRT   Air Training Corps
                                           Trent Wing & Cadets
Mr Fred Panton MBE   The Lincolnshire Aviation
Mr Harold Panton   Heritage Centre
The Panton Families   East Kirkby
Miss Sandra Morton M.Sc. MBA FIBMS CSci.
Squadron Leader Al Pinner MBE   Officer Commanding
              Battle of Britain Memorial Flight RAF Coningsby
Mrs Jeanette O'Connell   Public Relations Officer
              Battle of Britain Memorial Flight, RAF Coningsby
Flight Lieutenant Miles-Davey   Battle of Britain Memorial Flight
                                           RAF Coningsby
Flight Lieutenant Ed Straw   Battle of Britain Memorial Flight RAF Coningsby
Wing Commander Colin Reeves   Battle of Britain Memorial Flight
                                           RAF Coningsby
Flight Lieutenant Bill Williams   Battle of Britain Memorial Flight
                                           RAF Coningsby
Mr Rod Sanders   Visitors' Centre Manager Battle of Britain Memorial Flight
Mrs Margaret Trickett   Visitors' Centre Deputy Manager
                              Battle of Britain Memorial Flight
All other dedicated staff   Battle of Britain Memorial Flight RAF Coningsby
Mrs Mollie E Newbould   West Yorkshire
Mr Angus Newbould BA Hons   West Yorkshire
Mr Alan Chapman OBE   Wokingham
Mr Peter J Pennington B.Sc.   Histon Cambridge
Ms Catherine O'Brien   Journalist Golden Green Kent
Felix Hammett   her 10 years old son and school project writer
Mr Stanley Baldwin   Lincoln
Doreen Ainscough   Writer/historian West Yorkshire
Mr Bruce Smith   Edinburgh

Key to Photographs of Personnel Whose Names I Recall

PART ONE
CHAPTER TWO

Page 29
B Squad No 1 Air Observer Navigation School (No1 AONS) RAF
Prestwick November 1939

From left to right:
Back Row
1. Don Chadwick 2. Harry Bowers 7. Danny Hawthorn 11. Kirby
Centre Row
3. Alec Buckley 4. Bob Hay 5. Butterworth 6. Ron Hamer
7. 'Cruffy' Crawford 10. Heywood
Front Row
2. Julius Holland 5. Noel Hawthorn 6. Self 7. 'Nobby' Clarke
8. Gorman 9. Norman Giblin

CHAPTER SIX

Page 78
Le Kef Winter 1940/41

Back Row
1. Eric Shipley (Camp Echo Artist) 2. French Guard
3. Plt Off Ferguson 4. Bill Stevens 5. Fg Off Dai Davies 6. John
Riddick
7. 'Cap' Cooper 8. French Guard 9. Tony Randall 10. Plt Off Smith
NZ
Centre Row
1. Jock Burnett 2. French Guard 3. French Official
Front Row
1. Self 2. Wilbur Wright 3. French Guard 4. Ted Hart 5. French
Guard

PART TWO
CHAPTER NINE

Page 100
Mark 1 Latrine Laghouat

Back Row
3. Barney Todd 5. Sqn Ldr Brickell 6. Self 10. Jim Templeton
One on his own
Bill Stevens
Third Row
1. Wilcox
Second Row
4. Plt Off Ferguson 5. Ted Hart 8. (standing) H.C. Gibbins
Front Row
4. Wilbur Wright 5. 'Digger' Latter 7. Mick Steer

Page 108
Back Row
1. Bob Wilson 9. Jimmy Alexander 10. Tony Randall
Centre Row
1. Wilcox 2. Ted Clayton 8. Daffy Watson
Front Row
1. American pilot (see page 139) 3. Self

Page 114
Group Photograph Laghouat December 1941
Back Row
1. Macdonald?
Second Row
1. Bill Ballard 2. Sqn Ldr Brickell 5. (crouching) French Guard
6. 'Digger' Latter
Front Row
2. Pickles 5. Mick Cook? 6. 'Cap' Cooper 7. Mick Steer
CHAPTER TEN

Page 119
'AMENITY slit trench'

1. Sgt Macdonald 3. Plt Off Smith 4. Captain Montgomery 5. Lt Robairre